THE
GREAT WESTERN
RAILWAY

A Celebration

Tim Bryan

Ian Allan
PUBLISHING

For Ann, with love

*Although many of the engravings
(by J. C. Bourne) of the early GWR feature stations and
civil-engineering structures, none is so dramatic as this
view of Gooch 'Fire Fly' 2-2-2* Acheron *emerging from one
of the tunnels between Bristol and Bath. The locomotive was
built in 1842 and scrapped in 1866.*

First published 2010

ISBN 978 0 7110 3498 3

Published by Ian Allan Publishing

an imprint of Ian Allan Publishing Ltd,
Hersham, Surrey, KT12 4RG
Printed in England by Ian Allan Printing Ltd,
Hersham, Surrey, KT12 4RG

Distributed in Canada and the United States of America by
BookMasters Distribution Services

Code: 1005/B2

Visit the Ian Allan Publishing website at
www.ianallanpublishing.com

*Below: A poster issued by the company in 1935 to mark its
100th anniversary.*

 100 YEARS OF PROGRESS
1835 — 1935

CONTENTS

FOREWORD

As the only 'Big Four' railway with a pedigree stretching back to the 19th century, the Great Western was able to celebrate its centenary in 1935. The anniversary celebrated was not actually the opening of the line, perhaps because the original GWR opened in stages from 1838 onwards, culminating in 1841 with the completion of the main line from Bristol to London. Instead the company chose 31 August 1835, the date on which the original Great Western Railway Act was passed by Parliament.

This book aims to try and capture the essence of the Great Western Railway through a chronological survey of its history and development and a number of chapters covering specific areas of operation. Although the company ceased to exist as a legal entity in 1948 when it was nationalised, its legacy continued into the British Rail era, and is still with us today, through not only the current railway, but also the heritage railway world which, through preserving and operating GWR artefacts, continues to honour the achievements of the original railway.

In 1985 the exploits of perhaps the most famous main-line railway in the world were once again celebrated with a series of anniversary events to mark its 150th birthday. Having been involved in some of those 'GWR 150' events that year, the opportunity to revisit the history of the railway 25 years on was for me too good to miss. The millions of words already written about the Great Western mean that this book can only be a snapshot and summary of the highs and lows of a railway that dominated the lives of so many people during its existence, but hopefully the text and pictures will bring to life a story that, 175 years on, is still worth retelling. Isambard Kingdom Brunel called the Great Western Railway 'the finest work in England' and I am sure that he would have been delighted that his exploits were being celebrated so many years later.

Tim Bryan
Swindon, March 2010

Right: A famous GWR image. Seven 'King'-class locomotives stand outside Swindon running shed.

ACKNOWLEDGEMENTS

Franz Kafka once described writing as 'utter solitude', and although it is true that it can sometimes be a lonely experience, it would of course have been impossible to complete this book without the assistance and support of others.

Much of the background research for the book was carried out at the Swindon Central Library, and I am grateful for the assistance of Roger Trayhurn, the Local Studies Librarian and his team for their assistance and access to the local history and railway collections retained there. Grateful thanks are also due to Elaine Arthurs, Collections Officer at the STEAM: Museum of the GWR for her patience and good humour; she allowed me access to the library and archive collection there, as well as assisting me with the location and selection of images for the book. All the photographs except those credited separately in the text are from the collection of the STEAM Museum and I am grateful for permission to reproduce them here. I would like to acknowledge the work done by volunteers past and present at both the old GWR Museum and STEAM in preserving and cataloguing the amazing collection now housed at the museum in Swindon. I am also grateful to Alan Greer, Business Manager at STEAM, for his support in the early stages of the book.

Immersing myself in the history of the GWR after some years reminded me of the assistance and support of the many friends and colleagues I have encountered over the last three decades. There is not space to list them all individually here, but my thanks are due to members of staff at the old Swindon GWR Museum and STEAM, past and present members of the Friends of Swindon Railway Museum, the Great Western Society and Trust at Didcot, colleagues past and present at the National Railway Museum and finally ex-railway staff at Swindon and elsewhere who freely gave of their time and shared their experiences and knowledge.

My family have provided sterling backup during the writing process, and I am very grateful to my wife Ann, not only for reading and editing the manuscript but also for her love and support, as always.

STEAM — Museum of the Great Western Railway, Swindon
STEAM — Museum of the Great Western Railway tells the story of the men and women who built, operated and travelled on the Great Western Railway. The year 2010 marks the 175th anniversary of the creation of the GWR, and STEAM celebrates this milestone through its wonderful display of artefacts and photographs. The illustrations in this book heve been selected from many thousands of images that depict the GWR from the early years of construction, through to Nationalisation in the late 1940s and beyond. If you would like to find out more about the photographic collection at STEAM please telephone 01793 466646 or visit the museum's website.
www.steampicturelibrary.com.

INTRODUCTION

One hundred and seventy-five years on, the name of the Great Western Railway still evokes nostalgia and interest from both enthusiasts and those who know little about railways but still seem to have affection for the company and what it stood for. It is perhaps understandable in the busy modern age we live in to look back to an age when train travel seemed to evoke more positive feelings of comfort, adventure and even romance. Asked to write an appreciation of the Great Western when it was about to be nationalised, railway historian O. S. Nock described it as being greater than any other of the 'Big Four' railways and perhaps the 'greatest single institution in the West of England'. This may have been hyperbole, but, when Nock completed his book the reputation of the railway was still very high, even considering the difficulties the company had endured during World War 2. In the years since nationalisation the standing of the Great Western has, if anything, increased, especially since it ceased to exist, its independent streak and heritage ensuring its place in railway history.

Below: A truly atmospheric picture of Swansea High Street station c1900. Built in 1850 by the South Wales Railway, the terminus was named 'High Street' to distinguish it from the other six stations in Swansea, owned by five different railway companies

Perhaps the most significant aspect of the Great Western story was the longevity of the company itself; formed in Bristol in 1833, after the passing of the GWR Act in 1835 the railway was able to enjoy a history interrupted only by the passing of the Railways Bill in 1921, which created the 'Big Four' companies of the Great Western, London & North Eastern, London, Midland & Scottish and Southern railways. The process of amalgamation saw the GWR emerge as the only one of the four to retain much of its original identity and, most importantly, its original name. The absorption of pre-Grouping companies, particularly those in South Wales, gave it an enviable strength and stability that allowed it to weather the difficulties created by the Wall Street Crash of 1929. The long history and traditions of the GWR also gave it a confidence and swagger; indeed, some might regard its attitude as bordering on arrogance!

By the 1930s the GWR was an enormous enterprise. The network planned by Brunel had expanded far beyond the original London–Bristol main line opened in 1841 and covered large parts of the West Country, Wales and the West Midlands. At its height the company had more than 1,000 stations, from small wayside halts to great city stations like Paddington, Bristol Temple Meads and Birmingham Snow Hill. It also owned a good deal of other property — goods depots, docks and harbours, hotels and refreshment rooms. Away from the main trunk routes its branch lines ran deep into the countryside, providing a vital link between isolated rural communities and towns and cities across the network.

The Great Western always boasted that it was the 'Royal Road', Queen Victoria having been the first monarch to travel by rail when she took a trip on the GWR in 1842. For those travelling in its heyday, the GWR's express services were, for the most part, of the highest quality; holidaymakers travelling to Cornwall on the 'Cornish Riviera Limited' journeyed in luxurious carriages and could enjoy a delicious meal in the restaurant car. Its cross-country and branch-line services may have been rather less rapid, but punctuality was always a priority for the management at Paddington. Looking out of the window of a GWR express, the passenger would have seen many goods trains; the freight business, especially the

Above: *A wartime scene at Swindon Works. Neither the female worker holding a red-hot rivet nor her male counterpart operating the hydraulic riveter is wearing ear protection.*

movement of coal, was the railway's lifeblood, and great efforts were made by to generate and retain this business, even when the double blow of the Great Depression and road competition hit the company hard.

The Great Western's reputation amongst travellers also rested on its safety record. Although it was not immune from serious accidents, the company's widespread use of interlocking of signals and points, the introduction of track circuiting and, most importantly, the adoption of its own Automatic Train Control system put it at the forefront of developments relating to the safe working of trains. Great Western signalling was, like many other aspects of the company's operation, distinctive; its lower-quadrant semaphore signals dropped rather than being raised to indicate 'line clear'.

Many books have been written about the locomotives used by the Great Western during its long history; no other railway seems to have

Above: *The Great Western had an admirable safety record, but this photograph shows the aftermath of a serious accident which occurred on 3 October 1904 at Loughor Bridge, near Llanelli. 'Bulldog' No 3460* Montreal *was only eight months old when it and a pilot engine were involved in a derailment which claimed the lives of three enginemen and two passengers.*

Opposite page: *The Great Western's cathedral. Paddington station before the Great War.*

had so much attention paid to the efforts of its locomotive engineers, from Gooch to Hawksworth. Whatever their design, the GWR's engines had a distinct 'look', a family likeness that made them instantly recognisable. The Brunswick-green livery, copper-capped chimney, brass safety valve and brass nameplates are as evocative now as they were in the 1920s and '30s, when Great Western locomotives were making headlines all over the world. In the same way, the chocolate-and-cream livery used for its carriages was a unique feature that remained a constant, barring a few experiments with maroon (briefly) and all-over brown (wartime austerity).

The company's image was, in the inter-war period particularly, dictated by its publicity department, which, as the company developed, became ever more adept at publicising its activities through its corporate style, news stories or striking publicity material. The publicity department also helped promote services that were not really traditional railway activities; as well as a thriving hotel and catering operation the Great Western also had a large fleet of road

vehicles, a shipping fleet and an extensive docks business and in the 1930s even ran its own small-scale domestic airline service.

Above all, the reputation of the Great Western rested on its people. It is easy to concentrate on the efforts of the more flamboyant characters, like Brunel and Churchward, who blazed a trail across the railway world and turned bold schemes into reality, but, inevitably, it was the thousands of unknown Great Western employees who made the huge network run smoothly. The GWR was, for the most part, what used to be called a 'paternalistic' employer, providing support and assistance to its staff, for both philanthropic and pragmatic reasons; this benevolence was rewarded by a workforce that was intensely loyal to the company, maintaining its long-standing traditions and being extremely proud of its achievements. The term 'God's Wonderful Railway' was not invented by the GWR, but this interpretation of the company initials was one fully endorsed by staff, who were quick to praise its glorious past and defend its operation against 'foreign' companies.

Below: *The GWR ran more than just train services; this Guy motor omnibus, fitted with a John Buckingham body, is seen outside Torquay station in June 1927.*

CHAPTER ONE

BRUNEL'S GREAT WESTERN: 1835-1841

Rome was not built in a day, neither was the Great Western Railway' wrote an anonymous historian, more than 20 years after the line between London and Bristol had opened in 1841. By the 1860s the GWR's network already extended well beyond that original route, pushing into the West Country, Wales and the Midlands, and railways were well on their way to becoming an accepted part of the nation's landscape. From a modern perspective it is difficult to imagine the enormous revolution brought about by railways in so short a time; Benjamin Disraeli described their advance as 'absolutely prodigious', and although this industrial revolution 'outside factory walls' was largely bloodless it nevertheless marked an outpouring of energy and activity on a scale not previously seen.

Even by today's standards the pace of railway development was staggering. By the early 1860s — less than 40 years after the opening (in 1825) of the first important railway, the Stockton & Darlington — more than 10,000 miles of line were in operation. The sensation caused by the opening of the S&D led to many other similar schemes' being contemplated and promoted, and in Bristol this (and the subsequent success of the Liverpool & Manchester Railway, opened in 1830) served only to reinforce the belief among the business community that without a railway the city would lose ground to other commercial centres.

Even before the promotion of the scheme that eventually became known as the Great Western Railway a number of speculative schemes had already been proposed, but a lack of money — and the Bristol riots of 1831 —

curtailed any investment. Matters improved following the passing of the Reform Bill in 1832, and in the autumn of that year four Bristol businessmen — Thomas Guppy, George Jones, John Harford and William Tothill — determined to resurrect the promotion of a railway to London. By the end of the year they had convinced some of Bristol's most important commercial institutions — the City Council, the Chamber of Commerce, the Dock Company and the Society of Merchant Venturers — to investigate the proposal further, and by early 1833 a committee had been formed that included representatives from these bodies.

To move the project onwards the committee agreed to commission a survey of the route, the cheapest winning the job. It was a director of the Bristol Dock Company, Nicholas Roch, who introduced to the promoters of the railway the man who was to have such a significant effect on the subbsequent history of the GWR. Isambard Kingdom Brunel was a 26-year-old engineer who five years earlier had arrived in Bristol to convalesce after a near-fatal accident in the Thames Tunnel, where he had been working for his father, Marc Isambard Brunel. During his time in Bristol he had already gained something of a reputation, winning a competition to design a bridge over the Avon Gorge at Clifton and acting as consultant to the Bristol Dock Company, where he had met Roch.

In typical fashion, Isambard wrote to the committee, telling them that they were 'holding out a premium to the man who makes you the most flattering promises' and that he would survey only a route that was the best and not necessarily the cheapest. This was clearly a bold strategy and depended on the positive impression he had made on the promoters with his designs for the Clifton Bridge and Dock works. The gamble paid off, although his appointment was approved by only one vote.

Brunel was appointed Engineer on 7 March 1833, and he and his assistant, W. H. Townsend, agreed to carry out a survey of the route of the new line for £500. Within months they had considered two routes — one passing through the Kennet valley, Marlborough Downs and Vale of Pewsey, the other more northerly, via Bath, Swindon and the Thames Valley. Brunel chose the latter, as it allowed for better gradients and would also enable the railway to be extended in later years to Oxford, Gloucester and South Wales. After a successful public meeting in Bristol on 30 July 1833 committees of directors in both Bristol and London were created with the aim of both raising the capital to build the railway and obtaining an Act of Parliament.

In 1833 a joint meeting of the two committees agreed that the new line should be known as the Great Western Railway (rather than the Bristol & London Railroad), in the hope that the grander name might attract more capital from investors. Brunel was then instructed in September 1833 to carry out a more detailed survey with the intention of gaining Parliamentary assent the following year. Brunel entered into this task with characteristic gusto — and considerable diplomacy, for not everyone viewed the coming of the railway with enthusiasm. Whilst opposition to the new line was widely reported in newspapers, away from the city what one writer called 'the dogged resistance of the landed proprietary' made life difficult for Brunel and his team of surveyors, who resorted to a combination of diplomacy and cunning to gain access to land over which the railway was to run.

Slow progress in raising capital meant that powers were sought only for the Bristol–Bath and Reading–London sections of Brunel's railway, with the hope that, if this scheme were approved, further investors would provide the capital needed to complete the line. The trials and tribulations of the survey were nothing compared to what was to follow

Below: The route of the original Great Western Railway as shown in the company's second prospectus, issued in 1834.

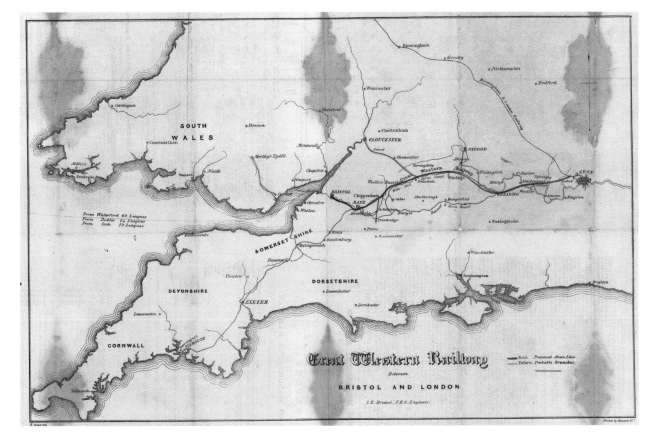

in Parliament when the bill was debated. The company had to endure a marathon 57-day committee session, during which every aspect of the proposed railway was discussed, and evidence taken from all manner of opponents and supporters of the GWR. Brunel bore the brunt of much of the questioning, but approval of the Bill by the Commons was followed by a decisive defeat in the Lords, one describing the railway as 'a fraud upon the public in name, in title and in substance'.

Another prospectus was issued, and strenuous efforts were made to raise enough capital for the new, complete scheme to build the railway, now at an estimated cost of £2.5 million. Public meetings to canvass support were held at locations along the route of the proposed line, and the efforts of the directors, Brunel himself and Charles Saunders, the GWR Company Secretary, ensured that by the early part of 1835 more than £2 million had been promised by investors, allowing a second bill for the construction of the whole line to be submitted to Parliament. After the prolonged discussions that characterised the first bill's passage through the House of Commons committee it was hoped that the new proposal would receive an easier ride. Despite support from the Committee Chairman, Reading MP Charles Russell, proceedings still extended to 40 days, Brunel once again taking centre stage, answering questions on many aspects of the proposed line. Eventually all objections were overcome, and the Great Western Railway Bill was finally passed on 31 August. The birth of Brunel's new railway had not come cheap; in October 1835, at the first half-yearly general meeting after the passing of the Act, shareholders were informed that of almost £89,000 so far spent by the company, £18,168 had been used to fund Brunel's survey of the route, land valuation and expenses for professional witnesses in Parliament. Moreover, a staggering £38,771 had been spent on solicitors' bills and other legal fees, although the directors noted that this expense 'may fairly be considered by no means disproportionate to the object attained'.

Running to 127 pages, the Great Western Railway Act 1835 includes a description of the land the new railway would traverse, beginning with the parish of Temple, 'otherwise Holy Cross in the City and County of the city of Bristol', and concluding with that of Hammersmith, 'wherein a certain field [lies] between the Paddington canal and the turnpike road leading from London to Harrow on the western side of the general cemetery'. The Act's 251 clauses also include details relating to the width of a bridge near Maidenhead, directions on preventing toll-keepers' misbehaving and specific instructions regarding the protection of springs, rivers and other watercourses.

Detailed lists of landowners and tenants affected by the construction of the GWR provide a fascinating snapshot of England's rural landscape before the coming of the railways. West of Swindon, in the parish of Wroughton, details were recorded of a 'Coppice, Pasture field, Green Lane, Cowhouse, Willow Bed, Brook and Orchard' close to Toot Hill Farm — land owned by the governors of 'Charter House School' but occupied by various individuals, including Thomas Spackman, John King and William Matthews. Closer to Swindon, sections of 'canal and towing path' belonging to the North Wilts Canal were also acquired by the GWR, whilst further east, in the parish of Stratton St Margaret, pasture fields owned by Merton College, Oxford, and the Trustees of the 'Hannington Poor', as well as various members of the aristocracy, were also listed as being needed for the building of Brunel's new line.

With the passing of the GWR Act, work on construction began almost immediately; as one contemporary writer noted, 'No efforts were spared by the directors and officials of the new undertaking to mature their project in the shortest possible time'. The first contract, for the building of Wharncliffe Viaduct, was awarded in November 1835, and the rest of the work was divided into contracts of various sizes and values, construction taking place at both ends of the line. From early on it was clear that the hiatus between the two GWR bills had enabled Brunel to formulate a clear vision of what he was to call 'the finest work in England'. This new railway was to be no carbon copy of other existing or planned lines; instead it was to be a completely new design, with innovatory architecture, motive power and track formation and, most importantly a radically different track gauge of 7ft — the 'broad gauge'. Giving evidence to the Gauge Commission in 1845, Brunel would argue that the decision to adopt this novel idea grew upon him 'gradually', but GWR directors did not hear of this important development until a month after the passing of the GWR Act, in September 1835, when in a special report he recommended that, with regard to track gauge, they should approve 'a deviation from the dimensions adopted in the railways hitherto constructed'. It is unlikely that many directors learned much from the highly technical report, which was full of references to friction, resistance and wheel sizes, although Brunel did outline some of the disadvantages of the new system, namely increased costs of earthworks, bridges and tunnels.

A further problem highlighted by Brunel in his report was the inconvenience of effecting a junction with the London & Birmingham Railway. Describing this as an inconvenience was an understatement, for it had originally been planned that the GWR and the L&B would share a station at Euston. The idea of two companies' sharing one large central station was a far-sighted one, but ultimately differences and misunderstandings with the directors and officers of the London &

Birmingham meant that the arrangement collapsed, the two parties being unable to agree terms. Whilst the adoption of the broad gauge is often cited as the cause of this rift, the fact that the London & Birmingham refused to offer the Great Western anything more than a five-year lease on land and buildings at Euston cannot have helped. Although directors of both companies met in November 1835 no agreement could be reached, and early in 1836 it was announced that the GWR would instead build its own terminus at Paddington, in West London. By August land had been purchased and a further bill deposited before Parliament for these new arrangements.

The Great Western station at Paddington was, initially at least, the poor relation to some of the grander designs produced by Brunel for cities like Bath and Bristol. Much capital had already been committed to the building of the line, so facilities for passengers at Paddington were somewhat modest, although a correspondent writing for *The Railway Magazine* in 1838 noted that its entrance gates and piers, with a gatekeeper's lodge in the centre, were substantial, and that the station was 'sufficient without any pretensions to

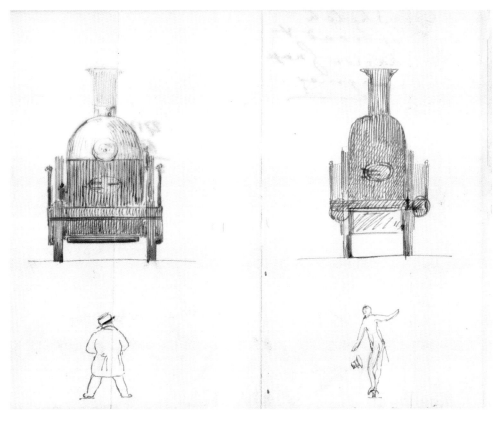

Left: *An early cartoon illustrating the differences between broad and narrow gauge.*

splendour'. Others were less complimentary, one writer describing the station as 'a dark and dirty wooden shed on the west side of Bishops Road Bridge'. Brunel eventually managed to design a London terminus fit for an important regional railway like the GWR, but it would be more than a decade before the company could afford it. Perhaps sensing that the facilities at Paddington were not to the liking of the directors, Brunel informed a meeting of shareholders held in February 1837 that the purchase of land to build the station would save the company £25,000 per year, as opposed to the rent of land and cost of joint working with the London & Birmingham. However, a critic writing in the 1860s felt that in the circumstances this forecast was somewhat 'sanguine'.

An unknown correspondent for the original *Great Western Magazine* in 1864 noted that there was 'nothing more thoroughly uninteresting to the general public ... than the details of the construction of a railway' and that as soon as the railway was constructed the process by which it became a railway was forgotten by those who travelled on it. Although it is probably true that passengers on the new line had little interest in the obstacles encountered in constructing the GWR, there is, even today, much to marvel about in the

story of the construction of Brunel's Great Western. It is easy to forget, as one speeds along the GWR main line at over 100mph, that the railway still in use today is the result largely of human toil. The navvies who built it were undoubtedly a tough bunch, with little or no mechanical help available to excavate cuttings and tunnels or build bridges, embankments and stations.

Many of the workmen employed by contractors building the Great Western had helped build canals in earlier years; the writer Samuel Smiles gives a fascinating pen portrait of a navvy, noting that they usually wore a white felt hat with its brim turned up, a velveteen or jean square-tailed coat, a scarlet waistcoat with 'little black spots' and a bright coloured kerchief round his 'Herculean' neck. Corduroy breeches retained by leather belt, tied and buttoned at the knee, completed the outfit, displaying a 'solid calf and foot' encased in strong high-laced boots. As the pace of work on the new line began to grow the navvies' powers of endurance were sorely tested, men often working 12- to 16-hour days.

It seemed that after the difficulties encountered in the Parliamentary stages, it was wiser to get on with the work as fast as possible, even though the cost was ultimately greater. Pushing out into Berkshire from the

Below: A view of the Great Western Railway's first terminus at Paddington, not long after it opened for business in 1838. The ticket office was situated beneath one of the arches of Bishops Road Bridge.

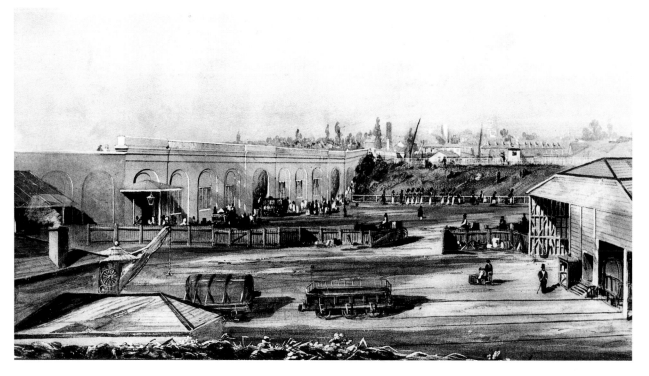

capital, the route of the railway followed the course of the Thames. Unlike the urban sprawl through which trains now run leaving the capital, a 19th-century travel guide describing the landscape and monuments close to the GWR main line noted that 'pretty and fresh is the country through which the traveller is hurried along the fine "broad gauge" which opens out boldly towards the sunny south-west'.

The story of Brunel's magnificent bridge at Maidenhead is described elsewhere in this book, and this great structure was still unfinished on 4 June 1838, when the first scheduled GWR passenger service ran to and from Paddington to a temporary station named 'Maidenhead' which in reality was at Taplow, more than a mile away. The opening of this first stretch of line had already been delayed, and the London terminus was barely complete, with Brunel's broad-gauge track laid without ballast. The first train, hauled by the locomotive *Aeolus*, left Paddington promptly at 8am as timetabled with three First- and five Second-class carriages but took no less than 90 minutes to complete the short journey; this inauspicious beginning was thought to have been as a result of the locomotive's suffering a leaking or collapsing tube at West Drayton, causing the fire to be put out. The locomotive of the next train was forced to push *Aeolus*'s carriages in front of it to Maidenhead, as well as hauling its own carriages. As railway historian Adrian Vaughan later reported, the train was not late, as the first GWR timetable neglected to record any arrival times for its trains!

The first timetable issued by the Great Western — a simple handbill printed at the post office in Maidenhead — reveals fares for the journey to London, ranging from 5s 6d (27½p) for a seat in a First-class coach to 4s (20p) in Second class. These fares undercut dramatically the cost of travelling the same journey by carriage which, the diary of George Henry Gibbs a GWR director revealed, could cost up to 10s. As well as researching coach fares the company had carried out censuses of road traffic at various locations in the months after the GWR bill received Royal Assent, in an effort to gain more information about likely competition for the new railway. Observers at Colnbrook and Hanwell recorded the passage of 123 'stage coaches', 143 'post chaises and private carriages' and 105 'mounted horses' in a one-week period.

The first timetable noted that passengers could join trains at Hanwell, West Drayton and Slough, where, initially at least, there was no station. The reason for this omission was that during the committee stages of the GWR bill, the authorities at Eton College had objected to the railway, claiming that it would be 'injurious' to the morals of the scholars there. As a result there were five clauses in the Act of Parliament relating to the College, the most important being that the company agreed not to site a station within three miles of it; in addition it was forced to build and keep in good repair a 'good and sufficient fence' to keep the boys away from the railway. If this were not enough, the company had also to employ several members of staff to patrol the line at this point, and this arrangement was still in place in the early 1860s. The Act stated that these men, who were to be paid by the company, were however under the control of the college, which retained the right to have them dismissed at any time.

Undeterred, the Great Western was forced to resort to unorthodox methods to provide passenger facilities for Slough residents, who had petitioned the Provost of Eton College to relax its opposition without success. It made use of a public house, close to the line, where tickets could be purchased, passengers climbing into carriages from the lineside. This imaginative but makeshift arrangement to circumvent the Act was soon challenged by the College in the Court of Chancery but was dismissed, as the actual arrangements did not break the letter of the law. It was almost two years before the College finally relented, possibly following pressure from the nearby Royal household at Windsor, and a proper station at Slough was finally opened in June 1840.

A different battle faced Brunel and the company further east at Sonning, where the excavation of a two-mile-long cutting proved to be a challenge of a different type. The contractor employed to complete this section of line, William Ranger, ran into trouble in the spring of 1838 when a combination of poor weather, waterlogged ground and lack of manpower meant that the work came to a virtual halt. Ranger ran out of money to pay the navvies, who promptly marched to the nearby town of Reading where eventually only promises from the mayor prevented a major breach of the peace. Ranger was dismissed in August 1838, and the company was forced to take over the contract, Brunel supervising the work personally. The completion of the cutting became an epic battle against the elements and the local geology, the combination of sand, clay and gravel leading to frequent landslips. More than 1,200 navvies and 200 horses toiled in a sea of mud for more than a year before the cutting was finally completed at the end of 1839.

The completion of work at Sonning enabled the Great Western to run trains from Paddington to Reading, and the first scheduled service ran on 30 March 1840, hauled by 2-2-2 *Fire Fly*, the first engine designed by the company's young Locomotive Superintendent, Daniel Gooch. Gooch had begun work for the GWR in August 1837, bringing some order to the motley selection of engines built for the company to specifications supplied by Brunel himself. His diaries record the fact that of all the engines delivered to the railway, only the Stephenson-designed *North Star* and six locomotives built by the Vulcan Foundry could be relied on. After the opening of the first section of line in 1838 Gooch wrote that 'for many weeks my nights were spent in a carriage in the engine house at Paddington, as repairs had to be done to the engines to get them to do their work next day'.

With the introduction of his 'Fire Fly' class Gooch could, he noted, be certain that they would not break down on the journey, but also that they could haul trains at high speeds. It is possible that reports of the engine reaching a speed of 56mph subsequently led to a rumour reported in the *Railway Times*. It was that a GWR driver obtained permission from Gooch to run one of his new engines as fast as possible, having previously obtained an agreement that in the event of any accident, provision should be made for his widow and children. The paper added that a distance of 28 miles was covered at a speed of more than 100mph. Perhaps nervous about the veracity of this story, the paper concluded: 'We give the rumour precisely as it reached us; we do not vouch for its truth.'

As spring turned to summer, further sections of line were opened; by June it had reached Steventon near Didcot, and just over a month later the company was able to announce that the line was complete to Faringdon Road near Swindon. The arrival of the GWR in this Wiltshire market town was the beginning of a proud railway history and is told elsewhere in this celebration. West of Swindon both Brunel and the hundreds of navvies toiling to complete the line had a far tougher landscape to cope with. The great engineer had made enormous efforts to ensure that the gradient between London and Swindon was as shallow as possible, managing to maintain a ruling gradient of 1 in 1320, leading to this stretch of line being nicknamed 'Brunel's Billiard Table' by company staff. After Wootton Bassett the route to Bath included a number of inclines, deep cuttings and embankments and probably the most difficult task on the whole railway, the excavation of a tunnel through Box Hill, near Corsham.

Some idea of the difficulties facing Brunel can be gauged by the fact that after Chippenham the railway ran along an embankment for two miles, and then continued through a cutting for a further three miles before reaching his greatest achievement on the line, the Box Tunnel. Driven through a 400ft-high hill consisting of oolitic limestone and Fuller's earth, the tunnel had been a source of controversy during the committee stages of the GWR bill. Many people were convinced that such a 'monstrous

Right: *This composite picture of Sir Daniel Gooch was probably created by the photographer at Swindon Works but serves to illustrate the two roles he played during a 52-year association with the Great Western.*

SIR **DANIEL GOOCH** BART

CHIEF LOCOMOTIVE SUPERINTENDENT
GREAT WESTERN RAILWAY COMPANY OF ENGLAND
1837 TO 1864

and extraordinary' tunnel would be dangerous, one critic arguing: 'The inevitable, if not the necessary consequence of constructing such a tunnel would be occasionally the wholesale destruction of human life, and that no cure, no foresight, no means that had ever been applied up to that time could prevent it.'

Contracts to build the tunnel were let early in 1838, the majority of the excavation being handled by Kent contractor George Burge, who was to be responsible for all but 2,820ft of tunnel, the remaining work being carried out by Brewer & Lewis, a local concern. It was hoped that the work could be completed by August 1840, but this ambitious target proved wildly optimistic. With a length of 9,680ft, it was the longest tunnel yet built, and the hard limestone through which it was driven proved to be a formidable obstacle. A ton of gunpowder a week was used to blast the limestone, but most other tasks were left to the navvies, who used more than a ton of candles each week. More than 3,000 navvies were employed on a shift system, and since there was a shortage of accommodation in the local area, many 'played Box and Cox', as one contemporary writer called it, those on night shift climbing straight into the beds of the day shift as they turned out of them in the morning.

Problems were encountered with flooding in the excavations, and the *Great Western Magazine* reported that the influx of water 'occasioned great expenditure of labour as well as considerable annoyance'. Extra pumps were required and Burge fell behind schedule, incurring the wrath of Brunel. The planned completion date of August 1840 passed, Brunel reporting to shareholders that five-sixths of

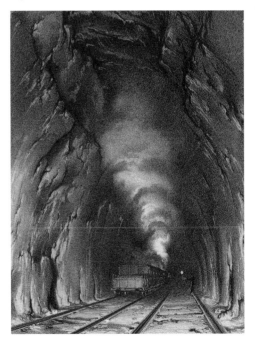

Above: *Photographs of early broad-gauge GWR locomotives are not common, and even this picture of 'Fire Fly' 2-2-2* Argus, *built in 1842 by Fenton, Murray & Jackson, has been heavily retouched at some stage. It also shows that the locomotive tender is fitted with a 'coffin' — a rearward-facing seat occupied by a guard who operated the train brakes when required.*

Left: *Although in later years the interior of Box Tunnel was lined with brick, this Bourne lithograph clearly shows the oolitic limestone through which the tunnel had been driven.*

Right: *A rather stylised drawing of the opening of the Box Tunnel on 30 June 1841. The caption also recounts the tale that on 9 April, Brunel's birthday, the sun shines through the tunnel — something that has never been conclusively proven.*

Below: *The overall roof of Bath station is clearly visible in this Bourne engraving of St James Bridge, along with a very tall disc-and-crossbar signal. Although the roof was removed before 1900 the station frontage remains largely unaltered today.*

Opposite top: *The magnificent 'mock' hammer-beam roof of Brunel's station in Bristol. The terminus was built on a viaduct, so passengers ascended and descended steps to and from the ticket office to the platforms. Railway staff can be seen pushing a carriage truck complete with a passenger's horse-drawn carriage down towards a traverser situated at the west end of the station.*

Opposite bottom: *The Great Western Railway was the result of not only Isambard Kingdom Brunel's civil-engineering genius but also the muscle of the navvies who blasted rock and shifted spoil to turn his ideas into reality. This J. C. Bourne lithograph shows the east end of Foxes Wood Tunnel, between Bristol and Bath.*

the tunnel was now complete and that it would be finished by February the following year. In the event it would be another 10 months before trains could run through the tunnel, after additional workmen and materials had been drafted in to assist with Gooch and Brunel personally supervising the final stages of the work.

The west portal of the tunnel served as a gateway to the West Country, and with the Bristol–Bath section of line already complete, the opening of Box Tunnel on 30 June 1841 meant that the Great Western Railway main line was finally complete although the *Railway Times* reported that passage through the tunnel was made 'with a degree of slowness and caution which is unusual in the case of finished works', suggesting that the tunnel was literally only just complete!

After almost six years of struggle, Brunel's vision had finally become a reality. In contrast to the events of earlier years, the opening of the line was marked with little ceremony; a directors' special left Paddington at 8am, arriving in Bristol four hours later. To have travelled such a distance so quickly was no mean achievement, but by 1841 the novelty of railways was beginning to fade, for the inhabitants of Bristol and London at least. The *Railway Times* reported the 'completion of this magnificent undertaking', qualifying its praise by noting that, whilst it would 'sink all differences of opinion on points of construction and management', it congratulated the company's directors 'on the successful completion and general results of their enterprise'.

CHAPTER TWO

ENGINEERING EXELLENCE

By the GWR's centenary in 1935 the company's Chief Civil Engineer was responsible for a huge network of more than 9,000 miles of track, and his department was responsible for the maintenance of not only the permanent way but also bridges, tunnels, embankments and cuttings. An article in *The Times* argued that the Engineering Department was in effect responsible for 'everything that is without movement' on the railway, so also built and maintained stations, goods and locomotive depots, offices and hundreds of miles of sidings. After the Grouping of 1923 the acquisition of substantial docks in South Wales added to this workload. It is hardly surprising, therefore, that at any one time the Engineering Department employed between 15,000 and 19,000 people, according to workload.

Although many of the bridges, tunnels and buildings maintained by the Civil Engineer's Department were relatively unglamorous and workmanlike, the GWR network included numerous landmark structures, many of which still form part of the working railway today. The construction of many played a vital part in the story of the GWR described throughout this book, but this chapter will highlight a number of the most important in more detail.

Given the enormous influence he had over the early development of the Great Western, it is not surprising that some of the most significant engineering achievements on the network were the work of Brunel. The construction of the London–Bristol line presented the great engineer with a number of difficult and different challenges; only a few miles from his Paddington terminus the railway had to cross the Brent Valley at Hanwell, where instead of using millions of tons of earth to construct a long embankment he designed an elegant viaduct that was 896ft long and 65ft high. Completed in 1837, Wharncliffe Viaduct took 14 months to build and consisted of eight semi-elliptical arches, each with a span of 70ft. The piers of the viaduct were sunk down through the gravel of the river valley into the London clay below and were styled to resemble the columns of an Egyptian temple, a motif Brunel used elsewhere on the railway. Named after Lord Wharncliffe, Chairman of the House of Lords committee that had considered the GWR bill, the viaduct was widened in the 1870s when the line was quadrupled and remains one of the most imposing structures at the London end.

Brunel had spent much time planning the route of the Great Western to ensure that its ruling gradient remained as gentle as possible. When the new railway reached Maidenhead he was faced with the challenge of crossing the Thames at a point where the river was around 300ft across. At the time the railway was under construction the river was still navigable, and sufficient clearance needed to be allowed for barges to pass under the bridge. Adrian Vaughan describes how Brunel designed the bridge on a piece of 12in x 10in cartridge paper, sketching out a bridge with two arches separated by a central pier resting on an island mid-stream. The result was a bridge with two of the flattest and largest arches ever designed, what Vaughan concludes was the 'greatest brick bridge ever built'. Writing in 1870, Brunel's son argued that the bridge was 'remarkable for not only the boldness and ingenuity of its design but also for the gracefulness of its appearance'.

When the plans for this amazing bridge became public Brunel faced much criticism from engineers and the press. The 128ft-wide flat arches could not possibly stand, they argued, and in 1838, when minor distortion of the brickwork was revealed with the easing of the centrings, this criticism intensified. Despite the contractor's admission that the problem had been due to the cement's not fully setting, at the insistence of GWR directors the wooden centrings remained in place long after repairs had taken place, giving the impression that they were supporting the bridge. Brunel agreed, in the knowledge that the centres had already settled and were not supporting the bridge at all. When a storm finally blew the centres down in the autumn of 1839 the bridge did not fall down, as the experts had predicted, and has remained standing ever since. Brunel would no doubt have been pleased to see that half a century later the company used his designs to widen the bridge to accommodate the quadrupling of the GWR main line, although the construction of a slightly smaller structure took a year longer than it had in 1838.

As his son argues in his biography of the great engineer, there is little doubt that, had Maidenhead Bridge been designed even a few years later, Isambard Kingdom Brunel would probably have used timber or iron to span the Thames at this point, and, as engineering technology improved, Brunel did indeed use such materials to good effect elsewhere. By the late 1840s he had designed an elegant 'bow-string' wrought-iron girder bridge to cross the Thames. This bridge was, however, on a short branch from Slough to Windsor and opened for traffic in 1849. More unconventional was a much larger bridge built to cross the River Wye at Chepstow, on the South Wales Railway. This four-span structure was a complicated project, not least because of the terrain. On the Gloucestershire side of the river the railway plunged through a deep cutting which ended with a sheer drop and cliff face to the river beneath. Over 120ft below on the other side of the Wye was a muddy river bank, which meant that foundations for the piers of the bridge were sunk through 40ft of slimy mud and silt, with the additional danger that the work might be overwhelmed by high tides.

The three bridge spans on the Welsh shore were supported by cast iron tubes which had been sunk through the mud until bedrock was reached. Once mud had been excavated from the tubes they were filled with concrete to form a very strong foundation on which the bridge could sit. The main 300ft bridge span was supported by two towers, one constructed of iron on a pier above the river, the other a stone structure on the Gloucestershire side of the river. In between Brunel designed a unique structure which consisted of two wrought iron tubes which ran between the towers, under which the bridge was suspended using struts and suspension chains. By far the most difficult aspect of the construction process was the lifting of the tubes into position. The 9ft-diameter tubes had been built on the banks of the Wye, and on 8 April 1852 were hauled into position below the towers. Timing the operation to coincide with the rising tide, Brunel supervised the delicate manœuvre of

Below: The baronial shield of Lord Wharncliffe is clearly seen in this photograph of the viaduct named after him. The massive brick bridge supports also demonstrate the Egyptian styling adopted by Brunel.

lifting the tubes firstly up to the level of the railway and then finally to the tops of the towers.

The unusual design of this bridge proved adequate for most traffic using the South Wales line for almost a century, especially since the opening of the Severn Tunnel had taken much of the heaviest traffic away from the route. However, the heavier and more frequent trains that used the bridge during World War 2 changed matters, and in 1944 part of the Welsh span began to flex, resulting in a speed restriction of 25mph (reduced in later years to 15mph). The Welsh spans were replaced in 1948, but in 1962 a brand-new bridge was constructed, replacing the Brunel structure after almost a century of service.

Within a few months of the opening of Chepstow Bridge in July 1852 Brunel had completed plans for a much larger bridge, also using wrought-iron tubes. As Engineer of the Cornwall Railway he had been faced with a number of major difficulties, the most serious being the terrain over which he was to build his railway. It was estimated that between Plymouth and Falmouth 42 viaducts would be needed to cross the many deep valleys that characterised the Cornish landscape; matters were not helped by the poor financial position of the company itself, which meant that many of these viaducts would be built from timber rather than masonry as an economy measure — a move that in years to come would cost the GWR dear.

Despite the difficulties Brunel had told a House of Commons committee in 1845 that 'The Cornish line is a thing I have looked forward to for some time. By far the greatest obstacle on the route of the line was the crossing of the River Tamar at Saltash, and when the idea of a train ferry was rejected in 1845 Brunel returned to the river to survey a new scheme which would carry the railway from Devon to Cornwall by means of a high-level bridge. Work on the line began after the passing of the Cornwall Railway Act in 1846, but a shortage of funds made progress slow. Brunel's final design for the bridge was subject to a number of challenges: at this point the Tamar was more than 70ft deep at high tide, and a clearance of 100ft was required to allow sailing ships to pass under the bridge. The design finally chosen called for a 19-span, 2,200ft-long bridge which consisted of two main spans, with one bridge pier in the centre of the channel and two further main piers on either bank. The other side spans varied in size, the largest being 90ft long.

Constructing a large central bridge pier in 80ft of water — the deepest underwater foundations yet built — proved a challenge in itself; Brunel tackled the problem by designing an 85ft-high iron cylinder that, once built, was floated to the centre of the river and then sunk in a vertical position. Once the water had been removed, workmen were able with the aid of compressed air and pumps to excavate to bedrock and then build a stone pier to 12ft above the high-water mark. By 1856 this work was complete, and the cylinder dismantled; at the same time the two great bridge trusses were built on the bank of the River Tamar. The trusses were of a unique design consisting of a wrought-iron arched tube and suspension bridge, each 455ft long and 56ft wide. In an operation supervised personally by Brunel, the first 1,000-ton truss was floated out on pontoons and secured to the base of the piers

on 1 September 1857, the whole being watched by thousands of people and accompanied by a military band playing 'See the Conquering Hero Comes'. The truss was then gradually lifted by hydraulic jacks, workmen building the masonry underneath until it was finally raised to the correct height — a process completed in May 1858.

The second truss was floated into position a month later, but Brunel's failing health meant that his assistant, R. P. Brereton, supervised the operation instead. By February 1859 the truss had been fully raised, and the bridge was completed by the addition of a girder structure carrying the track, which was suspended from chains which had been sold to the railway by the Clifton Bridge Company. On 2 May 1859 the bridge was formally opened by Prince Albert, but Brunel was too ill to attend the

Below: *Chepstow Bridge, viewed in the direction of Gloucester. The suspension chains can clearly be seen, with the wrought iron tubes above.*

Right: *Brunel's timber viaduct seemed an ideal solution for railways in the West of England, short of capital for expensive stone structures. Bridges like this one at Penryn were cheap to build, but eventually cost the GWR dear when heavier trains, and wear and tear necessitated their replacement.*

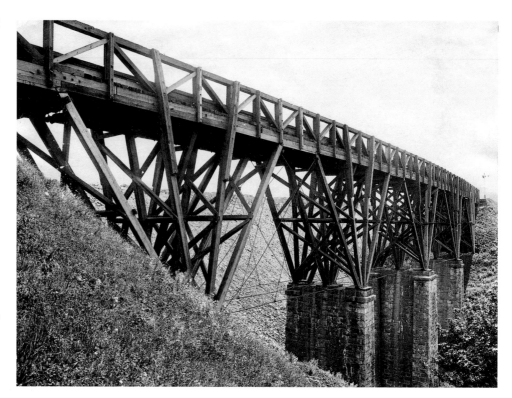

Below: *The Royal Albert Bridge at Saltash under construction. There is still much to be done; one bridge truss has been jacked into position, but the other Devon span is still under construction on the bank of the River Tamar. This was floated into position in July 1858, but it would be eight months before it was finally secured.*

ceremony, his only proper view of his creation being from a couch resting on a broad-gauge wagon run slowly across the bridge. Within months Brunel was dead, and in the half-yearly report of the directors of the Cornwall Railway issued in September 1859 it was noted that 'Considering the extraordinary difficulties which were overcome and the magnitude of the operation, it is believed that there is no engineering work in existence which has been more economically completed.' The bridge had cost £225,000, and biographer Stephen Brindle has argued that the Royal Albert Bridge at Saltash was unique in that it was Brunel's only major project 'to be completed on time, to budget and without loss of life during its construction.'

Less than 20 years after the death of Brunel, a man whose achievements had typified the pioneering spirit of the Great Western, the company completed a project that, for some, equalled or exceeded anything done in his time. The construction of the Severn Tunnel was truly the most difficult project ever undertaken by the company, and its completion was, argued company historian W. G. Chapman, 'outmatched by no experience in the long account of human endeavour'. Whilst one might well argue with this

Above: A very early photograph, c1870, of the Royal Albert Bridge in use, with a broad-gauge train leaving Saltash station.

Left: At track level the view from underneath one of the Saltash Bridge portals is very impressive, the massive tube and suspension chains being well in evidence.

Right: *A section and plan of the Severn Tunnel originally reproduced in the GWR Magazine.*

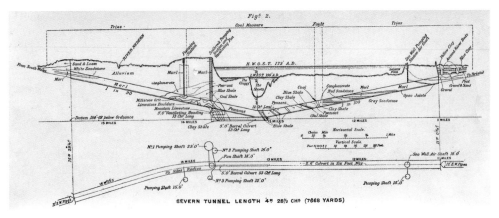

hyperbole, there is little doubt that the building of what was then the longest underwater railway tunnel in the world was a tremendous achievement, and its 13-year-long story was a battle with the forces of nature. In his 1888 account of the building of the tunnel, Sir Thomas Walker wrote: 'Sub-aqueous tunnels have recently become quite the fashion … the Severn Tunnel, with its ever-varying and contorted strata, and the dangers from floods above and floods below has been sufficient for me. One sub-aqueous tunnel is quite enough for a lifetime.'

The long circuitous route to South Wales had until the completion of the tunnel, been via Gloucester for the heaviest goods and mineral traffic, and for passengers via a ferry which plied a route between New Passage, near Aust, on the English side and Portskewett on the Welsh side. It was not until the 1870s that funds were available to allow the construction of a tunnel to finally take place. An Act of Parliament was passed in 1872 authorising the GWR to build a tunnel which would run from the old Bristol & South Wales Union Railway at Pilning, north of Bristol, under the River Severn to join the South Wales line at Rogiet (later named Severn Tunnel Junction). The tunnel was to be built at a location called the English Stones, where the Severn estuary was 2¼ miles wide. The major obstacle was an 80ft-deep channel named 'The Shoots', and to overcome this a 4 ½-mile tunnel was planned, running half under land and half under the river. The design aimed to carry the tunnel 35ft below The Shoots, which would entail a gradient of 1 in 100 on the English side, a short 538ft level section in the middle of the river and a 1-in-90 climb back into Wales.

Construction was supervised initially by Charles Richardson, an engineer who had been a pupil of both Isambard Kingdom Brunel and his father, Sir John Hawkshaw being retained as the consulting engineer. Work began in 1873 with the sinking of a shaft on the Welsh side of the river at Sudbrook. From there a tunnel or 'heading' was excavated eastwards towards the Shoots, to ascertain something of the detailed geology under the river. Progress was slow, and by August 1877 a 7ft heading had only been driven around 1,600 yards. Tenders had been sought for contractors to undertake the whole project, but uncertainties about what they might find led to high prices' being quoted. As a result the Great Western decided instead to carry out further investigations by the sinking of more shafts along the route of the tunnel.

At the same time work started in earnest, heading west from the first 'old' shaft. The method of excavating the tunnel was to drive two 7ft headings through the tough sandstone rock, one above the other. The upper and lower headings were ultimately linked together, and the complete tunnel was excavated to the correct profile. In October 1879 disaster struck, not in the workings under the river but in a heading rising to the west, when a large freshwater spring was struck, causing water to pour in at a rate of 6,000 gallons a minute. Pumps installed at Sudbrook simply could not cope with the deluge, and within 24 hours all the workings were completely flooded.

This disastrous setback could have been the end of the project, but, undaunted, GWR management under the direction of Gooch instead pressed on, putting Hawkshaw in charge of the work and appointing Thomas

Walker as principal contractor. Walker agreed to build the tunnel for £948,959, and the scene that greeted him when he finally took over the work in 1879 can hardly have been encouraging, most of the workings being under water. The most urgent task was to install more pumps, in order to raise water out of the headings at a faster rate than it was filling them up and to dam the source of the flooding. Attempts to block what had become known as the 'Great Spring' with an oak shield failed whilst Walker scoured Britain to find additional pumps that could be used to drain the tunnel. Extra shafts were dug, and when larger pumps finally arrived in July 1880 the struggle seemed to be easing, but the complete failure of one of the new pumps caused the shaft to fill yet again.

It took several months to acquire enough pumping capacity to begin again, and in October a further attempt was made to clear the workings. Levels dropped, but it was clear that whilst pumps could now hold water levels, more drastic action was required. It was discovered that during the first inrush of the Great Spring, an iron door in a headwall 1,000ft into the tunnel had been left open; closing the door and screwing down the valves of two pipes running through the wall would, it was hoped, stem the flow of water. The only way to do this was to send down a diver, and so Alexander Lambert, assisted by two colleagues manhandling his air hose, groped his way along the tunnel in total darkness, climbing over abandoned tools, wagons and other debris. It is hard to imagine the courage and mental toughness needed to carry out this task, especially when his first attempt failed, largely because of drag from the unwieldy air hoses he was using. Lambert finally succeeded when he used a new self-contained portable oxygen supply developed by Henry Fleuss RN. However, the navy man could hardly have filled Lambert with confidence when he declared that he would not do the job for £10,000! On 8 November 1880 Lambert finally reached the headwall, closed the door and screwed down the valves but was unfortunately unaware that one had a left-hand thread and thus stayed open. Despite this setback the battle was finally won, and with the blocking off of the Great Spring in early 1881 work on the tunnel could finally surge ahead.

The huge scale of this undertaking was apparent from the small settlement that sprang up at Sudbrook to service the project. As well as houses for the workforce there was a hospital, mission hall, post office and school. A large brickworks was also built to manufacture the staggering 76 million bricks eventually used in the construction process. By September 1881 headings from east and west had been joined up, opening the way under the river with a passageway of over 2¼ miles and allowing proper ventilation to be installed using a large fan at Sudbrook.

A further combination of misfortunes occurred in the autumn of 1883, when, on 10 October, the Great Spring made one further dramatic attempt to destroy progress, bursting in yet again and flooding the works at Sudbrook and under the river to a greater extent than before. To make matters worse, two days later pumps west of Sudbrook broke down; more catastrophic was the inundation of the workings at the west end by a tidal wave that sent salt water tumbling into the Marsh Shaft at a point where 83 men were working. By the time a boat had been lowered down the shaft to rescue the men the water was only 8ft from the top of the tunnel, and the workmen were trapped on top of scaffolding at the west end of the tunnel; rescue came in the nick of time!

The workings were once again pumped out, and by the end of 1883 the company could record that more than 2¼ miles of full-sized tunnel had been completed. Daniel Gooch was able to record an historic moment in his diary for 27 October 1883: the two main headings had finally joined, and a small hole had been excavated between the two halves of the work. Gooch reported that he was 'the first to creep through, and Lord Bessborough followed me … and the men gave us some hearty cheers'. The Great Spring was finally conquered by its diversion into a side heading and the sinking of a further shaft equipped with six 70in Cornish beam engines powering additional large pumps. By the 1930s it was being reported that between 16 and 25 million gallons of water daily were being pumped out of the tunnel, of which more than 60% originated from the Great Spring, the enterprising company selling the water to a variety of industrial users along the Monmouthshire coast to generate further income.

Right: *The village of Sudbrook. Built to house workers from the Severn Tunnel, the settlement also came to include a hospital, Post Office, school and mission hall.*

Right: *The English portal of the Severn Tunnel c1900, with a GWR 4-4-0 emerging into daylight with its passenger train after its four-mile journey under the river.*

The final length of brickwork was completed on 18 April 1885, and in September of that year Sir Daniel and Lady Gooch were guests of honour on the first train to run through the tunnel. Gooch recorded the running of an experimental coal train through the Severn Tunnel on 9 January 1886, noting that the tunnel had been 'a very anxious work for me', largely because of the costs involved, but that he had 'never lost hope of succeeding in the end'. The tunnel finally opened for goods traffic on 1 September 1886, passenger services being introduced three months later.

The additional work required to tame the Great Spring and other works had increased the cost of the Severn Tunnel from the estimate of £948,959 to £1,806,248, but the expense was soon justified, as traffic began to increase to the level where additional signalboxes at each end were required to speed it up; indeed, traffic would increase to the point that by 1913 more than 18,000 goods and mineral trains annually were passing through the tunnel, a figure that would increase further in future years.

The 4½-mile tunnel under the Severn, whilst successful, also presented the Civil

Engineering and Locomotive departments with new problems: the damp, corrosive atmosphere in the tunnel meant that rails corroded rather faster than elsewhere on the system. Even the powerful 40ft Guibal fan installed at Sudbrook struggled to remove smoke and fumes, and operating trains through the tunnel required great skills from footplate staff, for as well as poor visibility to deal with, the running of goods trains up and down the steep gradients was no easy task. If a coupling did snap, dividing the train, locomotive crews could break a 'tell-tale' cable run through the tunnel, alerting signal staff to their difficulties.

The creation of an enlarged GWR in 1923 saw the company taking possession of many more miles of permanent way and hundreds of bridges and structures, large numbers of which were in Wales. Amongst the most impressive was Barmouth Bridge, built for the Aberystwyth & Welsh Coast Railway, later absorbed by the Cambrian Railways. Almost ½ mile long, it was, according to the *GWR Magazine*, 'the most costly bridge the Cambrian have had to maintain'. This was because the bridge was largely a wooden structure of 113 closely spaced spans which have required replacing at regular intervals over many years, due mainly to the attentions of Teredo shipworms, which eat away at the timber piers.

At the north end the original bridge had a drawbridge structure which could be lifted to allow ships to pass through from the estuary to the open sea, but this was replaced in 1903 by a steel swing bridge built by the Cleveland Bridge Company, supported by cast-iron cylinders driven down to a rock foundation. A GWR publication noted that there was also a footpath along the bridge, used by 'thousands of holidaymakers who annually visit the Cambrian Coast, for the estuary it spans is one of surpassing beauty'. The 1935 GWR publication *Track Topics* reported that the bridge had also been used as the setting for a dramatic scene in the 1931 film *The Ghost Train*, wherein a train is seen to plunge from the viaduct, but the author, W. G. Chapman, reassures the reader that the effect was achieved by trick photography, providing 'a nice tidy end for the Ghost Train'.

Below: *A 1946 visit to the Severn Tunnel. The party includes F. W. Hawksworth (far right) and K. C. Grand (far left).*

Left: *A postcard view of the bridge at Barmouth, produced c1900 by a local photographer.*

CHAPTER THREE

THE BROAD-GAUGE EMPIRE
1841-1892

In January 1845 Brunel was given a handsome testimonial by the Directors and shareholders of the Great Western, Bristol & Exeter and other railways with which he had been professionally associated. It was certainly a gift worthy of both givers and recipient, the engineer being presented with 'handsome centrepieces and candelabra, side dishes and salt-cellars' valued at 2,000 guineas. Brunel was, however, not without his critics, and a correspondent in the original *Great Western Magazine* wrote in 1865 that many of his schemes were 'freely and, we might say, warmly criticised by those shareholders who, being opposed to the broad gauge, objected to the extra expense which it entailed'. Whilst few doubted the scale and quality of Brunel's designs for the GWR main line, the fact that the railway had been completed late, and for a cost far exceeding the £2.5 million estimate, was not forgotten by his opponents.

The Great Western's original London–Bristol route was only the first in a series of lines built by advocates of the broad gauge who, argued one writer, aimed 'to seize Devon and Cornwall'. Most were not built by the GWR directly but instead by associated companies, with its support. The first link in the chain was the Bristol & Exeter Railway, which, although planned as a logical extension to the Great Western, was an entirely independent company with no financial support from Paddington. Brunel was engineer for the railway, and, although the line was completed as far as Bridgwater by 1841, Exeter was not reached until 1844, when it was reported that the opening on 1 May was celebrated 'amidst tremendous rejoicings'. The same correspondent added that the Exeter public were 'almost wild with delight' and that the opening day was observed as a general holiday.

West of Exeter, Brunel was once again employed to design another broad-gauge concern, the South Devon Railway. The route for the new line ran along the bank of the River Exe to Starcross before hugging the coast past Dawlish to Teignmouth. From there the most direct route to Plymouth involved steep gradients as the railway skirted the slopes of Dartmoor. Still nervous of the capabilities of steam locomotives, Brunel proposed instead a radical solution — described by a later historian as a 'gallant experiment' — which was rather grandly called the 'Atmospheric Railway'. Although the idea of using of air pressure to propel vehicles was not new, its employment on railways was as yet untried and was considered very unorthodox. By the time of the first South Devon shareholders' meeting in August 1844 the only working atmospheric system in use was the Kingstown & Dalkey line near Dublin, but Brunel pressed on, persuading the directors of the company to accept the new scheme, abandoning the original plans placed before Parliament which allowed for a doubled-track line worked by steam locomotives.

Much has been written about this ill-fated experiment; instead of a double track, Brunel now proposed a single-track route with passing places, with a 15in cast-iron tube placed between the rails. At the front of each train was a vehicle attached to a piston inside the tube; air was pumped out from the tube in front of the piston, allowing atmospheric pressure behind it to push the piston along the tube, moving the train. In theory the system seemed to have advantages; there would be little smoke and steam, other than at pumping stations situated at regular intervals along the line, and, as the line would not be not worked by locomotives, curves could be sharper, and gradients increased. No doubt shareholders were also attracted by the reduced running costs of the line, there being no locomotives to purchase, maintain or stable. Brunel estimated that these savings might run to £257,000 initially, plus a further saving of £8,000 on annual running costs.

Despite the high cost of installation, South Devon shareholders were convinced by Brunel's arguments, and work began in earnest in 1845. Despite the physical completion of the line between Exeter and Teignmouth by May 1846 progress on the actual installation of the atmospheric system was painfully slow, and the line had initially to be operated by steam locomotives hired from the GWR. The first trains propelled by the atmospheric system finally ran in February

1847 over a 20-mile stretch of line between Exeter and Newton Abbot, but barely a year later the 'Atmospheric Caper', as it became known, was proving a liability to the SDR. Difficulties were encountered in maintaining an air-tight seal of the cylinder piston, and a leather flap affixed to the top of the pipe suffered badly in the salty atmosphere of the Devon coast. Moreover, the size of pumps specified by Brunel proved to be inadequate, and, because no telegraph system was installed, running trains became a complicated and difficult operation.

Further operational problems led to the suspension of the atmospheric system in September 1848. By January of the following year shareholders had voted to abandon it completely, leaving the company with a bill of more than £400,000, plus the expense of having to re-equip the line to run with conventional steam traction. The whole affair was a great embarrassment to Brunel, and his friend Gooch recorded in his diary that he

Below: A contemporary engraving showing the workings of the atmospheric railway system.

Bottom: One of a series of views of the South Devon Railway produced by a local artist. One of the pumping houses can clearly be seen on the left of the picture.

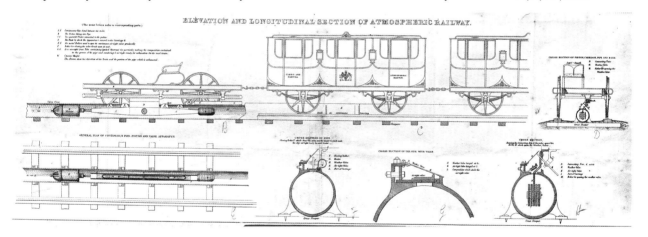

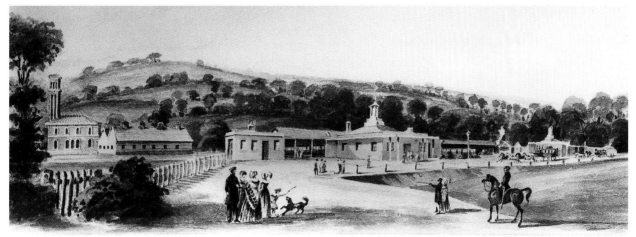

could not understand 'how Mr Brunel was as misled as he was'. Another professional colleague, the great George Stephenson, had pronounced the Atmospheric a 'great humbug', and events were certainly to prove him right.

Many critics of the great engineer also pointed to the folly of the broad gauge. Within months of the opening of the Great Western in 1838 he had been forced to submit to a series of reports on the suitability of the broader gauge, commissioned as a result of pressure from the 'Liverpool Party', a group of shareholders who had grave misgivings about his bold ideas. Many of the problems suffered by the railway were a result not of the actual track gauge but of the performance of its locomotives and the track itself, and despite highly critical comments from railway engineers Nicholas Wood and John Hawkshaw, with the help of Daniel Gooch (who improved the running of the GWR's locomotive fleet) Brunel was able to weather the storm and narrowly survive a vote on the gauge issue, by a margin of 7,790 to 6,145 votes.

During these early debates about the suitability of the broad gauge Brunel admitted that, although the gauge problem was 'undoubtedly an inconvenience', because the GWR was intended to penetrate an 'entirely new district in which railways were unknown'

it would not be a significant problem. In addition to the South Devon, which, even with its ill-fated atmospheric system, was still built with rails 7ft ¼in wide, more railways were completed to extend Brunel's broad-gauge empire; these included the Cheltenham & Great Western Union Railway, the South Wales Railway and the Cornwall and West Cornwall railways, as well as numerous smaller branch lines all over the network.

This extension of the broad gauge eventually led to what became known as the 'Battle of the Gauges', a dispute that would dominate the history of the company for nearly 10 years. The first signs of this conflict were provoked by ongoing criticism of what were called 'breaks of gauge' — places where the broad and standard gauge met. By 1845 there were 10 such locations, and at stations like Gloucester passengers were forced to disembark from their trains to transfer from one system to the other to complete their journey. The same process was repeated in a more laborious and complicated fashion for freight traffic, goods being unloaded and moved from wagon to wagon, often with delays of up to four or five hours. The arrangement was hardly convenient for either type of traffic but was a result of Brunel's assertion that the GWR was largely a self-contained regional network. Speaking some years later, he dismissed the idea of a national railway network with one uniform track gauge, arguing instead that the 'spirit of competition' between railways would do more good than the 'uniformity of system that has been much talked of'.

Apart from pure practicality, the gauge question was also linked to territorial ambition between railways; rivals like the London & North Western were unwilling to allow the Great Western to extend its empire into their territory, and the promotion of a number of new railways escalated a dispute that had been simmering gently for some years. The first such difficulty was the decision by the Bristol & Gloucester Railway, after pressure from Brunel, to adopt the broad gauge rather than standard as originally planned. The extension of a larger scheme, the Bristol & Birmingham Railway, to include the route all the way to Birmingham made matters worse, although the failure to come to a satisfactory deal eventually led to the line's being purchased by the Midland, ending for good Brunel's dream of running his broad-gauge trains to Birmingham.

Two other schemes promoted in 1844 raised the temperature in the battle. Both were new broad-gauge lines planned to run north of Oxford, deep into standard-gauge territory; the route of the Oxford, Worcester & Wolverhampton had the potential to generate considerable freight traffic in the industrialised West Midlands, whilst the Oxford & Rugby Railway was equally contentious, threatening LNWR and Midland Railway traffic to the east. The furore generated by these proposals led to the establishment by Parliament of a Royal Commission in 1845 to investigate the practicability of creating one 'uniform gauge' for the whole country, and whether future railway acts should make reference to a particular track gauge.

Three commissioners spent some weeks interviewing eminent railway engineers of all opinions on the pros and cons of the broad gauge. Despite being a personal friend Robert Stephenson did not hold back on his criticism of Brunel's gauge, calling it a 'great inconvenience' and singling out the 'break of gauge' problem as being of greatest importance. Well used to difficult questions after his experiences steering the GWR bill through Parliament in the 1830s, Brunel was nevertheless subjected to a total of 200 questions when called to give evidence in October 1845. Remaining defiant about his decision to adopt the broad gauge, he revealed that 'the impression grew upon me gradually, so it is difficult to fix the time when I thought a wide gauge desirable'. Indeed, questioned further, he argued that if beginning again he would 'rather be above than under seven feet

Left: *The now infamous drawing reproduced as part of the 'Battle of the Gauges' controversy in the* Illustrated London News, *showing the 'break of gauge' at Gloucester.*

now'. Brunel gave less satisfactory answers when grappling with the 'break of gauge' question, particularly when making proposals to speed the trans-shipment of goods, suggesting the use of containers which could be transferred from one railway to the other and the use of wagons with telescopic axles — ideas which did not come to fruition.

The final conclusions of the Gauge Commissioners were not published until 1846. As a preamble, the commissioners agreed that they could find little wrong with the broad gauge, which provided fast and safe trains for the 'convenience of passengers', due to the 'genius of Mr Brunel and the liberality of the Great Western Railway'. However, these platitudes could not hide the fact that the outcome of the commission was a recommendation that the standard gauge should be adopted as a uniform gauge for the whole country. By far the strongest evidence was the fact that by July 1845 there were only 274 miles of broad gauge as opposed to 1,901 miles of Stephenson's 4ft 8½in track; the economic argument for the easy movement of goods across the railway network was a reality that the commissioners could not ignore.

There was understandable anger and dismay amongst the supporters of the broad gauge, and Brunel and Gooch responded almost immediately by producing a 43-page rebuttal of almost all the commissioners' recommendations. Daniel Gooch's diary records that the two men, along with Company Secretary Charles Saunders, 'had some fun over it' and that they 'of course proved that the commissioners had come to quite a wrong conclusion'. Gooch did admit, however, that 'so far as the evil of the break of gauge was concerned, we had a weak case'. There is little doubt that the objections raised by the Great Western following the Commission led to some watering down of its recommendations; although 4ft 8½in was specified as the standard gauge the Act confirming this also had a clause allowing a 'special enactment defining the gauge' to be included in any future railway acts, allowing for some flexibility and the possibility of further broad-gauge lines' being built. Both the Oxford, Worcester & Wolverhampton and Oxford & Rugby lines were built, but there was now no question of the broad-gauge network being extended too far from its traditional heartland, and the domination it once enjoyed was gradually eroded.

By 1860 the superiority of the broad gauge began to come into question. Events of the previous year had not helped. In May 1859 Brunel, architect of the great experiment, died, and one of his most contentious projects, the Oxford, Worcester & Wolverhampton Railway (one of the lines which had triggered the 'Battle of the Gauges'), obtained Parliamentary sanction to abandon the broad gauge completely. The railway was already a mixed-gauge operation, able to run trains of both broad and standard gauges through the use of an additional rail. Abandoning the Brunel system, it joined with two other railways — the Worcester & Hereford and the Newport, Abergavenny & Hereford — to become the West Midland Railway.

Well aware of the strategic value of this new operation, the GWR leased the line in 1861; what was more significant was that as part of the deal it agreed to add a third, standard-gauge rail from Reading to Paddington. Supporters of the broad gauge could be in little doubt of what was to come when, in October 1861, the first standard-gauge train left Brunel's Paddington terminus. The provision of what became known as 'mixed-gauge' track then spread along the old main line to Swindon, Gloucester and as far west as Exeter

Right: *By the time this picture was taken in 1859 Isambard Kingdom Brunel was a shadow of the man who had blazed a trail along the route of the original Great Western Railway from London to Bristol.*

and Truro. By 1869 the dominance of the standard gauge in the Midlands was such that even the GWR stopped running broad-gauge passenger trains to Birmingham and Wolverhampton from Paddington.

Matters were also hastened by the re-appointment in 1865 as Company Chairman of Daniel Gooch, who had resigned the previous year after a turbulent period for the company but was persuaded to take up the reins once again. The finances of the railway were in a parlous state, and a high level of debt and declining share price meant that drastic action was required. Always a strong advocate of the broad gauge, Gooch as an engineer was above all a realist, being all too well aware that if the GWR did not generate additional business it would fail. If the only way it could do this was to embrace the standard gauge, which would enable it to capitalise from interchange traffic from other railways, then his personal feelings about the broad gauge were irrelevant.

Whilst the 'mixing' of the gauge and the acquisition of standard (or 'narrow' gauge, as the diehards called it) was a temporary fix to maintain the company's viability, it soon

became obvious that complete abolition was the only long-term solution. By creating a mixed-gauge railway the GWR had immediately increased its costs, for it had now to maintain locomotives and rolling stock of both gauges, provide additional transfer facilities (there were already more than 30 of these in 1865) and bear the expense of what had become a very complicated track system. One has only to look at photographs of the incredibly complex pointwork at junctions to realise that this arrangement must have been very costly to maintain.

When the decision to begin the process of complete gauge conversion was finally taken the company was still operating more than 1,500 miles of broad-gauge track using more than 700 locomotives; by 1867 the only 'pure' broad-gauge lines were the South Wales Railway, the main line from Exeter to Truro and various other branch lines. Although the GWR had had the chance to test the process upon conversion in October 1868 of the Princes Risborough branch, the modification of a minor 7-mile line probably did not provide too many lessons for company staff. A more ambitious operation was planned the

Above: Broad-gauge zenith. Mixed-gauge track is in evidence at Flax Bourton station as a 'Rover' 4-2-2 races through with an up express.

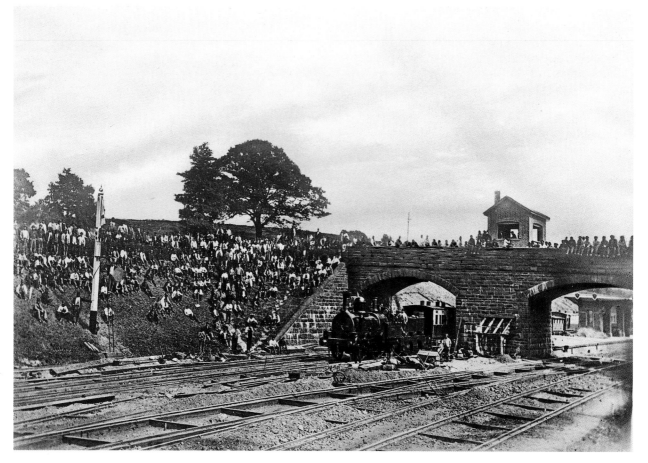

Above: A rare and historic photograph taken at Grange Court to record the conversion of the Hereford, Ross and Gloucester branch lines in 1869.

following year, when a 22½-mile stretch of line between Grange Court and Hereford was tackled. In advance of this, Gloucester station, the docks and the line between there and Grange Court had been modified by the addition of a third 'narrow'-gauge rail to aid the forthcoming conversion.

The route of the old Hereford, Ross & Gloucester Railway gave GWR engineers much experience, for it contained all manner of obstacles including tunnels, gradients and sharp curves; Christopher Awdry records that it also contained virtually the whole gamut of Great Western permanent way, including longitudinal-baulk road, cross-sleepered track, Barlow rail, Seaton rail, Vignoles and bracket-and-chair. Each type required different tools and equipment, making the process more difficult and time-consuming; just to complicate matters, not all station platforms were on the same side of the track, entailing more inconvenience to workmen slewing the track. Work began on 16 August 1869 and took a week to complete. A staff of

more than 300, drawn from as far afield as Milford Haven, was assembled, a special train of 40 vans being used as sleeping quarters during the operation. In true Victorian fashion, a First-class carriage was provided for the supervisory staff!

The work was divided into four-mile stretches, with a gang of 20 men for each quarter of a mile. The men and their equipment were dropped off in the morning by a broad-gauge train and collected at the end of the day by a standard-gauge train which moved them on to the beginning of the next section to be converted. Much was learned on this initial conversion, the first and most obvious lesson being that the process was aided by as much advance preparation as was possible, notably the prefabrication of pointwork and crossings; the second was that plenty of labour would be required and that a methodical approach, working section by section, seemed to serve best.

The success of the Hereford conversion was followed by that of the Wycombe Railway in the summer of 1870 and the Uxbridge branch in 1871. These were relatively minor projects compared to the events of 1872, when the pace of change increased markedly. The conversion of lines in South Wales was especially important to the Great Western, as so much revenue was generated from coal traffic in the area. In April 1872 the company issued a comprehensive 28-page book detailing the process, which illustrates the complexity of the operation. Work was carried out in two stages, the line from Grange Court to New Milford (and all branches in between) being tackled first, followed by the Swindon–Gloucester line and its branches to Cirencester and Cheltenham.

When work began, on 1 May, one broad-gauge track was retained on the main line as a temporary measure to enable train services to continue. An added complication to the process was the company's valuable coal traffic, instructions including one, relating to the Forest of Dean and Central Forest branches, that insisted: 'No goods or mineral traffic to be run after 26 April, especially those belonging to owners in South Wales that will have to be returned to them'. Much effort had to be expended in ensuring that coal wagons were either sent back to collieries before the conversion date or moved to outside contractors for scrapping or conversion. The instructions note that in the case of The Hon Y. H. Yelverton, owner of Carway Anthracite Colliery Company, his 10 wagons were to be sent to the Bristol Railway Wagon Works, whereas Mr Edwin Richards was quoted as stating that 'I am now altering them in my own yard'. One of the tasks of inspectors before work began in earnest was to travel up the line, checking stations and yards to ensure that no broad-gauge stock was left stranded. Another important factor was the fact that much of the GWR Locomotive Department's coal came from collieries on the Ely branch. The instructions noted that 'this branch must, if possible, be kept open for GW locomotive-coal traffic until after the broad-gauge working ceases, and narrow-gauge working must commence on it as soon as possible … so that the Swindon factory may have, as far as practicable, a continuous supply of coal'.

The South Wales conversion dealt with almost 500 miles of broad gauge when all the branches were included, and as a result the workforce drafted in numbered 5,000. Staff began with the up line, in a process that involved the sawing-off of transoms, slewing the baulk rail inwards, re-fixing, checking of gauge and re-ballasting. Once this was done — usually taking a week — they rested for a

Below: The huge selection of rail types, particularly the early 'bridge' type used by Brunel on the GWR, is illustrated in this display created by the company in 1897, not long after the abolition of the broad gauge.

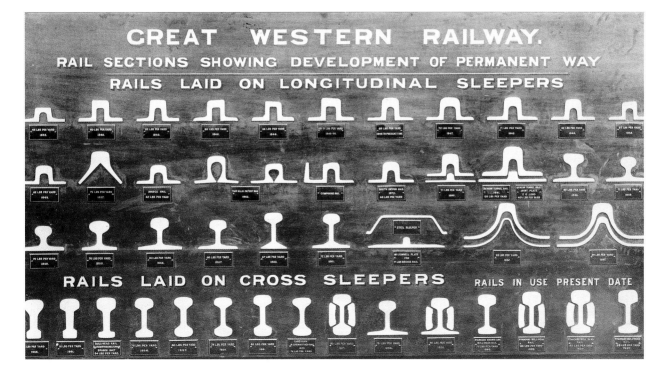

Below: *With the abolition of the broad gauge in South Devon the vacuum pipe used in connection with the atmospheric railway, which had thus far remained in situ, was removed and recycled — or, as here, retained as a souvenir of Brunel's ill-fated experiment. This rare photograph showing a section of the pipe is believed to have been taken at Paddington; other relics can be seen in the background. The author encountered the same section when he began work at the GWR Museum in the early 1980s, and it is now on display at the STEAM museum in Swindon.*

day and then turned their attention to the down line. Within a fortnight the line to New Milford in West Wales was converted, and the first standard-gauge trains ran from Paddington to Wales. There were specific instructions for locomotive drivers who were asked following the alterations to the track to 'run with great caution' and advised that they should 'never attempt to make up time or exceed the speed at which the trains are timed to run'. With the removal in May 1872 of the broad gauge on the Swindon–Gloucester line Swindon, ironically, now became a 'break of gauge' station.

Another major conversion followed; in June 1874 the old Wilts, Somerset & Weymouth line between Thingley Junction and Dorchester, including the Salisbury, Bathampton, Radstock, Wells and Bridport

branches, was tackled. The instructions issued for this conversion were along similar lines to those relating to earlier work, although the very rural nature of the lines in question is apparent from one instruction which stated that 'during the conversion no horses or carriages will be conveyed … unless special arrangements are previously made with the companies' agents'. The conversion of other lines followed in subsequent years, including the Barnstaple, Brentford, Calne and Marlborough branches.

Gooch noted in his diary for June 1874 that 'thus is the poor broad gauge gradually dying out' and that it now existed only on the London–Bristol main line and Windsor and Henley branches. He did not mention lines west of Bristol, largely because at this time they did not directly belong to the Great Western. Awdry notes that, these lines aside, the GWR had almost abolished the broad gauge by 1875, as it now operated barely eight miles of pure broad-gauge track, the rest of its 1,400-mile network being 'mixed' gauge. In that year a threat of takeover by the Midland precipitated the full acquisition of the Bristol & Exeter and South Devon railways by the GWR, adding to the company's portfolio more than 250 miles of broad-gauge line — something about which Gooch can hardly have been happy. In the next few years the pace of conversion slowed dramatically, and although some work was carried out and mixed gauge added in the west, a lack of finance, coupled with work on the Severn Tunnel, meant that progress on completing the rest of the network remained painfully slow.

GWR company historian E. T. MacDermot records that the complete abolition of the broad gauge was finally prompted by a resolution discussed in November 1885 by the board of the Cornwall Railway. At this meeting it was suggested that 'the time has arrived when it would be desirable that the gauge of the Cornwall Railway should be altered from broad to narrow' and that the GWR should take steps to accomplish this. This request led to the completion of a lengthy report by General Manager James Grierson, which highlighted the fact that there were still 182 miles of broad-gauge line to convert, although only 42 miles of this total was double track. Grierson estimated that the cost of converting this permanent way would amount to almost

£129,000. More expensive was the cost of converting or replacing locomotives and rolling stock. In 1885 there were still 170 broad-gauge engines, of which 73 were capable of being converted. Although more carriage stock had been built as convertibles, the state of the wagon fleet was less encouraging; only 800 wagons of a total of more than 3,000 were capable of being converted to run on the standard gauge. The estimate for conversion or replacement of all this stock ran to £413,250.

Faced with this considerable investment, GWR directors chose to do nothing further following the completion of the report in April 1886, as company finances prevented any further expenditure. Three years later Gooch, in his last General Meeting as Chairman, suggested that the end of the broad gauge could not be postponed too much longer, but he did not live to see its complete demise, dying on 15 October 1889. Plans were finally put in place for a final abolition of the broad gauge at a meeting in February 1891, with the aim of completing all work by the end of May the following year.

A precursor to the main event was the conversion of the 12¾-mile Chard branch line, effected in July 1891, but the following April a notice was issued by the company stating that both main line and branches would be converted to standard gauge over the weekend of 21/22 May 1892. This momentous news was reported in the *Swindon Evening Advertiser*, which noted on 14 April 1892 that 'On Monday May 23, the broad gauge, that great conception of Mr Brunel, will have ceased to exist.'

Detailed plans had been compiled well in advance, and in the light of experience gained with previous conversions, much preparatory work done beforehand; care was taken to retrieve every broad-gauge locomotive, carriage and wagon from the west, ready for despatch to Swindon. 'All kinds of odds-and-ends on wheels, recalling the early days of railway history, were unearthed from their resting places to join the procession', noted GWR historian Alfred Williams in 1925. Considerable advance work was also done the track, which involved sawing through transoms, removing ballast and ensuring that new rail and points and crossings were in position ready for installation well before the actual conversion.

As one contemporary writer reported, 'great expedition' was required in the two days scheduled for the final conversion. Because much of the track in Devon and Cornwall was single it was important that both passenger and goods services be

Above: No 3028 was one of a series of 10 Dean singles built as 'convertibles' — standard-gauge locomotives temporarily modified to run on Brunel's 7ft gauge.

suspended for the shortest time possible. To ensure the success of the operation more than 4,000 men were drafted in to carry out the work, having been transported on special trains from all over the GWR network. Men from as far afield as Chester, Crewe, New Milford and Swindon began arriving as early as Wednesday 18 May and were housed all along the line in good sheds, stations and tents. As dawn broke on the morning of 20 May thousands of men began work in fine weather, and this (and the meticulous preparations) meant that by the end of the first day most of the job had been completed, and a trial train was even run from Exeter to Plymouth. Further work was, however, required on the Sunday, but such was progress that the 177-mile conversion was essentially complete in 31 hours — 17 hours ahead of the 48 originally scheduled. Whilst trains began to run on Monday 22 May, a full passenger timetable came into operation the following day, goods trains running from the 23rd. At Swindon Works additional land had been purchased west of Rodbourne Lane, and this was used to store broad-gauge locomotives and rolling stock before scrapping or conversion.

The folorn sight of broad-gauge locomotives awaiting the cutter's torch marked the end of an experiment that from its inception had aroused huge debate. Although these arguments had been rehearsed on numerous occasions, most notably at the Gauge Commission of 1845, the final abolition of Brunel's broad gauge was still, for many, hard to accept. A few weeks after the final conversion an article in *The Engineer* reported that: 'We suppose that highly conservative natures are in a minority, even in the West, but, nevertheless all must feel a regretful interest in seeing the last of a bold experiment carried out in the teeth of vehement opposition, and brought to success, at least for a time.

Below: This picture is one of a series of familiar but famous views of the conversion of the broad gauge at Plymouth Millbay station in May 1892. In the case of complicated trackwork like this, crossings and points were built elsewhere to save time during conversion.

Right: *The broad gauge being converted at Saltash. The picture illustrates that, no matter how much advance planning and preparation had been done, the actual conversion process was extremely labour-intensive, especially in view of the time constraints imposed by the company on its staff.*

Below: *The forlorn sight signalling the end of Brunel's broad-gauge dream: the 'Dump' at Swindon Works in 1892. By the end, there were only 60 'proper' broad-gauge locomotives left, including the 23 'Rovers', which had been the mainstay of express services until the end. The legend that one of these locomotives had been buried intact in this area was disproved when the site was redeveloped after works closure. Neither a locomotive nor the stash of broad-gauge nameplates rumoured to be there was ever found!*

CHAPTER FOUR

PASSENGER COMFORTS

When the Great Western celebrated its centenary in 1935, amongst all the discussion of the huge engineering achievements of Brunel, Gooch and other GWR pioneers there was nevertheless a realisation that conditions for travellers on the railway had changed enormously since the opening of the Bristol to London main line. Even today, in an era when air travel makes it possible to cross continents in hours, it is hard to imagine the sense of wonder (or even dread) felt by passengers on the early GWR who could travel from London to Bristol in five hours on a train instead taking two or three days in an uncomfortable stage coach. Railway travel was nevertheless still an adventure for most people in those pioneering days, as trains lacked many of the comforts — like toilets, corridors or refreshments — we would now take for granted.

When the Great Western had first opened for business between London and Bristol in 1841 it had been assumed that many well-heeled passengers would travel with their own carriages, transported on flat wagons, and whilst some early engravings show this kind of arrangement where, as one contemporary writer joked, the owners of these stage coaches 'enjoyed the dust and flying sparks and ashes', the volume of business did not grow to the extent anticipated. Those who did travel this way, seated in their own carriages, were still expected to buy a First-class ticket, and the social profile of the passengers using the railway was still predominantly such that until the early 1840s, at least, the railway made no effort at all to carry Third-class passengers. Questioned by a Parliamentary committee in

1839 about the possibility of carrying Third-class passengers, Company Secretary Charles Saunders famously replied that 'the very lowest orders of passengers' would at some stage be allowed to travel by very slow trains, in inferior accommodation and at a very low price, and probably at night. In an early Bradshaw timetable the company gave notice that 'Third-class passengers will be conveyed by the goods trains' — a reference to the fact that the movement of these passengers originated with the activities of some road carriers, who, when they began sending goods by rail instead of road, followed their previous practice of also conveying with the goods 'persons in lower stations of life'.

These 'goods train' passengers travelled in what the GWR called 'uncovered trucks', and even when these were re-designated as 'Third class' they remained primitive, at best; as reported in the *GWR Magazine* they had bare wooden seats and 'sides and ends only two feet high'. The sides were later raised to 4ft 6in, but when the railway opened between Bristol and London in 1841 Third-class passengers were catered for with only one service each way, the journey taking between eight and 10 hours — twice as long as that taken by First- or Second-class travellers. In the depths of winter conditions for Third-class travellers must have been truly dreadful, albeit probably no worse than they had been for those who had braved the rigours of travelling on top of a horse-drawn coach in the days before the coming of railways.

It took both a tragedy and new government legislation to change the lot of Third-class passengers on the GWR. Nine passengers were killed in the first major accident to befall

Right: *A Great Western six-wheel Third-class carriage built by the company in 1845. Although lacking any windows, they at least did feature a roof, unlike earlier stock classed as 'uncovered trucks' by the railway.*

Below: *By 1848 Third-class stock had become somewhat more sophisticated, as this copy of a GWR drawing shows.*

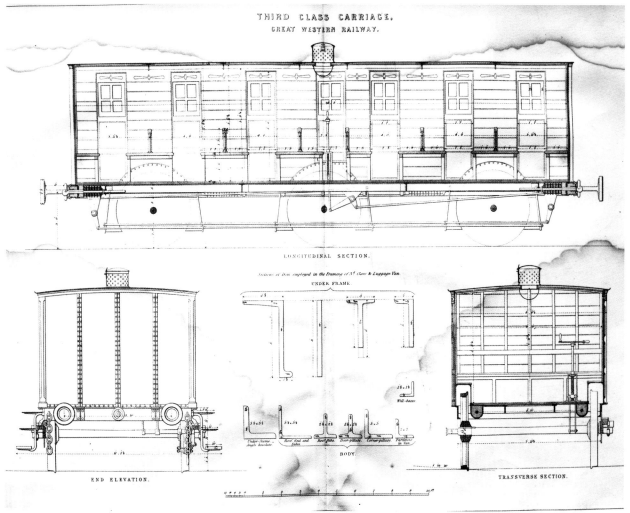

THIRD CLASS CARRIAGE.
GREAT WESTERN RAILWAY.

LONGITUDINAL SECTION.

END ELEVATION.

TRANSVERSE SECTION.

the company, near Reading on Christmas Eve 1841, when a train that had left Paddington at 4.30 that morning ran into a landslide in Sonning Cutting. *The Times* reported that the train had been carrying 38 passengers, 'chiefly of the poorer class', and those seated in the low open trucks were flung out all over the line, eight being killed instantly and twice as many badly hurt. One of the injured died later in hospital. 'Eight persons in an instant dashed to atoms and twice as many grievously wounded', argued an outraged letter writer to the *Mechanics Magazine*, adding that the Christmas Eve disaster was just one of a 'long train of disastrous accidents' on English railways. Within three years The Railway Regulation Act had been passed, a section of which was intended 'to secure to the poorer class of travellers the means of travelling by railway at moderate fares, and in which they may be protected from the weather'. The new bill, promoted by Gladstone, also forced railways to run at least one Third-class train each day, travelling at an average of not less than 12mph, and at a cost of no more than one penny per mile to passengers.

Soon after the passing of the Act the Great Western introduced eight new Third-class carriages resembling, noted a GWR writer in

1935, a modern milk van, with solid sides and no windows but fixed louvres and small sliding boards which could be opened or closed, allowing in some light and air. In 1892 an anonymous chronicler of the broad-gauge era claimed that 'there were only two doors to these caravans, one on each side, so all the passengers, save those nearest to them, had to climb over the seats to find places'. Less than 21ft long and just 8ft 6in wide, the carriages were not enormous but were capable, claimed the company, of seating 59 passengers and a 'brakesman' — all in all a cosy prospect, especially in the height of summer. In 1845 the company began building its own carriages, turning out larger six-wheeler Third-class iron-construction coaches; as Jim Russell noted in his book on GWR carriages, although they looked like prison vehicles they were a distinct improvement on what had gone before and had additional doors with windows.

Until the introduction (from 1877) of Swindon-built clerestory stock designed by William Dean, many First-class carriages were themselves still fairly primitive, although clearly more comfortable. The anonymous writer already mentioned argued that some First-class carriages 'were of practically the

Below: The horse-drawn origins of this 1846-built First-class carriage are clearly visible in this atmospheric photograph taken on an occasion when the carriage had clearly seen better days. The 18ft-long coach had a wooden frame and papier-mâché body panels.

same design as those first put upon the line' and goes on to give a rare insight into what travelling on the early GWR was really like. Inside, he continued, the carriages were 'low, dark, but with little space between the seats, and with the iron coverings of the wheels sticking up inside the doorways to trip you up … they by no means deserved the name the Great Western obtained for the roominess of its carriages'. Some coaches had a door in the middle, dividing the compartment into two snug little boxes, holding four persons apiece an arrangement 'which ought to have satisfied even the English love of privacy in railway travelling'. It should, of course, be remembered too that carriages were not steam-heated until 1893, and so until that time footwarmers — large oblong tins containing hot water — were supplied to passengers. Those in First class began making use of this innovation in 1856, but the service was not available to Third-class travellers for another 17 years, finally being introduced in 1873. As steam heating began to become more widely available on new stock, especially after the abolition of the broad gauge, the footwarmers were gradually phased out, the last being used in 1901. For the sentimental passenger, however, they remained available by request, but this antiquated anachronism did not sit well with the pioneering developments of the Edwardian era, and they were withdrawn for good in 1908.

The sensation of travelling in a broad-gauge express was described as 'majestic but lumbering' and inferior to the best standard-gauge trains of the day. Most railway writers of the period agreed that it was not carriage design but Brunel's baulk-road track that was chiefly at fault. A stretch of line several miles outside Exeter had been relaid with cross-sleepered track sometime before the broad gauge was changed and gave travellers the opportunity to judge the difference between the two types of track. Most agreed that the difference was very perceptible; instead of the clatter of wheels against the unconnected ends of the bridge rails (a clatter made worse by those ends' never being laid exactly opposite each other) the trains on the cross-sleepered rails ran smoothly and quietly. By the early 1890s most new carriages were being constructed at Swindon as 'convertibles', having only broad-gauge underframes, so

Above: A GWR chef conjures up yet another meal for hungry diners in the kitchen of a restaurant car on a GWR express in the 1920s.

that, as one opponent of Brunel's experiment remarked, 'it was scarcely possible to tell that you were not on the LNWR or GNR, instead of on the worn-out anachronism of the seven feet gauge'. Supporters of all things Great Western had a rather different attitude!

In the year that the broad gauge finally disappeared for good a more positive and far-reaching innovation was introduced on the Great Western; on 1 October 1892 the first corridor train to be run on the network was brought into use on the 1.30pm service to Birkenhead. The following year more corridor carriages were introduced on West of England trains to Torquay and Penzance. The general adoption of corridor services, the *GWR Magazine* rather primly observed, meant that 'it became possible to provide lavatory accommodation and greatly to improve the amenities of rail travel'. One of these amenities was the provision of food to hungry passengers who prior to 1896 had been unable to enjoy any hot food on their journey, unless they stopped *en route*. In May of that year restaurant cars were introduced on Bristol and Cardiff expresses, but it was not until 1903 that they were more widely adopted on trains elsewhere on the GWR network. The design and equipment used improved steadily, so that by the 1930s passengers on express and cross-country services had access to a variety of catering, from the traditional dining car to the art-deco-styled 'quick lunch' cars introduced in 1934. The latter featured a counter running the entire length of the buffet car, 12 'stand up rest seats' being provided. A steward was available to serve passengers with hot and cold snacks, sandwiches, drinks and cigarettes.

In its own guide to its Hotels & Catering Department, published in 1937, the GWR argued that it laid claim to a 'standard of efficiency' in its efforts to look after its passengers 'whether it applies to the modest sandwich and a refreshing cup of tea or a most

splendid repast served under ideal conditions by … attendants with the accompaniment of the choicest wines'. 'Today,' it continued, 'train meals are, perhaps, the greatest of all assets to modern travelling, and their production is the result of much careful forethought and ingenuity.'

Describing a trip behind 'Castle' 4-6-0 No 5018 *St Mawes Castle* on the 'Cheltenham Flyer' in 1934, W. G. Chapman gave his readers a peep behind the scenes of the restaurant car. When the 'inner-man calls for refreshment,' he noted, 'he will find an appetising meal, daintily served, awaiting him in the dining car'. Chapman further marvelled at the ability of restaurant car staff to produce a seven- or eight-course meal for up to 100 people, 'along with all the various dishes and their trimmings', in a small kitchen, preparation, cooking and serving all being carried out as the train hurtled along at over 80mph. Needless to say, the arrangement of the

Below: *A refreshment stall at Taunton station, pictured in January 1928.*

kitchen had been developed through years of experience so that everything was well placed, and so ovens, grills, hotplates, ice-boxes and glistening pots and pans, with an adequate supply of hot water, 'enable the small kitchen to produce magic results'. The final touch was the work of waiters who, under the watchful eye of a conductor, exercised 'some agility in moving up and down the car with hot soups, coffee and so forth as the train speed to its destination'. Feeding hungry Great Western passengers was big business: in 1933 more than 1.3 million meals were served in restaurant cars alone, this total including more than half a million 'luncheons', 154,000 dinners, 86,500 breakfasts and 26,100 'suppers'.

The 1937 Refreshment Department tariff records that breakfast on the train cost 3s 6d (17½p) and dinner 5s. For those not wishing to visit the dining car or those with smaller budgets a visit to one of the Great Western's station refreshment rooms was an alternative. Here, for a shilling, one could purchase a 'Light Lunch Box' which contained sandwiches, fruit and cake 'packed in a convenient form for passengers to take with them on a journey'. For the larger appetite breakfast, lunch or dinner 'baskets' could be had, the most expensive — the dinner basket — costing just 3s. This contained 'cold chicken and ham, bread, butter, cheese, salad'. A tea basket contained 'a pot of tea, coffee etc, bread and butter, cake or bun and fruit'. Clearly anxious about the loss of its elegant crested china and cutlery, the GWR noted that 'In view of the serious losses by breakage and otherwise of basket fittings etc the company ventures to solicit the co-operation of passengers to ensure their proper use, and to replace them in the baskets when finished with.'

Many travellers chose to take refreshment before or after their journeys and so took advantage of the facilities that were provided at most 'principal stations'. These varied tremendously in size; at Birmingham Snow Hill the restaurant was a large and grand affair, situated in what (before the station was modernised in 1913) had been the Great Western Hotel. The opulent Edwardian décor and starched white tablecloths harked back to its prewar glory when described by the GWR in 1937 as '*the* luncheon rendezvous of the city', and the enlarged 'Grill Room' in Livery

Street remained open until 10pm every night. In contrast the company had in 1936 opened a new and modern 'Quick Lunch and Snack Bar' at Paddington which could accommodate up to 38 diners who sat around a horse-shoe-shaped bar. 'Speedy and skilful service' was given by 'white-coated chefs', the company boasted, customers being able to choose from a menu of more than 100 items that included shellfish, soups, meat and poultry, as well as 'salads, waffles and gateaux'. Mirroring developments in the United States, a wide range of sandwiches were available, 'cut in the presence of the customer'.

The availability of government funding in the 1930s for major projects to alleviate unemployment enabled the company to modernise many of its major stations and

Above: A porter at Paddington presents a passenger with a Refreshment Department luncheon basket for her journey to the West Country.

Right: *A glamorous 'set piece' publicity picture taken at Paddington in May 1936 to mark the opening of the 'Quick Lunch and Snack Bar'. Through the window in the background two porters await the departure of a train.*

Below: *The interior of the Swindon Refreshment Rooms in 1901. Although by then the rooms had been in use for almost 60 years, the grandeur of the original Brunel design is still apparent.*

allowed developments like those at Paddington to be duplicated at places like Bristol, Cardiff, Leamington, Newport and Taunton. At the same time, at many larger stations the GWR took the opportunity to add a good number of platform tobacco and confectionery kiosks, where 'all kinds of cigars, cigarettes and tobaccos, a variety of smoker's requisites and fancy goods and also chocolates are offered at popular prices'. The 1937 guide to refreshment facilities on the GWR also noted that 'at Swindon Junction Station, also, the facilities for obtaining meals and refreshments are vastly improved', and we cannot leave this celebration of the GWR's history without revisiting the sorry saga of the Swindon Refreshment Rooms, even though it has been recounted many times.

The original arrangement agreed by the company to build refreshment rooms at Swindon in 1841 must initially have seemed ideal, given that Brunel's great railway was already proving far more costly than at first thought; the contractor, J. & C. Rigby, would build the station at its own expense in return for a 99-year lease on the rooms at a peppercorn rent of one penny a year. The GWR also agreed that all trains using the new London–Bristol line would stop at Swindon for 10 minutes to allow passengers to take refreshment, and that no other rival facilities would be provided at other stations *en route*.

Brunel provided Rigby's with a specification for the construction of the station and refreshment rooms. The First-class facilities were particularly grand, Brunel noting that they should be 'handsomely fitted out', and when completed the rooms were considered to be of an extremely high standard, being likened by a local newspaper to a 'first-rate hotel'. The rooms were formally opened in July 1842, by which time Rigby's had already sub-let the business to Samuel Griffiths of Cheltenham for a rent of £1,100 per annum and a lump sum of £6,000. This not inconsiderable sum helped offset the initial

Below: One of a series of pictures taken to record the occasion in 1895 when trains were able to run through Swindon without need for the compulsory 10-minute stop for refreshment. Another photographer captures the moment when the 'Cornishman' passes Swindon at speed.

outlay of £15,000 incurred by Rigby's in building the station and put the day-to-day management of the facility well beyond the GWR's control. This lack of control became all the more apparent when complaints about the standard of fare served at the rooms began to be directed with unerring regularity to the Great Western. After a particularly disgusting cup of coffee at Swindon Brunel famously wrote a letter of complaint to Mr Griffiths, and in his 1889 book *The Railways of England* W. M. Acworth recalled another irate letter from a customer. The traveller had written to Charles Russell, Chairman of the GWR, complaining that the only food available was 'pork pies (perhaps stale), sausage rolls and Banbury cakes' and that he and two friends had paid 7s 6d for pork pies and indifferent bottled liquor'. Not surprisingly, given that he had had only 10 minutes to complete his meal, 'one of my friends had an attack of indigestion on the road — and no wonder, after such a meal'. The Great Western made considerable efforts to try and improve matters, but to no avail, and the lease remained out of their hands, being sold outright for £20,000 to John Phillips in 1848. By the 1850s the quality of catering had improved, but as train speeds

increased, having to stop all expresses at Swindon became more and more inconvenient. It was not until three years after the abolition of the broad gauge that the company was at last able to buy back the lease, paying £100,000 — a sum equivalent to around £8 million in today's prices. Expensive though the buyout was, it did finally enable GWR expresses to speed through the Wiltshire town without stopping.

In the years between the two world wars travelling on the Great Western — especially on its premier train services like the 'Cornish Riviera Limited' or the 'Cheltenham Flyer' — could, for the well-heeled traveller, be a luxurious and exciting experience. In his book about the latter train W.G. Chapman remarked that 'There can be no finer prelude to a holiday and few things really more restful than a long journey by express train.' In the GWR's own 'Through the Window' publication describing the route between Paddington and Penzance the writer noted that the journey 'has about it a certain savour of romance, a spice of adventure, which no familiarity with railway travelling can destroy'.

When the Great Western celebrated the silver jubilee of the 'Riviera' in 1929 it marked

Below: *The operation of slip carriages necessitated the use of special lamps. This picture, showing just such a lamp, was actually taken on 9 September 1960 and shows Guard G. W. James checking the lamp of the last slip service.*

the anniversary by investing in new rolling stock which, it boasted, had 'many novel features and refinements calculated further to enhance the comfort of those who "Go Great Western"'. The new 60ft carriages were as large as the loading-gauge would permit, the extra space being used to improve legroom for the 428 passengers the train could hold. Although they were largely of steel construction, the interior featured wood from all over the world, including mahogany and teak from Borneo and the Honduras. Another new feature of the carriage stock was the use of 'Vita' glass, which, the railway argued, demonstrated its desire to 'ensure the well-being of its patrons', the new glass admitting 'health-giving ultra-violet rays from the sun which ordinary window glass excludes'. GWR publicity extolled the virtues of UV rays (or, as it preferred to call them, 'health' rays'), which 'in some extraordinary way promote the mystic ingredient in our make-up known as Vitamin D'. Since the benefits of sunlight were one of the reasons passengers travelled to the 'sun-drenched beaches of Cornwall and Devon', passengers would, the GWR hoped, 'literally commence their sunlight treatment *en route* to their holiday destination'.

Travel on the 'Limited' also highlighted another peculiarly unique GWR operating procedure, that of the slip coach. By the summer of 1934 the train consisted of 14 carriages, sometimes increased to 16 on busy Saturdays. The core of the train, which worked right through to Penzance, comprised just eight coaches, including two dining cars. In addition there were six 'slip' coaches — two for Weymouth, two for Newquay, one for Falmouth and one for St Ives. Each had its own 'Slip Guard', who rode in the front vehicle of the section to be slipped; when the train approached the place where the 'slip' was to be

Below: On long train journeys having enough to read is essential. This view of the bookstall at Paddington can be dated from the date on the advertisement for the Graphic *magazine hanging above the stall. The latest is dated 16 August 1913. There is much GWR publicity material for sale, including travel guides, timetables and the company's own staff magazine.*

made the guard operated a lever which separated the couplings between the carriages. Once separated, the carriage was brought to a stand in the station using limited vacuum braking and a hand brake; considerable skill and judgement were therefore required to ensure that the carriage did not come to a halt outside the station or overshoot it. Special large lamps, manufactured at Swindon Works and fitted with up to three lenses, were fixed to the back of expresses that included slip carriages, to help signalbox staff identify them and ensure that they had the correct number of coaches in the formation. For the passenger, booking a ticket and seat on the 'Limited' ensured that — in theory, at least — they would be sitting in the appropriate portion of

the train to reach their desired destination, although in the hustle and bustle of Paddington station before the train's departure at 10.30am there were also plenty of staff to make sure that passengers and their luggage were in the right place!

It is a great pity that there are very few first-hand passenger accounts of travelling by the Great Western; its trains were featured in works of fiction, notably Agatha Christie's *4.50 from Paddington*, but the experiences of everyday travellers can be gleaned only from fragments in miscellaneous sources. A short article in the special 'GWR Centenary' supplement to *The Times* in 1935 provides a few tantalising glimpses of passenger habits which to the modern reader may well now appear

Below: Another publicity photograph of Great Western travellers produced by Paddington in the 1930s. The elegant scene was, however, probably posed at the rather less glamorous General Stores Building at Swindon Works.

anachronistic. The English obsession with class was very apparent, the writer observing that in one month that year railways had carried 1 million First-, 113,000 Second- and 61 million Third-class passengers but that 'the satisfaction derived from a superior class of travel is but transitory'. It was noted that men tended to travel First-class if they could afford to do so but that 'womenfolk when paying for themselves tend to travel Third as a rule'. The introduction of carriages with an open saloon in lieu of compartments had allowed travellers 'to abandon the national habit of splendid isolation', and this new boldness was also apparent in GWR dining cars, where passengers 'do not hesitate to ask for just what they want', the writer concluded. Moreover, in view of modern claims that Britain is now overwhelmed by litter and that things were better in the past, the revelation that in 1935 'the Englishman remains insistent on his right to throw his rubbish where he pleases — on the floor, under the seat, or on the luggage rack' is somewhat surprising.

Above: A heavily re-touched photograph of the interior of a 1936 carriage compartment. Close scrutiny of the picture reveals that the lady is reading a copy of Shipping Wonders of the World!

CHAPTER FIVE

The Giant Awakens: 1892-1914

Even before the addition of constituent and subsidiary lines at the Grouping in 1922/3 to make a much greater Great Western, the company was an operation of some substance and one of the pre-eminent railways of Great Britain. This had not always been the case, and after the pioneering years of development steered by Brunel and Gooch the broad-gauge experiment began to go sour, and the GWR lost ground to other rivals. Following the decision of the 1845 Gauge Commission Brunel's dream of a broad-gauge empire began to fade; his death in 1859 did not see the end of his bold ideas but marked the beginning of a slow decline, halted only when the 7ft gauge was abolished in May 1892.

During those twilight years the GWR was seized by a torpor triggered by conservative leadership and a lack of finance. Gooch had become Company Chairman in 1865, when the railway was close to bankruptcy, and presided over lean years precipitated by both an economic depression and the huge cost of converting the broad gauge. The cautious approach adopted during those years had a long-term effect from which the railway would take some time to recover. One writer described the GWR in this era as a 'slumbering giant', and it was not until the early 1890s that matters really began to improve significantly. One important factor was that many of the staff who had started their career in the earliest days of the GWR began to retire or pass away. Gooch wrote in his diary entry of 18 May 1885 that 'Death has been busy amongst my friends the last few weeks,' recording the passing of Sir Watkin Wynn, an old GWR director, and that of William George Owen, formerly Chief Engineer, who had joined the company in the

1830s. Gooch was almost 70 when he remarked with some regret that 'Year after year fewer of my old friends are left', and within four years his own death finally severed one of the last major links with the earliest days of the Great Western company.

Although by 1889, the year Gooch died, The GWR had the greatest route mileage in England and the second-largest volume of traffic, its express services were slow and small in number, many running to the same timings that had applied more than 20 years earlier. 'The Great Western is a very solid line, and makes its progress in a stolid style; doing some great things and many small, but all alike with the immovability of Jove', noted H. S. Foxwell. Much of this torpor could be attributed to the attitude of GWR management, typified by G. N. Tyrell, Superintendent of the Line until 1888, who was described as 'cautious, anxious, scared of speeds of over 40mph'. His replacement, N. J. Burlinson, was a very different character, introducing new trains and accelerating existing services to compete with rival companies. A major milestone was the introduction in March 1892 of the first corridor train, the 1.30pm from Paddington to Birkenhead, complete with toilet accommodation for all three classes. The following year similar trains began to run to the West Country.

With new management, ideas and ambition began to permeate through the railway at every level. Much of the credit for the progress made in the years before the Great War can be attributed to two men who guided the GWR at the highest level during the period. Speaking in 1899, General Manager J. L. Wilkinson argued that his aim was to make the GWR 'the biggest railway in every respect in the kingdom ... we want to make our big undertaking *the* undertaking of the country'. Although Wilkinson had joined the GWR as a boy in 1863, rising through the ranks to become Chief Clerk to Goods Manager in 1876, he had left the company in 1885 to become General Manager of the Buenos Aires Railway in Argentina. Eventually tempted back by the GWR directors, Wilkinson was finally promoted to the top post in 1896. However, like many Great Western staff at the highest level, Wilkinson was to die 'in harness' in 1903, having ultimately been responsible only for laying the foundations of what would truly be a 'golden age' for the company.

Wilkinson's replacement was James Inglis, a Scot, born in 1851, whose background as engineer made him eminently suitable for the task facing the Great Western. Although he began his career on the South Devon Railway, Inglis had become an independent consulting engineer in 1878, working on dock and railway projects in the West Country for more than a decade before joining the GWR as Chief Engineer in 1892. Eleven years later he was appointed General Manager and Consulting Engineer, overseeing what one writer has described at the Great Western's 'great leap forward'. The General Manager and the board of directors realised the urgent need to change

Left: *James Inglis, General Manager of the GWR from 1903 to 1911.*

the reputation of the Great Western; despite being such a large concern, apart from Brunel's old main line it had hardly any really direct route to any town of importance on its network, one historian noting that, where a Great Western route competed with another railway, the GWR's was usually the longer. Indeed, its rambling network, combined with its sluggish trains, led it to be ridiculed in the press as the 'Great Way Round'.

Before much effort could be expended in shortening its routes the Great Western had a more urgent task: in order to allow increased

Below: *Improvements to the main line had begun even before the end of the broad gauge. Work to quadruple the route as far as Didcot is well in evidence in this view, recorded on 15 May 1892.*

train speeds, miles of track had to be replaced,
particularly on the main line between
Paddington and Penzance. When conversion
took place the old baulk road had been slewed
to the standard gauge, but there was simply
not enough time or money to replace it
immediately. However, if higher speeds were
to be achieved the problem needed to be
addressed quickly, and as a result more than
500 miles of baulk road was replaced by cross-
sleepered track within five years of conversion
from the broad gauge. For a company still
reeling from the expense of gauge conversion
the statistics make sobering reading: more
than 1.2 million sleepers, 67,000 tons of
bullhead rail, 47,000 tons of track chairs and
1,200 tons of bolts and fishplates were used to
upgrade the permanent way, hundreds of staff
being employed to carry out the work.

In parallel with this project the company
carried out an ambitious scheme to quadruple
Brunel's main line as it ran through the
Thames Valley. This had begun in 1874, when
two new tracks were laid on the stretch
between Paddington and Taplow. This was
completed by 1882, and work resumed in 1890,
when the widening was completed as far as
Didcot, the process being finally completed six
years later. At the London end, at least, the
work wiped out much evidence of the original
Brunel main line, the old broad-gauge stations
at Slough and Reading being completely
flattened and replaced with new, larger
facilities. Widening of important structures
like Wharncliffe Viaduct and Maidenhead
Bridge involved the construction of additional
spans replicating the original Brunel designs.

In the West Country much of the old main
line was widened from single to double track;
there had been over 90 miles of single track
between Exeter and Penzance and so a
programme of gradual replacement was
instituted, having a significant effect of
journey times from London to Cornwall.
Starting in 1894, most of the railway had been
doubled by the beginning of the 20th century,
a process that also meant the replacement of
many of the Brunel timber viaducts that had
characterised the railways in the west.

This essential but rather less glamorous task
was complemented by more dramatic projects
designed to shorten the GWR network, a
process that involved the building of many
entirely new lines, the first major work carried
out for some time by the company with the
exception of the construction of the Severn
Tunnel. Such expansion was unparalleled and
involved the building of more than 250 miles
of new railway and the doubling of a further
90 miles of secondary lines in a period of just

10 years. The new lines included a direct route to South Wales, new 'direct' services around Swansea, a new route to the West Country via Westbury and a shorter line from Paddington to Birmingham, while another new railway was built to link Birmingham and Bristol.

The hard economics of the situation were inescapable: Brunel's railway, whilst well laid out to provide gentle gradients on his lines running out of Paddington, had left his successors with a number of difficulties which by the end of the 19th century were beginning to cost the railway dear. Severe gradients on lines in the West Country, South Wales and the Midlands slowed trains, and the additional cost of providing banking locomotives was one the company could ill afford. In addition, trains were slowed at various locations where congestion through sheer weight of traffic impacted on both passenger and goods services. Nowhere was this more obvious than at Bristol, where GWR expresses to Cornwall had to compete for space with coal trains from South Wales bound for the South Coast.

The need to improve the movement of trains to and from South Wales was the driving force behind the first major development of the period, the Bristol & South Wales Direct Railway. It might have been assumed that the opening of the Severn Tunnel in 1886 and the consequent shortening of the distance between London and South Wales might have improved matters, but despite the heroic efforts required to complete the project (described in Chapter 2) many of the potential benefits of the tunnel were diminished, initially at least, by the fact that trains still needed to run via Gloucester and the steeply graded line to Swindon. The alternative route for London-bound trains was that via Bristol, which although 15 miles shorter was in practice no quicker because of the congestion in the area.

The huge demand for coal from South Wales was both a long- and short-term spur for the company to improve matters. In 1913, one writer described the journey from London to South Wales on the GWR, noting that as the trains passed through South Wales 'one sees the results of the underground labours of the miners in the long trains of trucks loaded with hard steam coal which brings great wealth into England if not to the miner'. Although in the broad-gauge era rival companies like the London & North Western and the Midland had made inroads into the movement of coal, the GWR still dominated the business. In 1900 it shifted a staggering 30 million tons of coal, coke and minerals, having increased its share of this traffic by a third in only six years; in the preceding decade, however, there had been much criticism of the company for its lack of progress in improving the movement of coal, especially from business interests in South Wales. This criticism led to the promotion in 1895 of a brand-new line, the London & South Wales Railway. This highly ambitious scheme proposed a new railway that would run from South Wales via a new bridge at Aust, striking west across Gloucestershire and Wiltshire, running parallel to the GWR main line and connecting with the Midland Railway and the Midland & South Western Junction Railway before finally linking up with the Great Central and Midland railways in two separate junctions at Great Missenden and Hendon respectively.

The Great Western had fortunately progressed sufficiently with their its plans that this highly speculative scheme came to little. Much work had already been done to design a new railway from Wootton Bassett, west of Swindon, to Patchway, near Bristol, where it joined the existing railway from Bristol to the Severn Tunnel. Once Parliamentary Assent had been granted, in 1896, the rival scheme was dropped, and work began apace, the 30 miles of new railway being completed within five years. The new line served as a model for future schemes: it had few substantial curves, being driven 'fairly straight across country', as one GWR observer noted, and, even though its route took it through the Cotswolds, its gradients scarcely exceeded 1 in 300, ensuring that high-speed running was the norm. A further aid to this was that four of the seven stations on the line had four running lines, allowing slower local services to be overtaken by expresses without delay. The new route opened throughout in July 1903, bringing immediate improvements to journey times; although the distance travelled had been cut by just 10 miles, the time from Paddington to Newport was reduced from four hours to two hours 55 minutes.

The growth of coal traffic from South Wales was matched by increases in passenger numbers on the Great Western in general.

Right: *A postcard view of Chipping Sodbury, one of the new stations on the new direct line to South Wales, completed in 1901.*

Right: *A postcard view of Chipping Sodbury, one of the new stations on the new direct line to South Wales, completed in 1901.*

Below: *An evocative GWR poster, probably issued c1900.*

Business had grown steadily in the final decade of the 19th century, such that the number of passengers using the railway had almost doubled to exceed 80 million by 1900. This new demand was generated largely by the growth of holiday traffic to resorts in Devon and Cornwall but also by increased business from shipping companies, whose transatlantic liners had begun calling in larger numbers at Plymouth. There was fierce competition between the GWR and LSWR for this business, for although the Great Western held a vital contract to carry mail from Plymouth to the capital, it had no such arrangement for passenger traffic, and as a result the years before 1910 saw the company making huge efforts to reduce the time taken to speed mail and passengers from Plymouth to Paddington. The story of these trains, culminating with the record-breaking run by *City of Truro* in 1904, has been repeated many times over the years, and although the trains themselves were often lightly loaded (sometimes with as few as three carriages after Bristol) they cemented the importance of high-speed express services on the railway.

A tragic accident at Salisbury in 1906 brought an end to the competition between the two companies, and despite the success of the Ocean Mail expresses the fact remained that this business — and the more important West Country holiday traffic — needed to bypass Bristol if train speeds and journey times were to improve. The process of creating a new main line to the West was a clever blend of upgrading existing secondary lines and building new bypass or 'cut-off' railways to connect them. Brunel had speculated about the possibility of a direct line to the West Country as early as 1847, but the idea never become a reality in his time.

In 1897 the GWR began work to upgrade the Berks & Hants Railway, doubling almost 20 miles of line between Hungerford and Patney & Chirton, from where it then built a new 20-mile railway to Westbury, bypassing the old line to Devizes. This 'cut-off' had only two intermediate stations, the intention being largely to accelerate through traffic. Along with this new line stations like Westbury were modernised and extended, and elsewhere platforms were lengthened, bridges widened and other improvements carried out. The Stert–Westbury section, like other new stretches of line built at this time, was constructed with fast running in mind, having easy gradients, few curves and only two intermediate stations. Upon completion of this short cut-off in 1900 the GWR continued with a more ambitious avoiding line, from Castle Cary to Langport. This project involved the construction of 32 miles of new track and the doubling of a further 24 miles of single line across a landscape that changed from rolling countryside at the London end to the low-lying Somerset Levels in the West.

The Castle Cary cut-off was completed in July 1906, and from this point all trains from Paddington to the West Country were switched to the new route; GWR timetables and publicity reflected this change, trains to Devon and Cornwall being advertised as running 'via Castle Cary', although few passengers would have been aware of the place, as trains sped through the station without stopping! The completion of these fast 'cut-off' lines in Wiltshire and Somerset was further augmented by other complicated and expensive improvements in the West Country. The doubling of the line between Dawlish and Teignmouth, the final section of the old South Devon Railway, entailed the eradication of another unwanted legacy of Brunel's 'Atmospheric Caper'. This 1½-mile section had been left until last, as it involved the enlargement of no fewer than five tunnels and the construction of a new sea wall at Dawlish, all while trains continued to use the line. The final section of the main line from Devonport Junction to Penzance had also been doubled in stages, the last section being completed in 1906, whilst further east the line between St Germans and Saltash was bypassed entirely, a new deviation line replacing the old route, a 5-mile stretch of which had included six of Brunel's old timber viaducts.

Hand in hand with improvements to the West of England main line was a determined effort by the GWR to attract customers to what

Left: *In addition to the major work required to build new cut-off lines in the West of England to speed trains on the GWR main line to Devon and Cornwall, considerable expense was incurred with the widening of the route along the coast between Exeter and Plymouth. This view shows a GWR service bursting out of Parsons Tunnel between Dawlish and Teignmouth.*

it called the 'Cornish Riviera'. Under the direction of James Inglis, the company used a variety of methods to publicise both the Royal Duchy and the train services that linked it to Paddington. Much effort was expended to extol the mild climate enjoyed by Cornwall all year round, a contemporary poster of the period promising travellers a 'guarantee' that in Cornwall 'there is in depth of winter a mild and gentle climate rivalling that of the resorts of France and Italy and of a far more equable nature, the Duchy being a veritable winter haven'. The publication of a string of travel books by the company began in 1904 with the issue of a 52-page title, *The Cornish Riviera*; great emphasis was placed on the benefits of Cornwall as a 'winter health and pleasure resort', a number of scientists being quoted in a chapter devoted entirely to its climate. Costing just 3d, the book sold an amazing 250,000 copies, being modestly described by the GWR as 'the most popular travel book ever issued by a railway company'.

Urging its passengers to desert damp and foggy London for the mild climate of Cornwall, the Great Western was also not averse to using jingoism to sell the county with the message 'See Your Own Country First', arguing, with the flimsiest of evidence, that the Cornish Riviera was as warm as the French or Italian Riviera if mean temperatures were taken into consideration. Another important

publishing 'first' for the GWR was the production in 1906 of *Holiday Haunts on the Great Western Railway*. In its introduction the company described its purpose, namely to 'impart to holidaymakers of all classes — noble and simple, rich and poor, strong and weak — such information as will enable them to secure a maximum of change, rest, pleasure or sport, at a minimum of expenditure and fatigue'. The book contained a description of features and places of interest in each county served by the railway, followed by a directory of accommodation for each resort, augmented by advertisements. *Holiday Haunts* was an instant success; within two years it had expanded from 334 to 580 pages, and by the time publication was suspended during World War 1 more than 100,000 copies were being sold each year.

Whilst the driving force for improvements on the West of England main line had been the lucrative and growing holiday business, the upgrading of the GWR route from London to Birmingham — the final link in its route modernisation in the years before the Great War — was motivated by the need to generate passenger and freight business in the West Midlands. The new route to Birmingham was once again a combination of new lines and the upgrading of existing track, but importantly also involved the construction of the Acton & Wycombe Railway in partnership with the Great Central. This 38-mile railway cost more than £1 million to build and was completed in April 1906, running through Buckinghamshire to Wycombe, where it joined the existing Banbury– Oxford Line. This new cut-off improved matters, but still entailed trains' continuing to Birmingham via Oxford, so a further new line was authorised; the final cut-off to be constructed before the World War 1 ran from north of Princes Risborough to Aynho, on the Oxford–Birmingham main line. Unlike the Wycombe line this railway was a purely GWR affair, and the heavy engineering works required to build a high-speed railway of this type did not come cheap. As well as a major tunnel, the line also included large cuttings and a 7-mile embankment that utilised millions of tons of clay and rock excavated from elsewhere on the line. It also included stations with the now standard GWR arrangement for most cut-offs whereby local trains used platforms away from the fast lines used by through expresses. With the completion in 1910 of the Aynho cut-off the Great Western was able to advertise and run fast two-hour expresses from Paddington to Birmingham, enabling it to compete directly with the LNWR and, as a by-product, improve the timings of trains to locations far beyond the second city, such as Birkenhead and the Cambrian Coast.

Just as Bristol had been a bottleneck for trains to the West Country before the opening of the new West of England main line, the Great Western station at Birmingham Snow Hill had much the same effect on traffic running north and west. Built in 1854 and extended in 1871, Snow Hill station was cramped, grubby and congested and was hardly a great advertisement for a company taking such giant strides to improve its services and lines, especially once two-hour services had been inaugurated. The new station planned by the GWR was almost twice the size of the old one, and the task of demolishing the existing structure and

building the new terminus took more than seven years. By 1913 the new station at Snow Hill was complete, and included two large platforms that were more than 1,100ft long and capable of accommodating two trains each at any one time. A new overall roof replaced the old broad-gauge structure, and spacious booking facilities were complemented by refreshment rooms described by the *GWR Magazine* as 'the most handsome and elaborately fitted'. As well as handling express services from Paddington, along with considerable local traffic, Snow Hill was the terminus for another cross-country route planned and built before the Great War. The Honeybourne line, opened in August 1906, was constructed through what the GWR called the 'Garden of England' and connected Cheltenham and Honeybourne, south of Stratford, allowing it to run expresses direct from Bristol to Birmingham.

Birmingham Snow Hill was not the only major station to be modernised, and Brunel's great terminus at Paddington was also

Below: The scene at Platform 7 at Birmingham Snow Hill in 1913 after the major reconstruction there. The modern station was a huge improvement on the old broad-gauge-era terminal it replaced.

extensively refurbished. New electric lighting was installed, improving visibility within the murky confines of the trainshed, and Platform 1 was lengthened considerably. Already an enormous station, with a staff of more than 500, Paddington witnessed an increase in traffic levels that led ultimately to the construction in 1913 of an additional roof span to cover three brand-new platforms. The new roof matched the work of Brunel in many respects but at 109ft was longer than his original structure and was constructed of steel rather than wrought iron. At the same time engineers took the opportunity to replace all the cast-iron columns supporting Brunel's original trainshed, it having been discovered that the roof had begun to shift horizontally — so much so that columns supporting the most northerly span were 5½in out of true. However, this, along with other improvement work, was interrupted by war and was not completed until the mid-1920s.

On a much smaller scale the GWR also built new halts in rural and urban locations to attract new passenger business; many of these were served by steam railmotors built to compete with trams and horse buses.

The company was also the first railway to operate feeder bus services from its stations. In August 1903 it began running 'Road Motors' from Helston to The Lizard, in Cornwall. With the creation of its Road Motor Department, based in Slough, the company began to expand its operations, soon afterwards inaugurating a further route, from Penzance to Newlyn. These services, the company argued, 'proved a great convenience to the inhabitants of towns and villages remote from the railway, as also to tourists'. The success of experiments in Cornwall led to the company's purchasing more vehicles and operating further services, in Wales and the Midlands; by 1910 many of the vehicles had run more than 60,000 miles and were also being used for pleasure trips as well as scheduled services. By the 1920s the company was operating 37 routes and carrying more than 4 million passengers annually by bus.

Another £1 million was invested in the construction of a new deep-water port at Fishguard, in West Wales. This remote location had originally been the intended terminus for Brunel's South Wales Railway, but for many years New Milford remained the most

westerly point on the line and the place where ferry traffic departed for Southern Ireland. Constructing the harbour at Fishguard required considerable engineering; miners and quarrymen blasted away the cliffs to excavate the quay and dock facilities, reusing the waste rock to build a large breakwater. More than 1,000ft long, the quay could handle three ships at any one time; as well as having a well-equipped passenger station Fishguard boasted excellent facilities for the unloading of livestock, the Irish cattle trade being particularly lucrative. Although initial plans were aimed at building a new, modern ferry port to service Irish cross-channel traffic, it soon became apparent after the opening of the facility in 1906 that the railway had more ambitious ideas. When the *Mauretania* called at the port two years later the GWR hoped that Fishguard might become an ocean terminal and a serious rival to Liverpool, attracting transatlantic liner traffic. This expectation was never to be fulfilled, due partly to a lack of capital to extend and deepen the harbour to accommodate ocean liners, and the outbreak of the Great War effectively put paid to the GWR's ambitions in this area.

Above: Although this picture of Fishguard Harbour was taken in 1928, the extent of the operation at the port can clearly be seen. The breakwater in the distance was constructed from rock blasted out of the hill to the right of the picture. The funnels of one of the company's steamers are visible above the station buildings.

Right: *An official postcard issued and sold by the GWR showing the departure of one of its 'Ocean Expresses', perhaps carrying passengers from the SS* Mauretania, *in 1908.*

Right: *The era before the Great War was characterised by construction and redevelopment. This picture features staff at Paddington re-laying track on the lines leading into the great terminus.*

The major changes to stations and lines were matched by dramatic improvements to Great Western train services. These new, faster trains were themselves the result of great change at the heart of the Great Western, Swindon Works. The appointment in 1902 of G. J. Churchward as Locomotive Superintendent marked the beginning of a renaissance in locomotive development for the company. Innovative designs to cope with the new demands placed on the traffic department were produced, Churchward's 'standard' locomotives ranging from powerful 4-6-0 'Saint' and 'Star' classes for express services to more humble '28xx' 2-8-0 freight engines built to haul coal trains

through the Severn Tunnel from South Wales. Passenger comfort was not overlooked, and Churchward and his team also designed and built new and more luxurious carriages used on some of the company's most prestigious expresses, such as the 'Cornish Riviera Limited'.

This 'busy period', as one GWR writer noted, also saw considerable change at the works at Swindon. By 1914 the factory employed 12,000 staff, and there had been much investment to re-equip the workshops with the facilities to allow them to build Churchward's new locomotives and rolling stock to the highest standards. New workshops constructed after 1900 were modern and fitted out with the most up-to-date machine tool, cranes and power. A new, larger erecting shop was built before World War 1, but a further extension to what became known as the 'A' Shop was not finally completed until after the conflict. This 257,000sq ft extension became necessary as Churchward's locomotives became ever larger and more powerful and completed a process of redevelopment that left Swindon at the forefront of railway engineering, both in Britain and in the wider railway world.

In 1913 the Great Western celebrated the 75th anniversary of the opening of the first stretch of line, between Paddington and Maidenhead, and the same year marked almost the end of the period of rapid growth that had followed the final abolition of the broad gauge in 1892. In two decades the GWR had been transformed into a railway of the highest standard, with a staff of over 73,000 and more than 1,000 stations in England and Wales. With a fleet of more than 3,000 locomotives, it was able to run more than one million passenger trains annually, and by 1910 its carriage and wagon stock amounted to a staggering 86,549 vehicles (not counting the horse-drawn and motor vehicles and shipping fleet), making it the pre-eminent railway of the era. The optimism and confidence generated by this 'Golden Age' were, unfortunately, short-lived, for in 1914 the tension that had been building in Europe finally manifested itself in the outbreak of World War 1, a conflict that would dramatically change the fortunes of both the company and many of its staff and leave it with an unwanted legacy from which it would take years to recover.

Above: *A composite image of senior GWR staff taken after Frank Potter had taken over as General Manager in 1912.*

Left: *A fascinating picture of G. J. Churchward. The great man is being photographed in one of the workshops, as evidenced by the wood block floor, with a crude black sheet hung behind him as a background. The official version of the picture would have been cropped to remove all this interesting detail!*

CHAPTER SIX

SWINDON WORKS

When the Great Western Railway was first promoted in the early 1830s Swindon was a small market town 'set upon the summit of a moderate hill' at the western end of the Vale of the White Horse. In later years the company would put a more positive gloss on the place in those early days, one of its historians describing the old Swindon as 'an ancient market town of some note'. It was true that it dated back more than 800 years and had been mentioned in the Domesday Book, but, with a population of barely 2,500, it had been in danger of losing ground to other local towns, like Highworth and Wootton Bassett, before the coming of the GWR.

One less-than-sympathetic writer reported that the main amusements for the population of old Swindon in 1840 were 'dog fighting, bull-baiting and the skull-cracking game of backsword or single stick'. The last local tournament of backsword was held in 1841 to celebrate the opening of the Great Western, a 12-guinea prize going 'to the man who had fairly broken his opponent's head and saved his own', but it is unlikely that the agricultural labourers undertaking this violent pastime had any real idea of how much the coming of the railway would change the place. With construction of the railway well underway it soon became apparent that the company would require a workshop facility to repair its locomotives and rolling stock. Daniel Gooch had already spent many long nights in the engine house at Paddington, trying to keep the fleet of locomotives built to Brunel's specification running in less-than-ideal conditions, and, as the railway expanded with the addition of the Bristol & Exeter and Cheltenham lines, the need for a works intensified.

Brunel and Gooch visited Swindon in 1840, identifying land situated in a triangle between the new GWR main line and the new Cheltenham line. Gooch's diary records that the area was still 'only green fields' in the valley below the old town. Swindon was an ideal location for a works, for, in the early days at least, locomotives were changed for the steeply graded section west of the town towards Chippenham and Box, and it was already a junction for the line to Gloucester and Cheltenham. In a report to Brunel written in September 1840 his locomotive superintendent also noted that the nearby Wilts & Berks Canal could also be used to deliver coal and coke to the works, and also as a source of water if required. In February 1841 the establishment of a works at Swindon was authorised by GWR directors, and work began almost immediately on its construction, to designs produced by Brunel.

The Works opened on 2 January 1843. Although it was initially intended as a repair shop for GWR locomotives and rolling stock, within three years the factory had produced the first Swindon-built engine. In a response to the furore created by the 'Battle of the Gauges' and the establishment of the Gauge Commission described in Chapter 2, Gooch was instructed to build a 'colossal locomotive, working with all speed'. Within 13 weeks Gooch and his staff had produced *Great Western*, a powerful 2-2-2 that first steamed on 1 April 1846. With a staff numbering less than 300 when it opened, the works grew steadily. The acquisition of standard-gauge railways, like the Shrewsbury & Chester, and the leasing of the West Midland Railway naturally led to Swindon's both building and repairing what the company insisted on calling 'narrow-gauge' locomotives.

Until the 1860s the Great Western had no centralised location for the construction or repair of its carriage and wagon fleet; broad-gauge carriages were built by private builders and maintained at Paddington, whilst standard-gauge stock was built at Saltney and Worcester. In 1865 serious consideration was given to the establishment of a carriage works at Oxford, but the purchase of 22-acre site there was abandoned following objections from both 'Town and Gown' (who less than 50 years later were to allow the building of the Morris car factory) and more practical considerations regarding flooding in the area around the proposed facility. With the re-appointment of Gooch as Company Chairman the issue was discussed once again, and as there was already enough land at Swindon to accommodate a carriage works it was decided to consolidate all operations there. By the end of 1869 the operation was in full swing, the first new Swindon-built carriages entering traffic in June of that year.

By 1876 the number of Swindon employees had grown to more than 4,500, and by the outbreak of the Great War this figure had almost trebled to 12,000 — a figure that, with the addition of other Locomotive Department staff, would increase to almost 14,000 in the 1930s. Although after the 1923 Grouping (when the company absorbed smaller railways like the Taff Vale and Cambrian) the Great Western also maintained works at locations such as Caerphilly and Wolverhampton, Swindon remained its principal works, and a booklet produced by the company in its centenary year (1935) boasted that Swindon Works was then 'one of the largest establishments for the construction and repair of locomotives, carriages and wagons in the world'.

Certainly the scale of the works at Swindon was staggering, the complex covering an area of 323 acres, of which 73 acres were roofed buildings. A 1949 article describing the activities of the workshops in the early British Railways era estimated that a thorough viewing of the locomotive works alone would

Below: A very early view of the core of the original Swindon Works, taken c1860. The building in the centre of the photograph now forms part of the STEAM museum complex. In the background can be seen open countryside, soon to be swallowed up as Swindon rapidly expanded in the industrial age.

Above: A much later, aerial photograph of Swindon Works, taken in 1967, before the closure of the Carriage & Wagon Works. The extent of the 323- acre site is apparent, the General Offices complex being visible in the triangle formed by the GWR London–Bristol main line and the Gloucester branch, curving away to the right of the picture.

involve a walk of 7½ miles, and that, as a result, the organised visits to Swindon Works usually run on a Wednesday afternoon provided only 'edited highlights' for the thousands of schoolboys and trainspotters who visited. In a similar vein, what follows provides a mere glimpse into just some of the activities carried out at Swindon Works and is by no means a complete portrait of the huge complex. Situated on the north side of the London–Bristol main line, the Locomotive Department employed around 7,000 staff and was reached by a long subway running under the busy lines that ran west of Swindon Junction station. Before the construction of this subway, in the 1860s, staff had to climb up the embankment and take a risky walk across a level crossing to the works. Given the sheer scale of the operation, workshops on the Locomotive side were identified with letters, while in the Carriage & Wagon Works numbers were used.

Between the two world wars the works at Swindon had become almost self-sufficient, taking in raw materials like iron, steel and timber and producing almost everything

needed to run the railway, with the exception of signalling equipment (built at Reading) and catering and hotel equipment. The 1935 guide noted that more than 1,000 locomotives were being repaired annually and that the factory was turning out an average of two new engines per week. The development and design of locomotives and rolling stock took place in the vast General Offices (situated just west of the station), a three-storey building that contained the offices of the Chief Mechanical Engineer and his staff, the Drawing Office and hundreds of clerks and other administrative staff who dealt with more mundane but equally vital tasks, including ensuring that the men were paid on time.

The start of many works tours and the beginning of the construction process itself were the foundries. The largest was the Iron Foundry, situated in a spacious building next to the main line. The 'J1' shop was divided into sections, one producing larger castings such as locomotive cylinders, chimneys and smokebox saddles, the other mass-producing components such as brake blocks, brake cylinders, firebars and steam-heating radiators.

Two furnaces, operating on alternate days, were used to produce enough metal for casting. In the 1930s the Foundry was producing around 10,000 tons of rough castings each year, requiring 1,200 tons of coke and more than 70 tons of limestone. A huge amount of work was required before each day's 'melt' took place. Just how labour-intensive the process was is exemplified by the procedure for making a cylinder casting for a locomotive. The production of moulds using wooden patterns fabricated elsewhere in the works took three days; in the 1940s red Kidderminster sand was used for moulds, some also containing sea sand and oil, especially if mass-produced items were being cast. Before the use of more modern additives horse dung was also used to help bind together the mould. Once a mould had been produced it was allowed to dry thoroughly for a week, assembling of the mould ready for casting taking a further two days before the actual day of casting. Two further days were then required to allow the casting to cool properly before it could be knocked out and cleaned ready for machining.

When casting was in progress the Iron Foundry was a dangerous place, the molten metal being transported from the furnaces to the moulds using large 'prams' — heavy, ladle-like containers that were wheeled up and down the building. Close by was the Chair Foundry, which by 1935 was producing almost 10,000 tons of track chairs (used to fix rails to sleepers) each year. This too was a dirty and dangerous place and had changed very little in 20 years when Jack Hayward became a clerk there in the 1950s. He describes how, although there were louvres in the roof, even between casting pours the air was filled with 'a grey haze and acrid stench', and when molten metal was poured the smoke filled the building, making it impossible to see from one side of the foundry to the other. In addition, local people often complained about the filth that drifted from the foundry, ruining their washing. The men who worked in foundries day and night had to breathe this sulphurous mixture for days on end, and Jack Hayward rightly described them as 'Hell's Kitchen'. To produce the non-ferrous fittings found on Great Western locomotives Swindon also had a brass foundry, which manufactured castings of gunmetal and phosphor bronze. In the 1930s its output was more than 1,700 tons annually.

Only a short walk from the Iron Foundry, at the centre of what had been the original works complex, was the Steam Hammer Shop. The inside of this workshop was no less dangerous and unpleasant than the foundry, for it contained steam and drop hammers that literally made the ground shake. In latter years the largest hammer in use had a 5-ton rating, but an earlier and heavier 10-ton steam hammer was said to be so powerful that it could be heard four miles away, its operation affecting the activities of the machine shops close by. When it was finally removed it was discovered that its foundations included huge cast-iron blocks, wooden baulks and brick filling a space the size of a large cottage. The man controlling the movement of the hammer — the 'Hammer Driver' — traditionally demonstrated his skill to visitors by using the great machine to crack walnuts or to bring down the hammer precisely enough to crack the glass of a gold watch but not damage the watch itself! Fred Richens records that smiths

Below: *A casting being poured in the Iron Foundry. The trilby-hatted foreman keeps a close eye on proceedings.*

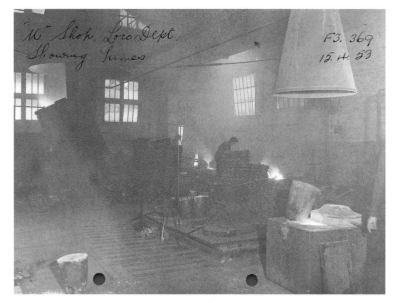

Top: The quality of this Swindon print is not good, but it is included because it illustrates graphically the poor conditions endured by staff in its foundries even in the 1950s.

Above: A well-known and atmospheric picture of the steam-hammer gang hard at work forging a locomotive connecting rod. It is a pity that the picture cannot evoke the noise and vibration involved!

employed in the Hammer Shop and other 'hot shops' normally wore trousers and waistcoats made from moleskin, this being particularly resistant to sparks; if they were not available after a visit to the pawn shop, 'a pair of policemen's trousers was regarded as an adequate substitute for the real thing'.

One area not always visited by works tours was the 'V' Boiler Shop, a large workshop producing the most important and financially valuable component of a GWR locomotive. In the Churchward era much progress had been made in the production of powerful free-steaming boilers, the basic design of which would be utilised until the end of steam-locomotive production at Swindon in the

1950s. Much of the credit for this progress could be attributed to the efforts of the staff who worked in the boiler shop. In the early part of the 20th century writer Alfred Williams described boilersmiths as an 'exclusive order', and, given the conditions in which they worked, there is little doubt that their skills were unique in the factory. Describing his apprenticeship in the works some 40 years later, Swindon apprentice A. E. Durrant described boilermaking as 'more of an art than a science'.

Two distinct tasks were required: in the first, 'platers' prepared the steel boiler plate, marking it up, cutting and bending it into shape; Durrant described how these men operated massive rollers, men who 'with a chalk mark here and there produced the final result almost by sleight of hand!'. By the 1930s more equipment had been installed in the boiler shop, including a large hydraulic flanging press, which, the company guide to the factory noted, worked at a pressure of '750lbs per square inch'. Massive drills 'of the most up to date type' were also used to make holes in the plate ready for the second stage of the process, whereby the boilers were riveted together. In today's Health & Safety-conscious age it is difficult to imagine just how noisy the boiler shop must have been; with up to 80 boilers being worked on at any one time, the sound greeting a visitor to the shop must have been staggering. Accompanying the sound of pneumatic riveting would have been that of men drilling, grinding and hammering, as well as operating all the machinery already described. Alfred Williams wrote that the efforts of 'four or five hundred boilersmiths … hammering and battering away' on the shells and interiors of boilers sounded as if 'hundreds of hammers are falling, banging and clanging perpetually, with an indescribable noise and confusion'. Looking at old photographs of the shop, it is clear that few if any workmen wore any noise protection, save some cotton waste stuffed in the ears, with the result that most staff working there suffered problems with their hearing for the rest of their lives. The Swindon expression that a boilersmith was 'a fitter with his brains knocked out' was not far from the truth!

The Boiler Shop backed on to Rodbourne Lane; this road had marked the western end of the works until the 1890s, when the company purchased further land on the other side of the road to store broad-gauge rolling stock brought to the works for conversion or scrapping. Once this process was complete the land was used to build impressive locomotive-erecting shops to replace outdated broad-gauge-era facilities elsewhere on site. Boilers were therefore trundled along a tunnel excavated under the road, large hydraulic lifts being situated at either end.

The company described its Erecting Shop at Swindon as its 'principal shop'. Certainly by the 1930s it was probably one of the largest and most impressive facilities of its kind in the world. Covering an area of over half a million square feet, this huge workshop served as a locomotive-assembly factory for the GWR, component parts being supplied from workshops elsewhere on the site. What became known as the 'A' Shop complex had been built in two phases; the first, completed in 1904, included not only a large erecting shop but also a spacious machine shop. There were machining facilities elsewhere in the works, most notably the 'R' Fitting & Turning shop (situated in a building now occupied by the STEAM Museum), but the 'A' Shop facility concentrated on the production and repair of larger parts, such as connecting rods, valve gear and cranks.

The second and larger part of the 'A' Shop, known in the factory as the 'A' Shop Extension or 'New Shop', was completed in 1921, following an independent investigation commissioned by the GWR board, which had begun to question Swindon's requests for significant additional capital. These requests came a result of the larger more powerful engines now being designed and built; new 'Saint'- and 'Star'-class locomotives, proving so important in the company's renaissance, were simply too large and heavy for cranes and equipment, even in the 1904 extension. The Locomotive Superintendent finally got his way, and the enormous new extension proved more than satisfactory for future production, surviving until closure of the works in 1986.

The 'A' Shop was one of the most photographed locations in the factory. Locomotives were assembled in a large area with 60 bays, each 100ft long and equipped with a pit. Traversers gave access to each bay, and there were also four large cranes, capable

of lifting completed locomotives; these made the process of wheeling an engine much easier. As well as the erection of new locomotives the shop dealt with heavy and intermediate repairs; the 1935 guide noted that more than 400 locomotives were dealt with each year, and by 1950 this figure had risen to more than 500. The complex also contained a separate Wheel Shop. The process of wheel production was a complex and time-consuming one. After being placed on the axle by a powerful press, wheel tyres were heated in a gas furnace and then shrunk onto the cast wheel centres. Huge lathes were then used to turn the tyres to the correct profile, a 'quartering' machine being employed to drill out the hole for the crank pin, which was fixed in place using a hydraulic press. The final operation involved the use of a large balancing machine to ensure that wheels ran smoothly in service. During the

Below: *The riveting of a GWR locomotive firebox in the 'V' Boiler Shop. Despite the fact that the workman is using a pneumatic rivet gun, he is wearing no ear protection.*

course of year more than 6,000 locomotive and tender wheels passed through this section.

The final part of the locomotive-construction process was the testing of engines; many express locomotives turned out of the great 'A' Shop could be rostered on 'running in' turns which tended to be local trains between Swindon, Bath and Bristol. They could also be run on the Engine Test Plant, built in 1903 and situated at the eastern end of the erecting shop. Locomotives could be run at speeds up to 90mph, and data, revealing power output, fuel and water consumption, extracted. Locomotives ran on five sets of rollers, which could be braked, and locomotive crews working on what was nicknamed the 'Home Trainer' worked hard under the watchful eye of the technical staff. For data on the performance of GWR locomotives 'on the road' the company also used a dynamometer car, built by Churchward at the same time as the plant. Both the carriage and the plant, whilst regularly in use in GWR days, found themselves 'in greater use than at any time in their history' in the early BR years. A 1950 publication produced by the works noted that although the equipment had been 'altered and adapted from time to time to keep pace with the march of progress' they were capable of dealing with the most powerful locomotives in Britain. Pictures show not only GWR locomotives under test on the plant but also BR Standard and LNER types.

Although the Carriage & Wagon Works employed fewer staff, with 5,000 on the complement in the years after the Great War, the range of occupations was no less varied. Originally situated to the south of the main line to Bristol, the Carriage Department by the 1930s also occupied a great swathe of land, workshops and sidings to the north of the station. The process of building a carriage began with the raw material, timber logs and even whole trees. These were delivered to the factory and processed in two sawmills, where they were converted into a more manageable size — 'planks, boards or scantlings', as one writer noted — for use in carriage- and wagon-building. Both mills had extraction systems to remove wood chippings and sawdust, which was piped into a boiler which generated enough steam to heat workshops and also to power nearby drying kilns, used to speed up the seasoning process; photographs taken prior to their introduction show large stacks of timber left to season outside the workshops. One unusual sub-section of the sawmill was the Saw Doctors' Shop; here most of the saws and cutters used in the factory and on the railway generally were sharpened, tensioned and set.

In contrast to the Locomotive Works, where workshops were identified not merely by name but also by a letter, on the carriage side the workshops were arranged numerically. As in the Locomotive Works, however, a series of smaller workshops formed links in a complex production process, providing component parts for the final assembly of carriages and wagons. Underframes for both carriages and wagons were fabricated in 13 and 13A Shop, situated close to the old canal that bisected the site, whilst many of the smaller components were manufactured next door, in the Fitting & Machine Shop. Known by the GWR as the 'Show Shop' of the Carriage & Wagon Department, 15 Shop was responsioble for the machining of brake fittings, axleboxes, drawgear, steam-heating apparatus and auto-coach controls and the manufacture of many other unusual items such as platform trolleys, ticket machines and loading gauges.

Despite the modernisation of the workshops in GWR days, old-fashioned trades like blacksmithing still survived into the 1950s. An article on the factory published in 1950 revealed that a team of 109 'men and boys' were still employed in the Smiths' Shop; machine tools had begun to make an impact, however, and the manufacture of three-link wagon couplings had been much improved by

Opposite top: The 'A' Erecting Shop in 1927. The image is one of a series produced to illustrate the construction of the new 'King'-class locomotives at the works. There is a wealth of detail to be seen: workmen's coats hang on a makeshift coat rack on the left of the picture, whilst a large hydraulic riveter is being used on the locomotive on the right. Just below the smokebox of the locomotive on the left are the tell-tale signs of white asbestos, used for lagging.

Opposite lower: The 'AW' Wheel Shop at Swindon Works in the early 1950s.

Below: A Swindon Drawing Office picture of the Works Test Plant, taken on 17 August 1935. The locomotive under test is 'Star' No 2931 Arlington Court, *built in 1911 and destined to be withdrawn in 1951.*

Above: *The view from one of the windows of Newburn House, official residence of the Locomotive Superintendent. At the time this image was captured, Churchward would have lived there, and his dog can be seen sitting outside a kennel in the garden. Behind the wall huge logs of timber are being seasoned ready for use in the carriage works beyond.*

Left: *A very young- looking apprentice bundling up firewood in the old Saw Mill at Swindon in 1934. Scrap timber was used for this purpose, and the completed the bundles were then sent to GWR locomotive sheds all over the system.*

the introduction of new welding equipment, boosting production to 400 couplings per week. Situated at the heart of the Carriage & Wagon Works complex, north of the station, was 18 Shop. This large building housed numerous steam hammers, drop hammers and hydraulic presses used to manufacture larger carriage and wagon parts such as axleboxes, brake rodding, frames and other items which in earlier years had been produced by hand.

Hundreds of carriages and wagons passed through the works each year for repair and maintenance. No 24 Shop, where this activity took place, was a relatively new building; completed in 1924, it covered a staggering 7 acres, and its 28 tracks could accommodate more than 200 carriages at any one time. One common maintenance task involved checking the wheels of both wagons and carriage bogies. The nearby Wheel Shop also dealt with the manufacture of new wheels and contained much the same equipment as its namesake in the Locomotive Works — furnaces for the shrinking of tyres onto wheels, lathes for tyre profiling, and balancing equipment. By the 1950s the shop also contained two Hughes Supersonic Flaw Detectors, machines that could identify flaws in vehicle axles before they went into service.

Great Western carriages had been constructed largely of wood until the Great War, when steel panelling began to be introduced. Despite this a large proportion of wood was still used in GWR coaches, especially the interior. Craftsmen in the 7 (Finishing) Shop made components like corridor, toilet and gangway doors, seats and tables, luggage racks and internal panelling. Once produced, the fittings were sent to the 10A Shop — where, the company noted, 'women only are employed' — for French-polishing. Elsewhere varnish or lacquer was also applied to parts before these were returned for assembly in the final product.

The Carriage Trimming Shop was another 'show' shop, making and fitting all upholstery for carriages. In the main part of 9 Shop staff produced upholstery for carriage seats as well as pads for axleboxes, hosepipes, belts for machines, carpets, curtains, mattresses for hotels and leather items such as window straps, horse-box reins, pouches for signalling tablets, water column bags and even staff briefcases. In 1935 the company guide to the works reminded readers that 'female operatives' worked next door in 9A Shop, where their more precise sewing skills were employed in delicate work such as the manufacture of bed linen, flags, towels, cushions, luggage rack netting and window blinds. The amount of raw material used was staggering; in 1957 alone more than 67,000 yards of moquette, 165,000 yards of canvas and 37,000 yards of carriage-blind material were processed. Final assembly of carriages took place in 4 Shop, the Carriage Body Shop; the completed underframes were wheeled into position, whereupon the coach body frames were constructed, and interior partitioning and doors added. The wood panelling and upholstery already described was installed, and the carriage was then moved the short distance to 8 Shop, where it was painted, varnished, lettered and 'finished off with the company's monogram'.

The Carriage & Wagon Works carried out a variety of other less-well-known tasks for the GWR and, later, BR. The Carpenters' & Cabinetmakers' Shop was responsible for making a great deal of equipment used on the railway as a whole; the skilled craftsmen employed there made chairs, desks and other office equipment and almost all the furniture and equipment used in stations and depots on the network. The station platform seats, signs, trolleys and carts and ticket racks now prized by railway enthusiasts were all made and repaired in 12 Shop. Swindon was also the location for the company's Laundry, which washed more than a million articles every year. Linen from Great Western hotels, ships and stations was returned to Swindon in wicker baskets and shipped back after cleaning. In 1954 a British Railways guide to the factory reported that the laundry was now equipped with a modern dry-cleaning machine for curtains and chair and cushion covers.

The self-sufficiency mentioned earlier extended further than the processing of raw materials to produce finished locomotives and rolling stock. To a great extent the Swindon factory also provided all the services it needed, generating its own electric power until supplies became available locally for the town as a whole. A gasworks for the factory was built as early as 1844, but a far larger installation was built to the north of the works in 1878 and subsequently enlarged even further in 1920 with the construction of a gas-holder with a capacity of four million cubic feet. Although Daniel Gooch had originally thought that water for the works could be obtained from the Wilts & Berks Canal, this supply soon proved inadequate, and reservoirs were built close to Swindon station. The need for a more secure supply of water led to the GWR's sinking a well at the works in

Left: *Swindon worker Albert Blanchard at work on one of the machines used in 18 Shop in the Carriage & Wagon Works.*

Above: *The interior of the Carriage Body Shop in the 1880s. The picture was one of a series taken by a local photographer either on a Sunday or during a lunch break, there being no staff in evidence. In the background is what is thought to have been Brunel's horse-drawn carriage which survived for many years at Swindon before being broken up.*

1885. Although this was sunk ostensibly to search for water, there were also suggestions from local geologists that a seam of coal might be found, but none was discovered, and the water that sprang from the well was found to have five times the normal level of salt. This situation was clearly unhelpful, although the workforce was convinced that the well was connected with the sea, specifically at Weymouth, where many went on their annual 'Trip Holiday'! Eventually the company was forced to build a pipeline to a well at Kemble, some miles to the north, on the Swindon–Gloucester line, and the works retained this independent supply until closure in 1986.

The works also provided its own supplies of steam, compressed air and hydraulic power to operate equipment such as hand tools, steam hammers and workshop heating systems. A large boiler house fitted with eight separate boilers provided pressurised steam, any excess being used to power a series of accumulators providing hydraulic power. The accumulators were housed in a building that was also known to staff as the 'Hooter House', for on its

roof were the now-famous steam hooters used to summon men to work. The problem of ensuring that all workers got to the factory on time had troubled the company from the earliest days. In the years after the works opened in 1843 a large bell was mounted on the roof of one of the workshops and tolled morning, noon and night. Whilst the workforce and the town remained a modest size this was adequate, but as the workshops began to expand rapidly in the second half of the 19th century more noise was needed, and a steam hooter was provided. What Fred Richens called the 'voice of the GWR at Swindon' was, as he remembers, the reason workshop staff rarely overslept — or, indeed, anyone else in the town!

At 5.20am the hooter was sounded for 10 long minutes, this being followed by another three-minute blast at 5.50am, and, in case anyone had not yet stirred, it blasted out for a further minute at 6am. This assault on the ears was not universally welcomed, especially by Henry St John, fifth Viscount Bolingbroke, whose country house, Lydiard Park, was some miles to the west of the works. Following complaints to the GWR in 1868, his Lordship managed to persuade the company to build a screen around the hooter to reduce its power — a measure that in turn brought complaints from workers and its eventual scrapping. Undeterred, in 1873 he obtained an injunction banning the use of the hooter, arguing that it produced a 'loud, piercing, roaring and distracted noise' and that it was damaging his health. Despite a petition signed by over 4,000 local people, including GWR factory hands, farm labourers and working men and women from surrounding towns and villages, the licence for the hooter was revoked. This was not, however, the end of the matter, and further local protest and public meetings led the local board to reconsider its position. The fact that the noble Lord spent only two months each year at his Wiltshire seat did not play well, and the injunction was revoked. A new and, some argued, louder hooter was installed, and this continued to sound right up until closure of the works in 1986.

This description of the huge range of activities carried out at Swindon gives only the most superficial impression of what the place must have been like in the age of steam. It is well known that Swindonians described a job in the railway works as working 'inside'; generations of workers followed their fathers or other relatives into company service, and behind the high walls of the factory the skills and traditions were jealously guarded. Discipline in the works was tough, the bowler-hatted foreman having almost complete power over the workers in his charge. A glance through the 1904 Rule Book for workmen employed at Swindon illustrates just how stringent rules were; 'making an article of the wrong dimensions, or finishing work in an inferior or unworkmanlike manner' could result in a fine of 2s 6d or even instant dismissal. Any workman found 'playing, idling or quarrelling during working hours' could also be fined, and smoking, especially in the Carriage & Wagon Works, was also strictly forbidden.

The 1904 rules also noted that staff worked a 54-hour week, averaging nine hours a day, beginning at 6.00am and finishing at 5.30pm every day except Saturday, when work ceased at midday. Until 1872 a 57½-hour week had been worked, and its abolition was greeted by

celebrations and a parade by the workforce. After the Great War the working week was reduced further, to 47 hours, with a start time of 8am — a welcome relief to staff, especially on dark winter mornings. Although the hours were still long, and working conditions not always good, what the company called 'esprit de corps' was strong within the factory. The close-knit community was very solid, and generations of workers toiled in the factory for well over a century, so that when it finally closed in 1986 there were still many with a genuine family connection to the Great Western era.

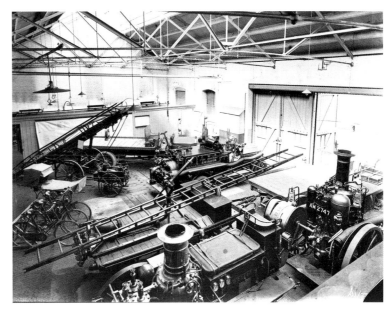

Below: *A vast array of fire-fighting equipment on display in the Swindon Works Fire Station in Bristol Street. This picture was probably taken when the company acquired a new Dennis fire tender in 1912.*

Bottom: *Lunchtime on a beautiful summer's day – 24 July 1928. Just some of the 12,000 men employed in the factory walk down Rodbourne Road, stopping the traffic including the tram, itself full of railway staff.*

CHAPTER SEVEN

GREAT WESTERN SWINDON

When Great Western directors authorised the construction of 'an engine establishment at Swindon' in 1841 the phrase 'at Swindon' actually meant land some distance from the old market town on the hill. Fields to the west of Swindon station, described by local writer Richard Jefferies as being 'covered with furze, rushes and rowan', became the site not only of a large railway works but also of a brand-new township known as New Swindon. It would be almost 60 years before the two towns were joined together, albeit separated (as one anonymous writer noted) 'by marshy land and a social cleavage as complete as though imposed by an impassable mountain barrier'.

With the construction of the railway workshops well underway, GWR management soon realised that accommodation would be needed for the influx of workers required to run the new factory. There was no tradition of railway engineering in north Wiltshire, and as a result Daniel Gooch and Works Manager Archibald Sturrock began recruiting skilled workers from other parts of the country, especially those where railways already had a foothold. Trevor Cockbill's *A Drift of Steam* chronicles the origins of many early residents of New Swindon, clearly illustrating that many staff were brought from engineering centres all over Britain. James Fairburn, who was recorded as living in New Swindon in 1842, hailed originally from Dundee and had come south to work for Daniel Gooch at Paddington before being transferred to Swindon. Records show that, as well as many other Scots, large numbers of men from Lancashire and the North East were brought to the town,

although, as Trevor Cockbill observes, they were also recruited from many other locations, including Bristol, London and South Wales.

With the arrival of these men and their families imminent, the company authorised the construction of an estate of cottages south of the London–Bristol main line. There were scarcely a dozen houses within the vicinity of the new works, and, being some distance away, the old settlement of Swindon was hardly suitable for housing large numbers of incomers. What became known as the Railway Village consisted initially of eight streets, all named after locations on the GWR — Bath, Bristol, Exeter, Faringdon, London, Oxford, Reading and Taunton. Until recently it had been thought that the cottages were designed by the architect Matthew Digby-Wyatt, but the discovery of original drawings for the village has revealed that they were in fact the work of Brunel himself.

The houses were of several types and ranged from 'two up, two down', with the addition of a scullery, to smaller one-bedroom cottages; although small by modern standards they were well-constructed, and all had their own tiny garden, privy and wash house — facilities lacking in many houses in other industrial towns. The houses were built from local limestone, augmented by stone from the Box/Chippenham area. Larger three-storey corner houses were added as the village grew in phases. The 'railway village' was completed in the 1860s with the addition of larger three-bedroomed cottages known as 'Foremen's Houses', only higher-paid men being able to afford the rent. However, the rapid growth of the workforce meant that overcrowding was not uncommon. An 1844 survey highlighted one extreme example in which a two-roomed house was occupied by 11 people — a husband, wife, five children and four lodgers! An 1861 census return for 1 Faringdon Street (nowadays a restored railwayman's cottage and museum) showed that this larger three-bedroomed house was occupied by engine driver John Hall, his wife Jane, one daughter and four sons ranging in ages from 6 to 20 years old.

The construction of a gasworks at the railway factory allowed the village to be lit by gas, although legend has it that, in the interests of economy, lighting was switched off three days before and three days after a full moon. Each cottage also had a water tap, although the water was not always fit for drinking; instead, fresh spring water sourced from the nearby village of Wroughton was supplied from a horse-drawn tanker, at a halfpenny a bucket. Until the installation of mains drains in the latter part of the 19th century poor sanitation also meant that incidences of diseases like smallpox, typhoid and scarlet fever were high. Matters were not helped by the fact that many villagers kept chickens, rabbits and even pigs in their tiny back yards!

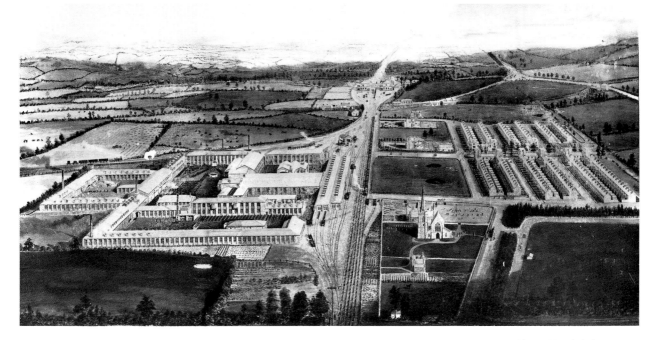

Above: *New Swindon as portrayed by Snell in 1849. Snell was a draughtsman employed in the works and his watercolour, now preserved at STEAM, shows not only the new factory but also the main elements of the railway village, although the Mechanics Institute and hospital were yet to be constructed.*

Left: *The photographer has set up his camera outside the entrance to the railway works in Bristol Street, and some of the cottages in what the GWR later called the 'Railway Estate' can be seen in this 1930 view.*

The overcrowding and shortage of accommodation was a particular problem for the single men attracted to the town to work in the factory; whilst many lodged with other families, this was not an ideal arrangement, and instead the company decided to build a 'model lodging house' equipped with 100 bedrooms, each large enough to fit a bed, chair and chest of drawers; it would also have communal features like a kitchen and washing facilities. The Barracks, as it became known, finally opened in 1855, but the watchmen — employed to keep order in the building — and the primitive cooking facilities proved unpopular with the young men lodging there, and new tenants were sought. A solution emerged with the opening at the works in 1861 of the Rolling Mills; 20 Welsh families moved into the building, but constant disagreements made life difficult for the works manager, who was called upon to adjudicate on their squabbles, which were often in a language he could not understand! Eventually the Welsh-speaking community moved out, and in 1863 Thomas Ellis, the Rolling Mills Foreman, set up a company to build an estate of houses for his workforce. Enough money was generated to allow the construction of two rows of cottages and a chapel close by, in an area known then as 'Welsh Buildings' (and now appropriately named Cambria Place).

The old Barracks building fell into disuse but after rebuilding in 1867 became a Wesleyan Methodist Chapel. Used as such for 90 years, it closed as a result of dwindling congregations and was subsequently (in 1962) converted into the Great Western Railway Museum — a joint venture between Swindon Corporation and the British Transport Commission. The museum closed in 1999 prior to the opening of the new STEAM Museum, and the building now serves as a youth centre — a pleasing return to something akin to its original function.

There is little doubt that the building of one of the earliest model villages was both a far-sighted and expedient move by the Great Western, but there were drawbacks for the inhabitants of New Swindon. The absolute power of the company naturally meant that occupation of a cottage was dependent upon keeping a job in the factory, and any transgression of the rules described in the previous chapter could have serious consequences for workers and their families. In 1847 an early slump in the fortunes of the company led to the formation of an organisation that would prove vital to the continued well-being of residents — the GWR Medical Fund. In response to an appeal to the directors by Daniel Gooch the company agreed to provide rent-free accommodation for a doctor who would attend railway workers and their families. This proposal was not entirely philanthropic, however, as the doctor would also be available to give medical aid to 'those to whom accidents may occur in the works and or on the Company's premises'.

The Medical Fund was set up shortly afterwards and was run by a committee of management and men, its objectives being 'to provide medicine and attendance to the men employed in the works of the GWR at Swindon and their wives and families'. Workers paid for this service through a deduction from their wages, which varied from 4d for married men earning more than £1 per week to 'three ha'pence for a boy earning less than ten shillings a week'. The rule book for Swindon staff stated that 'every workman is required, as a condition of Service, to become a member of the GWR Medical Fund Society' and also reminded staff that membership of the Sick Fund, set up by the workforce to provide sick pay, was also compulsory.

With the establishment of the fund Swindon staff and their families received a level of medical care above and beyond that enjoyed by many industrial workers of the time. As the 19th century progressed, the range of services offered grew in size and sophistication: in 1859 a 'Keeper of Lime Brushes and Invalid Chair' was appointed at a salary of £1 5s per year, and the practice of supplying lime and brushes for disinfecting toilets continued well into the 20th century. In 1872 the GWR Hospital opened, funded partially by the Great Western, which gave £130 towards the cost of converting what had once been an armoury. The new hospital consisted of a four-bed ward, operating theatre, surgery, mortuary and nurses house; to ensure its long-term future the hospital was given an endowment of £2,000, half this sum being supplied by the Medical Fund, the other half donated by Gooch from his own pocket. The society decreed that the hospital should be for accidents only and not for 'general diseases', as well as being free to all members of the society. It also served as a first-aid facility, dealing with accidents in the factory, of which there were many in the 19th century in particular. Until the establishment of St John Ambulance at the works in the 1880s, emergency care given by workers could be very rudimentary, and the dressing of open wounds could involve the use of rather unconventional treatments, including tobacco juice, axle grease or even cobwebs, none of which was particularly hygienic or effective!

In 1892 the GWR Medical Fund opened its largest and most comprehensive building in Milton Road. Its headquarters was supplied with gas and water from the works, piped through a tunnel which ran from the works to the cellar. The building contained doctors' consulting rooms, a dispensary and dental, eye and therapy departments, as well as two new swimming pools filled with hot water

Left: *The GWR Medical Fund Hospital c1900. To the right, its walls covered in ivy, can be seen the Faringdon Road Wesleyan Chapel, built as a lodging house for railway workers.*

Left: *The doctor's waiting room of the new GWR Medical Fund headquarters which opened in 1892. Male and female patients were kept separate and the board on the back wall lists the medical staff in attendance. It was said that the roof utilised old broad-gauge rail in its construction.*

from the works. In 1899 washing, Turkish and Russian baths were installed — a welcome addition, as most railway cottages did not have bathrooms or hot running water, and many families were forced to share a tin bath, filled with water heated in a copper, every week. The cradle-to-grave nature of the GWR Medical Fund was further reinforced by the final, more sombre service offered, that of the undertaker. For members the use of a 'shillibeer' and horse was free, but any dependants had to be paid for; for any worker killed whilst on duty the coffin, made by carpenters in the Carriage & Wagon Works, was supplied free of charge. With the creation in 1948 of the National Health Service the Medical Fund ceased to exist, departing (as its historian noted) 'trailing clouds of glory', having provided railway employees and their families with unrivalled medical care for exactly a century.

When the works opened, in 1843, a group of employees joined together to set up what became known as the Mechanics' Institution. The body was formally constituted the following year, its aim being 'to disseminate useful knowledge and encourage recreational amusement amongst all classes of people

HAIRDRESSING ROOMS

employed by the company at Swindon'. Even before obtaining its own premises the Institution began assembling an extensive library, while classes and much less serious social events, like dances and concerts, were held in the works itself. Without the direct influence of the GWR, staff created the New Swindon Improvement Company to build a facility that would house baths, reading, lecture and refreshment rooms, a market and shops. Land was leased from the company in a square at the centre of the railway village, and the Mechanics' Institute was opened in 1855.

Initially the complex included an octagonal market situated on the south side of the building. Housing stalls and shops, this was also the location of a rather dubious 'Hole-In-The-Wall' beer house, which, although serving excellent ale, broke most if not all of the licensing laws, closing not long after it had opened. More sober members of the Institute could enjoy its library, which even as early as 1844 contained more than 130 books, and catalogues issued over the years reveal just how comprehensive it was. By the end of the 1880s, as New Swindon expanded, some of the amenities originally offered by the Institution were now being provided elsewhere. The baths moved to a different location, and the shops and market had been overtaken by the development of larger and better-stocked shops in the centre of town. The market was duly demolished, and the Institute building extended by the addition of a larger theatre and dance hall, which opened in 1892. The enlarged facility provided both educational activities, such as lectures and debates, and entertainment, in the form of concerts, dances, drama and even opera.

The Great Western also tried, in the earliest days of the works, to cater for the spiritual welfare of its workforce. When George Henry Gibbs, a director of the company, died in 1842 he left a bequest of £500 to build a church and school at Swindon. The construction of both eventually cost almost £8,000, and much of this total was raised through contributions from GWR shareholders, a shortfall of almost £3,000 being provided by the company. St Mark's Church, designed by the architect George Gilbert Scott, was capable of seating 800 worshippers and opened in 1845. The nearby GWR School, situated in Bristol Street, offered

children of railway employees a good standard of education; discipline was, not surprisingly, tough. Schooling was not free, however, the first child in a family being charged 4d per week, and subsequent children a further 3d each. Soon after the school opened there had been some controversy when the vicar of the nearby church attempted to make church attendance compulsory for school pupils, but after some opposition from a workforce containing many non-conformist Christians the idea was abandoned.

Opposite the church and school was another important New Swindon landmark, the GWR Park; purchased in 1844 from local landowner Col Villett, this was known for some years as 'The Cricket Field', and it is rumoured that the great W. G. Grace once played there. In 1871 the field was turned into a more formal park, with landscaping and a large new pavilion. Many older Swindonians remember the park for a different reason, for it was the location for the annual GWR 'Juvenile Fête', organised by a committee of the Mechanics' Institution. Children of employees

Top: *The Mechanics Institute at New Swindon showing the octagonal market attached to the rear of the 1855 building. This structure was swept away when the building was extended in 1892.*

Above: *The extended Mechanics Institute featured a large and well- equipped theatre used for all manner of productions and activities. Five rather self-conscious models pose for the camera at a fashion show held in the theatre in the 1930s.*

Right: *A very early picture of the GWR School in Bristol, taken by local photographer J. B. Protheroe. The spire of the railway church, St Mark's, can be seen in the background.*

Above: *This view of one of the fêtes held in the GWR Park features a famous GWR face. In the centre of the picture, behind the lady with flowers in her hat, can be seen William Stanier, later to achieve fame as Chief Mechanical Engineer of the LMS.*

were issued with a ticket which gave them a turn on one of the fairground rides provided. More importantly each child received a slice of cake, made to a secret recipe and sliced and packed in greaseproof paper. The fête was one of the social events of the year for railway families, and the scale of the event is nowadays hard to imagine; for the 1904 fête more than 30,000 people crammed into the 10½-acre park.

The other social event that bound together the railway community at Swindon was the 'trip' holiday. Organised once again by the Mechanics' Institution, it began in 1848 with the running of a special train to Oxford for 500 workers and their families, paid for by the GWR. These day excursions continued until the 1870s, when the company gave staff a week's holiday, which was, of course, unpaid. During the dark nights of winter the annual ritual of Trip Week (and later Trip Fortnight) was much anticipated by adults and children alike, and preparations were made months in advance. By the end of the 19th century the 'trip' had become a huge operation, trains being run all over the network. Although staff and their families were carried free to holiday destinations, the length of their holiday depended on their income and savings, and many families could afford only a short break before returning to a deserted town. Many shop owners, knowing that railway families would be away on Trip Holiday, closed their premises for the duration, and so many people left the town that, as one railwayman put it, 'you could fire a gun up Regent Street and not hit anyone'. The most popular location visited by railway families was the Dorset resort of Weymouth, nicknamed by Swindonians 'Swindon by the Sea'; however, some men preferred other locations, such as Weston-super-Mare, where there was less likelihood of meeting factory staff with whom they worked all year round!

By 1900 the town of New Swindon had spread out in all directions from the original railway village. Waves of red-brick houses, constructed by speculative builders, filled in the gap between the old and new towns, and housing grew up around the newly extended Locomotive Works in Rodbourne. Similarly, in Gorse Hill, housing was built and occupied largely by staff working in the Carriage & Wagon workshops, and for many years there was a rivalry between the two communities, particularly amongst children, mirroring a general feeling of disdain between the two departments in the factory itself.

More houses were built up the hill towards Old Town. The residents here tended to be supervisory staff like foremen, whose higher wages allowed them to buy or rent larger houses away from the dirt and grime of the factory, and only the most senior and well-paid factory staff could actually afford to live in the Old Town. The snobbery between old and new continued well after 1900, when the two communities were formally amalgamated to form the Borough of Swindon. It was no coincidence that the first Mayor of the new Borough was G. J. Churchward, the appointment cementing the influence the company would have over the economic, social and political life of Swindon until well after World War 2.

Left: *The coat of arms of the town of Swindon, created after the joining of 'old' and 'new' Swindon in 1900. This crest was fitted to 'Castle' No 7037* Swindon, *the last locomotive of this design to be built at the works, in 1950.*

Below: *Trip Morning in July 1934. GWR staff and their families make their way past the carriage works to board trains to holiday destinations. Most trains left from the works since there was simply not enough space at Swindon station to despatch the 25,000 people moved promptly without disrupting scheduled services.*

CHAPTER EIGHT

GREAT WESTERN INHERITANCE:
1918-1929

The enormous upheaval caused by four long years of war left the Great Western Railway in a very run-down condition. Those workers not called up for military service were exhausted, and the company needed substantial investment to return its trains, lines and stations to prewar standards. The editorial in the January 1919 issue of the *GWR Magazine* noted that 'war conditions have rendered necessary many departures from former principles and high standards' and that 'facilities and conveniences that have been withdrawn cannot be restored immediately'. If anything highlighted the stresses and strains inflicted by the Great War it was the loss of the 'able and popular' General Manager, Frank Potter. Worn out after guiding the railway through such a difficult period, he had travelled to St Ives in April 1919 to recuperate but passed away there suddenly three months later. Shocked though the company was by this loss, it nevertheless faced a much greater problem, as time was also needed to recruit new staff to fill gaps left by those killed or injured in the conflict. That said, when the company carried out a census of its staff in 1921 the number of people it employed was found to exceed 92,000 — a huge total compared with the 161,000 employed by the whole of British Rail in the 1980s

Despite the war the GWR found itself in a comparatively strong position in contrast to some of its closest rivals; it owned and operated in excess of 3,000 miles of line on which there were more than 1,000 station. The railway also ran a number of luxurious hotels, notably the Great Western Royal Hotel at Paddington and the Tregenna Castle Hotel at St Ives. To work this great empire the company had more than 3,000 locomotives, 8,000 carriages and a staggering 78,000 goods and mineral wagons. It also ran a large fleet of road vehicles, horse-drawn and motorised, and to operate its ferry services to the Channel Islands and Southern Ireland it also maintained a sizeable fleet of steamships, tugs and tenders.

The 1919 *GWR Magazine* editorial noted that 'Rumours are current as to the intentions of the government in regard to the railways, which have now been under control for nearly four-and-a-half years.' This was hardly surprising, for in the years immediately after the war the combined working deficit of the 100 or so independent companies that made up the national railway network was a staggering £41 million and increasing. The success of the quasi-nationalised framework of the Railway Executive used during World War 1 meant that after 1919 full-scale nationalisation was seriously considered by the new coalition Government led by Lloyd George, but was ultimately rejected in favour of a scheme that involved the amalgamation of railways into four large companies, each serving, in the main, one geographical area of the country. Government control of the railways continued until August 1921, when a new Railways Act was passed. Reporting the implications of the new arrangements to staff in January 1921, GWR General Manager Charles Aldington noted that, whilst there would be a period of uncertainty until the ramifications of the new Act became clear, 'it is hoped that the Great Western will not lose its identity'.

In reality there was little likelihood of this happening; by virtue of the size and importance of the Great Western there was little doubt that the company would be the pre-eminent partner in the 'western group' of the new 'Big Four' companies. In the hiatus before the arrangements were finally confirmed there was some discussion regarding the make-up of the western group, and even a proposal to have a separate group for Welsh companies only. At one point a number of GWR directors argued that it should be the only constituent of the new grouping, the other railways being absorbed. Not surprisingly this somewhat arrogant attitude was challenged by larger Welsh companies such as the Barry Railway, which argued that its dividend of 10% was higher than that paid to GWR shareholders. In its heyday the Taff Vale Railway had paid dividends as high as 17½%, and as a result the enlarged Great Western Railway that came into being on 1 January 1922 consisted of the original GWR company and six constituents — a clever arrangement designed to ensure recognition of the history, prestige and traditions of the larger independent companies, these being the Alexandra (Newport & South Wales) Docks & Railway, the Barry Railway, the Cambrian Railways, the Cardiff Railway, the Rhymney Railway and the Taff Vale Railway.

Over the next 18 months a further group of subsidiary railways was also absorbed into the new railway, and these included the following:

Brecon & Merthyr Railway
Burry Port & Gwendreath Valley Railway
Cleobury Mortimer & Ditton Priors
    Light Railway
Didcot, Newbury & Southampton Railway
Exeter Railway
Forest of Dean Central Railway
Gwendraeth Valleys Railway
Lampeter, Aberayron & New Quay
    Light Railway
Liskeard & Looe Railway
Llanelly & Mynydd Mawr Railway
Mawddwy Railway
Midland & South Western Junction
    Railway
Neath & Brecon Railway
Penarth Extension Railway
Penarth Harbour Dock & Railway
Port Talbot Railway & Docks

Princetown Railway
Rhondda & Swansea Bay Railway
Ross & Monmouth Railway
South Wales Mineral Railway
Swansea Harbour Trust
Teign Valley Railway
Vale of Glamorgan Railway
Welshpool & Llanfair Light Railway
West Somerset Railway
Wrexham & Ellesmere Railway

The Great Western was the only pre-Grouping railway to retain its original name under the new arrangements, and under the terms of the 1921 Act became the 'Amalgamated Company' for the western group. This avoided the need to rearrange existing capital funding or dissolve the original company. It also meant that it was able to move forward far more quickly with the amalgamation process than could its rivals, expanding and modifying its existing management structure to absorb the smaller companies it had acquired. Speaking at the GWR's Annual General Meeting in 1922, Company Chairman Viscount Churchill told shareholders that he was sure it would 'bring

Below: *Company seal of the Barry Railway Co. The GWR retained all the company seals of railways absorbed throughout its history, and these are now preserved as part of the National Collection.*

joy to the hearts of many who loved the Great Western that the old name and identity is to be retained'. The takeover of the six larger independent concerns and 26 smaller companies increased the network mileage by 560 and also added a further 3,365 miles of single track, including sidings. A further 18,000 staff were added to the GWR payroll, whilst the working capital of the company increased by a staggering £36 million. Despite the obvious increase in costs, Viscount Churchill was able to reassure shareholders that he was 'satisfied that it should be possible to effect considerable savings as a result of the amalgamation'.

An amusing cartoon appeared in the *South Wales Echo* in November 1922 headed 'A Survival of Title' and featuring a member of Great Western Railway staff shouting: "Hooray! Never even blew me cap off!" A caption below noted: 'None of the companies which survive the amalgamation upheaval have come out of it with such enhanced prestige.' It was hardly a surprising that a Welsh newspaper should take such interest in this issue, since the six largest constituent companies joining the GWR were situated there. With the exception of the Cambrian Railways they were all built to serve the coal-mining and industrial heartland of South Wales, and most had lines which ran up and down the valleys, moving coal from pit to port, often crossing the Great Western's original South Wales main line. The company was more than aware of the considerable inheritance it had received in South Wales, and of the potential benefits it might bring to the region. Viscount Churchill, concluding his survey of the whole issue of amalgamation for shareholders in 1922, argued that 'the inclusion of Welsh railways in the Great Western undertaking would enable improvements to be made in the operation of the railway, and thereby benefit the trade and commerce of the Principality'.

Five companies covered a large area of the South Wales valleys, and the oldest, the Taff Vale Railway, was only a year younger than the GWR itself, having been formed in 1836 and also had I. K. Brunel as its Engineer. Described in the *GWR Magazine* as 'one of the brightest gems in the sceptre wielded by the Great Western Railway', the TVR was the largest railway in South Wales, and its history and fortunes were dominated by the growth and development of the coal-mining industry. Other than in some parts of the Vale of Glamorgan, reported the *GWR Magazine*, the Taff Vale Railway could never claim attention as a line for the tourist and holiday seeker. It serves an essentially industrial area, which has a dense a population as any district in the British Isles.

The Taff Vale Railway system consisted of 23 branch lines, mostly on tributaries of the River Taff and serving the colliery districts of East Glamorganshire where Welsh steam coal was mined. Some idea of the dominance of coal traffic can be gleaned from the fact that before the Great War the railway was shifting more than 20 million tons of 'black gold' over less than 100 miles of track, giving it the heaviest traffic density of any railway in the United Kingdom. To accommodate this it needed large areas of siding, and in 1922 it was calculated that the TVR could store almost 13,000 wagons around its lines, Penarth Junction having the largest capacity (2,494). To export much of the coal extracted from mines in the Rhondda the TVR had its own 26-acre dock at Penarth, modern equipment allowing the shipment of up to 4 million tons each year.

Next in size and importance was the Barry Railway, a company that had grown as a result of the huge increase in coal traffic in the Victorian era. By the early 1880s there was a severe lack of dock facilities in South Wales to enable the coal being mined in the valleys to be exported. The passing of the Barry Dock and Railway Act of 1884 permitted the construction of new docks at Barry and gave greater impetus to the development of further collieries in the Aberdare, Merthyr and Rhondda valleys and the lines connecting them. At the Grouping the Barry Railway's main- and branch-line mileage was 88, plus a further 161 miles of sidings. The extensive and busy docks at Barry had over 100 miles of sidings and in 1913 exported a record 11 million tons of coal; by 1921 this total had dropped to just over 5.5 million tons.

The Rhymney Railway had been incorporated in 1854, and its trains brought coal from pits in Merthyr, Aberdare, Dowlais and Rhymney itself down through Caerphilly (where it had its own locomotive workshops) to docks at Cardiff. When it was absorbed by the GWR it had a locomotive fleet numbering

Above: *Taff Vale inheritance. Two TVR locomotives stand at Cardiff West Yard in 1926. The 0-6-0 saddle tank on the left, No 796, was built in 1873, while nearest the camera on the right is 0-6-2 No 481, built 1891.*

Left: *Another pre- Grouping locomotive, Rhymney Railway 0-6-0 saddle tank No 612 was built by Sharp Stewart in 1884 and is seen at Swindon in 1927, having been placed on the sales list following its withdrawal.*

123 and a track mileage of just over 170. As with other South Wales railways, its best year for coal exports had been 1913, when it shifted 7.4 million tons. The Rhymney always struggled in comparison with its rivals, largely because it did not have its own dock facilities, and its lines also featured some of the most challenging gradients in South Wales. As one writer diplomatically put it, 'The equipment of the line, particularly in regard to stations and other buildings, has never been on a lavish style, which is putting the position somewhat mildly'.

The most easterly of the South Wales companies was the Alexandra (Newport & South Wales) Docks & Railway Co. Although this was originally promoted as a purely dock company in Newport, in the 1880s it also acquired a line of its own to Pontypridd, which it used to gain business from collieries in the area. The docks at Newport covered an area of more than 125 acres and by the time of the Grouping were well equipped, with the most modern cranes and loading equipment. Newport also had a healthy trade in imports and exports besides coal, ensuring that it was still performing relatively well financially after the Great War. With a route mileage of just 19 and a locomotive fleet of 38 at the Grouping, it was a well-run company, having paid a dividend of 5% in 1921.

The smallest of the principal constituent companies was the Cardiff Railway. This too had begun life as a dock company, responsible for the running of the Bute Docks in the Welsh capital, but had expanded in 1897 and made plans to build lines away from the coast. Although more than 10 million tons of coal was exported from its docks in the boom year of 1913, Cardiff was seen as the largest general-cargo port in South Wales, handling large quantities of food as well as iron and steel, timber and livestock. By the Grouping the route mileage of the Cardiff Railway was still only 11, excluding the miles of sidings it maintained, but its income in 1921 nevertheless exceeded £193,000.

From the above it can be seen that the absorption of other railway companies in South Wales had a very important effect on the GWR, making it the largest dock-owner in the world. By running ports at Cardiff, Swansea, Newport, Barry, Penarth and Port Talbot the Great Western took on a business that handled more than 50 million tons of goods a year, of which 75% was coal. The remaining 25% included practically every kind of commodity imported or exported by Britain. The principal exports were steel rail and plate, petrol and other chemicals, whilst imports included pig iron, timber, flour, fish, vegetables meat and other foodstuffs.

In comparison to the South Wales lines, the largest constituent company was very different. With lines covering nearly 300 miles of rural Wales, the Cambrian Railways operated quite differently from companies like the Taff Vale. Much of the rambling network was single-track and built through difficult terrain, many routes having steep ruling gradients like the 1 in 52 near Talerddig, where the line was almost 700ft above sea level. The sheer size of the area served by the company presented its own difficulties, and staff working at many of its 100 stations were a long distance from its headquarters at Oswestry. As befitted the Cambrian's rural network, milk was one of the largest sources of freight business, more than 3 million gallons being moved by rail in 1921.

Of the remaining subsidiary companies absorbed by the GWR the majority were located either in Wales or the borders, and most were small independent local lines which even by the early 1920s were struggling to survive; an example was the Neath & Brecon line, a 52-mile railway with only 15 locomotives; in 1921 it returned a profit of £39,342, but with only limited resources it was never going to make large sums of money. Completing the collection were two further cross-country routes — the Didcot, Newbury & Southampton Railway and the Midland & South Western Junction Railway. Both companies operated services linking the South of England and the Midlands, but neither had paid a dividend to shareholders in 1921 or seemed likely to do so in the foreseeable future.

Despite inheriting some poorly run railways the Great Western found itself in a better position at the Grouping than did the other three 'Big Four' companies. The fact that most of the railways absorbed were already within the geographical territory of the existing GWR it made life easier, and even with all the absorbed lines the new Great Western was still less than half the size of the largest

'Big Four' company, the LMS, which had taken responsibility for many miles of Scottish railways. The addition of relatively stable South Wales companies was clearly an advantage, although, as the effects of the Wall Street Crash in 1929 began to unravel, the financial position of the GWR was not as straightforward as originally thought.

A vital asset to the Great Western in the post-Great War era was its new General Manager, Felix Pole, appointed in 1921. Pole was truly a company man, joining the GWR at Swindon as a 14-year-old in 1891. Beginning his career in the Signal & Telegraph Department, he moved to the General Manager's Office in 1904 and edited the *GWR Magazine* before becoming assistant to General Manager Charles Aldington in 1919. Two years later he was appointed to the most important job in the company apart from that of Chief Mechanical Engineer. It seems that his appointment was not a surprise, and that he had almost been destined to do the job; the *GWR Magazine*, reporting his appointment, noted: 'The expected has happened … years ago we wisely wagged our heads and said that one of these days Mr Felix J. C. Pole would be General Manager'.

Knighted in 1924, Pole oversaw the process of creating a new unified GWR, harmonising the working practices inherited from absorbed companies brought under its control. To cope with these changes in South Wales a new Cardiff Division was set up, and to aid integration many of its new managers were drawn from pre-Grouping companies. Another new area, the Central Wales Division, was set up to operate the lines formerly run by the Cambrian Railways and the Brecon & Merthyr and Neath & Brecon railways.

Pole was very keen to promote the GWR whenever possible, and in 1923 the GWR scored a major public-relations coup with the introduction of its new 'Castle'-class locomotive. With a tractive effort of 31,625lb, this was billed by the company as 'the most powerful locomotive in the country'. The appearance of the new design was accompanied by a vigorous publicity drive from Pole and his team at Paddington, who arranged that the first locomotive, *Caerphilly Castle*, should be displayed alongside Nigel Gresley's new 'A1' Pacific at the British Empire Exhibition in 1924, its diminutive appearance

Left: *Sir Felix Pole, General Manager of the GWR 1921-1929.*

causing further debate when it was revealed that it was in fact more powerful than the LNER design.

The 'Castle' was the first major design to be produced at Swindon under C. B. Collett, who had been appointed Chief Mechanical Engineer of the GWR in 1922 following the retirement of G. J. Churchward. The 'Old Man' had retired as he approached the age of 65, but in reality his authoritarian management style had become increasingly out of step with the changed labour situation, particularly the rise of trade unionism, after the Great War. It is also likely that Felix Pole wanted to stamp his authority on Swindon and reduce the power of the Chief Mechanical Engineer. Not a universally popular choice amongst the men in the factory, Charles Collett had been an able deputy to Churchward, and although he did not have the same strong personality traits possessed by his predecessor there was little doubt that he was a capable locomotive engineer who in the following 20 years would produce numerous examples of what are now seen as 'classic' GWR designs.

With the other railways receiving much condemnation by the press, Collett and Pole might well have thought that the introduction of the 'Castle' class would help to lay strong foundations on which the GWR could build. In an attempt to sustain the South Wales coal trade, on which the fortunes of the company depended so heavily, the GWR board

Right: *A very rare picture, showing LNER Class A1 Pacific No 4474 arriving at Exeter St Davids on 25 April 1925 whilst participating in that year's Locomotive Exchanges.*

Right: *The 'Cornish Riviera Limited' passing Westbury behind a 'Castle' 4-6-0, as portrayed in a 1920s postcard.* Author's collection

introduced another innovation which it hoped would boost trade. For many years collieries had used 10-ton wooden wagons to transport coal from pit to port, and there were more than 100,000 of these in use in South Wales. Before the Grouping, with six rival companies, most with their own dock facilities, it had been difficult to reconcile the various and differing interests involved, but following their amalgamation the GWR was able to improve matters. To speed the handling and despatch of coal at ports it proposed the replacement of the old stock with new 20-ton steel wagons. The new design was 50% cheaper than the old wooden type and had doors at each end, making it easier to unload. Pole wrote to colliery owners in September 1923, suggesting this new course of action, and within a year the first wagons were in operation. By November 1925 more than 1,000 were reported to be in use, and more under construction.

The company did, of course, now have the advantage of owning the dock facilities from which coal was exported and was thus able to make swift modifications to the tipping equipment at each port, at a total cost of almost £2 million. The *GWR Magazine* reported progress on this scheme in 1925, noting that more than 25 new coal hoists were already in operation at Barry, Cardiff, Newport, Penarth and Swansea, and another 23 under construction. The company invested further large sums in its dock facilities, improving locks and pumping equipment and providing additional generating capacity for both electricity and hydraulic power, the latter being used extensively for operating cranes and capstans. The GWR also offered a 5% discount for those using the new 20-ton wagons, with the result that within a year 11 colliery companies had started using them. In a bid to increase traffic further the company extended the scheme to other traffic types, in particular roadstone, tarmacadam and limestone, the last-mentioned (for blast furnaces) a load carried extensively by the railway in the industrial heartland of South Wales.

The years following the end of the Great War were characterised by labour unrest and political uncertainty. A miners' strike in the autumn of 1920 was followed in 1921 by serious industrial unrest. In April another miners' strike, triggered by pay cuts of as much as 50%, ended when workers from other unions failed to come out in sympathy, forcing miners back to work. Unemployment had also begun to rise steadily, reaching 1½ million by the end of 1922. In January 1924, as the first Labour Government took office, the Great Western Railway was brought to a halt by a two-week strike of locomotive crews, followed shortly after by a national strike of dock workers. The absorption of the various Welsh railways, which had seemed such an asset in

Below: The sheer scale of the coal business in South Wales is apparent from this view of just one of many marshalling yards in the region which is full of loaded coal wagons.

Above: *The modern lines of the new 20- ton coal wagons introduced by the GWR in the 1920s.*

national subsidies on coal should be removed. Given the close links between miners and railway unions, it seemed likely that that railway staff would be drawn into a strike, and, in contrast with its stance in previous disputes, the TUC supported a co-ordinated national strike affecting such trades as transport, building, engineering and printing. What later became known as the 'General Strike' began on 3 May 1926. The day before, Sir Felix Pole had written to all staff warning them to 'hesitate before you break your contracts with the old company, before you inflict grave injury upon the railway industry and before you arouse ill-feeling in the railway service which will take years to remove'.

Ignoring Sir Felix's warning, most staff went on strike, and the action was solid, more than 80% of staff ceasing work. On the first day only 194 trains were operated across the whole network; on each subsequent day volunteers and workers who did not strike ran an increasing number of train services, so that by the last day of the strike, 14 May, more than 1,500 trains ran, although this still represented a mere shadow of the normal service. Although support for the dispute had remained largely solid, staff began returning to work before the end of the dispute, and on 6 May the company issued a statement that men would be taken back 'provided they could be usefully re-employed' but that supervisory staff could not be readmitted. Three days later a further circular noted that, once 50% of staff in a station had resumed duty, any further staff wishing to return should be handed a notice which read: 'You are hereby re-engaged on the understanding that you are not relieved of the consequences of having broken your contract of service with the Company.'

On 12 May the TUC called off the General Strike, and men began returning to work. It soon became apparent that the unions' call for 'one back, all back' was not going to be recognised by the railways, and not all staff would be re-employed straightaway. Whilst unions suspected that the company was using the strike as an opportunity to root out what it classed as troublemakers and agitators, the management of the 'Big Four' companies were not to be bullied and, despite the threat of further strike action, forced union leaders to sign a humiliating agreement in which they

1922/3, must have seemed less so as coal production dramatically slumped in 1925. Speaking to shareholders in February 1926, the Company Chairman reported that freight business for the previous year had decreased by more than 6 million tons — a drop which was due almost entirely to a decrease in coal traffic. The drop was even more significant when figures were compared with the last year before the war (1913), which revealed that traffic had dropped by more than 11 million tons in just over a decade. This situation was clearly unsustainable, and to cut costs the GWR was forced to consider far-reaching measures. These included reducing pay and the suspension and sacking of staff; following negotiations between Felix Pole and staff representatives it was reluctantly agreed that the redundancy route should be followed, casual and temporary staff losing their jobs first.

Whilst Great Western staff and management had come to an unpalatable but pragmatic agreement, the same could not be said for colliery owners and miners, who found it much harder to agree. In the summer of 1925 a coal strike had been narrowly averted after last minute Government intervention and the introduction of a national subsidy for the industry, subject to the deliberations of a Royal Commission. 'Not a minute on the day, not a penny off the pay' was the motto adopted by miners, and when the Commission reported in March 1926 it seemed inevitable that a strike would take place, as its principal recommendations were that wages should be cut and hours increased, and that were required to accept that in calling the strike 'they committed a wrongful act against the companies' and that they should 'not again instruct their members to strike without previous negotiations'.

In such a climate it is surprising that the repercussions of the General Strike lasted for years, the bad feeling that existed between those who went on strike and those who remained at work continuing even after World War 2; old GWR office staff recall seeing staff ledgers with names appended 'L' or 'D' — 'loyal' or 'disloyal'. More significant for the Great Western was the fact that, whilst its own workers had returned to work, the miners did not, the mines remaining closed until the winter. This loss of business had a catastrophic effect on the company's fortunes; the GWR's own historian, E. T. MacDermot, argued that the coal industry was 'utterly ruined' through a combination of 'avarice and greed' on the part of the colliery owners and 'stupidity' on the part of the miners' leadership. Whoever was to blame, the quantity of coal carried by the GWR in 1926 dropped by more than 20 million tons, and by the end of the decade the total handled was well below prewar levels, many of the overseas markets for Welsh coal having been lost forever.

A further worry for GWR management was the growth of road competition in the years after 1918. The extensive use of motor lorries during World War 1 had proved their value, and many servicemen returning from the war set up their own road-haulage businesses. To make matters worse, the railway was legally a 'common carrier', having to transport any item offered to it by customers, whereas lorry owners could pick and choose the loads they carried. There was also resentment that companies like the Great Western, as large land and property owners, paid vast sums in local rates, a considerable percentage of which was reinvested in the upkeep of roads. GWR Chairman Viscount Churchill reminded shareholders at the 1925 Annual General Meeting that the railway had paid more than £1.5 million in rates the previous year, whereas the owners of heavy lorries paid only a fraction of this amount in duty. The widespread use and ownership of lorries by non-unionised small haulage companies was also seen as a significant factor in the eventual collapse of the General Strike, as motor transport was used to replace rail services suspended due to strike action.

Belatedly the Great Western took steps to compete with the growing haulage industry.

Left: *Paddington station during the General Strike of 1926. There appears to be little activity at the great terminus, but volunteer workers used to unload trains are standing on the platform, as are soldiers guarding the premises.*

Above: Raw sugar being unloaded from the SS Author *at Cardiff Docks in the 1920s.*

In the 1920s the existing country lorry service, introduced in 1908, was extended, although its impact was limited, there being only 120 vehicles in use by 1930. More significant was the rural distribution service. Specialised collection and delivery contracts were agreed with large customers, guaranteeing delivery times, usually within a 30-mile radius of larger stations. By 1930 more than 1,300 lorries were operated by the company, and the use of horse-drawn drays to handle local deliveries from stations was in decline, although as late as 1937 more than 1,700 horses were still being used for this purpose.

Following a study of the company's branch-line network the GWR's directors and shareholders were told by the Chairman in 1925 that many of its branches did not cover their costs, even when their contribution to the rest of the network was taken into account. The alternative was, he argued, closure for some lines, and the introduction of buses to maintain services for travellers. Having introduced its first 'Road Motor' services in 1903, the company did indeed expand its motor-bus network in the 1920s, and in addition to short- and long-distance bus routes it ran tourist services and 'Land Cruises'; however, perhaps fearing a backlash from its shareholders and the press, it did not embark on a programme of closing branch lines, this process being postponed until the Beeching axe fell in the 1960s.

A highlight in an otherwise gloomy period for the company was the introduction in 1927 of the 'King'-class locomotives and, specifically, the exploits of No 6000 *King George V* during its visit to the United States of America. The locomotive's attendance at the centenary celebrations of the Baltimore & Ohio Railroad in the autumn of that year was a public-relations coup and enabled the company to revisit Brunel's original idea of the Great Western as a line of communication between

Britain and the United States, boosting tourist and freight business at the same time.

The situation for the GWR and the other 'Big Four' companies had not improved appreciably by 1928, and in that year further drastic measures were proposed. Management had worked hard to reduce costs all over the system, but the economies achieved were just not enough. As the wage bill was the largest item on the balance sheet of any railway, representatives from all the 'Big Four' companies and the Metropolitan Railway met with railway unions to discuss how costs could be reduced to protect the industry. Given the background of industrial unrest experienced most recently during the General Strike, the negotiations were long and difficult. Ultimately, however, the unions reluctantly accepted a pay cut of 2½% for all grades from Directors and Chairman downwards. That this was reversed only in 1930 — and then only for a brief period — illustrates how serious the situation was for the Great Western and the other companies.

Much of the credit for the completion of such an important agreement must go to Sir Felix Pole, a man known for his hard work, eye for detail and as described in the *GWR Magazine*, his 'accessibility to all classes, whether peer or porter'. However, eight difficult and stressful years at Paddington had clearly taken their toll, and, perhaps aware that many of his predecessors had died 'in harness', he left the company in July 1929 to become Chairman of Associated Electrical Industries. His successor as General Manager was Sir James Milne, another GWR 'company man' who had begun his career at Swindon Works in 1904. Within months of his appointment the world economy was plunged into turmoil by the Wall Street Crash of October 1929. In the last three years of the 1920s the company had been able to pay shareholders a dividend of 6%, but, as the effects of the slump intensified, unemployment increased dramatically, receipts fell, and many of the small gains made in the latter part of the decade were eradicated.

Above: *The visit of No 6000* King George V *to the United States for the centenary celebrations of the Baltimore & Ohio Railroad was widely seen as a publicity triumph of the highest order for the GWR. Pictured on 22 November 1927 are William Stanier, Driver Young, Fireman Pearce and Miss Bruhl (dressed as Britannia), along with two Swindon staff who also travelled with the locomotive.*

Below: *Another publicity picture, issued to mark the construction of* King George V. *Works staff stand inside its chimney, whilst to the right, the chimney of broad-gauge replica* North Star *has been used for comparison.*

CHAPTER NINE

GREAT WESTERN LOCOMOTIVES

Writing in *The King of Railway Locomotives*, one of the Great Western's 'Books for Boys of All Ages', W. G. Chapman noted that the GWR 'King' class boasted 'a noble and distinguished ancestry' and that 'the evolution of these super-locomotives may be traced back to the *North Star*, one of the first engines delivered to the Company', adding that 'Many of the characteristics of *North Star* will be found in locomotives performing useful service today'. This continuity in locomotive development continued for another two decades after the publication of his book; indeed, such was the continuity and tradition of the Locomotive Department that, by the time of nationalisation in 1948, the office of Locomotive Superintendent or Chief Mechanical Engineer had been held by only eight men over the course of a 113-year period. Belying this remarkable statistic was the fact that Great Western locomotive design developed through a slow and steady evolution rather than the rapid change seen on other lines. With the exception of its first Locomotive Superintendent, Daniel Gooch, all were 'company men'; even C. B. Collett, who had begun his career away from the GWR, had spent considerable time in the company's service before being appointed to the top post.

Daniel Gooch was not appointed until August 1837, by which time Isambard Kingdom Brunel had already taken some important decisions that would have a profound and far-reaching effect on GWR locomotive development. The most radical was the decision to adopt the broad gauge, and the ramifications of this dramatic initiative was to distance GWR locomotive development from the mainstream for some considerable time. Brunel had also made some unorthodox decisions about the motive power for his new railway; having issued a broad specification for locomotives to a number of the leading manufacturers of the day, he ordered what one railway historian described as 'an extraordinary collection of freak locomotives' which in some cases could hardly propel themselves, let alone haul a train. Harry Holcroft, who worked as an assistant to Churchward in the early years of the 20th century, described them as 'miscellaneous in character, unsatisfactory in performance', but one could hardly blame the manufacturers, for they were merely following Brunel's specifications, which resulted in locomotives with small boilers and cylinders and large driving wheels. Gooch's first task after taking up his new position was to visit the various factories where locomotives were being built for the GWR, and his diaries reveal that what he saw was not to his liking, recording that he was 'not much pleased with the design of the engines ordered'.

Matters did not improve when delivery of locomotives commenced; Gooch spent much time in the sheds at Paddington, repairing locomotives to keep the embryonic railway operating. Two from this initial order stand out as being particularly unusual; each was built by R. & W. Hawthorn and had the 'engine' (*i.e.* cylinders and motion) and boiler on separate frames. *Thunderer* had four driving wheels, driven by gearing, whilst *Hurricane* had a boiler carried on a six-wheel frame and another 2-2-2 frame carrying the 'engine'. The driving wheels on this strange-looking locomotive were an enormous 10ft in diameter. Neither of these engines was successful, and *Thunderer* was withdrawn within two years, having run just 9,882 miles.

Gooch was, however, fortunate that not all the locomotives purchased by the company were completely useless. In his diaries he noted that 'The North Star and the six from the Vulcan Foundry were the only ones I could at all depend on'. The Vulcan Foundry locomotives, built by Charles Tayleur, were 2-2-2 designs; *Aeoleus*, *Bacchus* and *Vulcan* arrived in 1837, and *Apollo*, *Neptune* and *Venus* the following year. The acquisition of *North Star* was a stroke of luck for the Great Western. The locomotive had been built by Robert Stephenson & Co in Newcastle for a 5ft 6in-gauge railway in New Orleans, but when this scheme fell through it was an easy task for the locomotive and a sister, *Morning Star*, delivered 14 months later, to be modified to run on Brunel's broad gauge. Both proved powerful and reliable, *North Star* being described by Gooch as his 'chief reliance'. The inadequacies of the Brunel designs led to GWR directors' requesting a report from Gooch on each locomotive, and, shocked by its conclusions, they asked Gooch to produce his own design to improve matters.

The design prepared by Gooch was the 'Fire Fly' class, a 2-2-2 tender engine, heavily influenced by *North Star*, with sandwich frames outside 7ft driving wheels. Since the construction of the new railway was continuing apace, and many more locomotives would be required, orders were placed with seven manufacturers. Once Gooch had completed the original drawings they were lithographed, and thin iron templates produced and supplied to the locomotive-builders to ensure that all locomotives were built to the same specification and had interchangeable standardised parts. The first locomotive, *Fire Fly*, built by Jones, Turner & Evans, appeared in March 1840, and a further 61 were built. When the railway opened, in 1841, 18 'Sun'-class locomotives were built, these being a smaller version of the 'Fire Fly' design, fitted with 6ft driving wheels for lines west of Swindon, where gradients were steeper. All these early passenger locomotives were given names, beginning a tradition that continued into British Railways days, and were fitted with nameplates with brass letters on a steel background — another feature perpetuated by Great Western locomotives until the company's demise.

When, in 1845, a Royal Commission was called to examine the question of a nationwide uniform track gauge, it was one of Daniel Gooch's 'Fire Fly' class, *Ixion*, that took part in the trials held to examine locomotive performance. On one run between Paddington and Didcot this reached a top speed of 60mph hauling an 80-ton train, whilst one of its rival, standard-gauge locomotives could manage just 53¾mph with 50 tons. Perhaps in a bid to influence the commissioners, Brunel asked Gooch to build a more powerful locomotive as soon as possible. Another 2-2-2, *Great Western* was essentially an enlarged 'Fire Fly' and was also the first locomotive to be built at the company's new workshops at Swindon. Much midnight oil was burned during the 13 weeks of its construction, but the locomotive, nicknamed 'Lightning' by the workers, was powerful and fast, hauling a 100-ton train between

Left: So many photographs taken by the company show locomotives in pristine condition. This picture, from the collection of Swindon Inspector Harry Flewellyn, shows Gooch broad-gauge 4-2-2 Amazon *in grubby working condition. Flewellyn's notes on the back of the picture record that the 1851 locomotive ran 729,840 miles before withdrawal in 1878.*

Right: *A 0-6-0 goods locomotive designed by Daniel Gooch and built at Swindon in February 1855,* Zetes *was also used for banking duties on heavier trains. The locomotive would finally be withdrawn in December 1877.*

Paddington and Swindon at an average speed of 59.4mph.

An extra set of leading wheels was soon added to *Great Western* for more stability, and within months a larger and more powerful 4-2-2, *Iron Duke*, had appeared, complete with standard features that would be repeated in many future designs. As well as having a round-top firebox, it had the safety-valve assembly decorated with the addition of a polished brass cover. These locomotives would haul expresses on the London–Bristol main line until the 1870s, when they were extensively rebuilt. The growth of the broad-gauge network, in spite of the unfavourable outcome of the Royal Commission, meant that more and varied motive power was required, and to cope with the increase in goods traffic no fewer than 102 Gooch-designed standard goods engines were built at Swindon in the period from 1852 to 1863.

When expansion northwards of the broad-gauge network was curtailed the GWR began acquiring standard-gauge lines in the West Midlands and North Wales. In the late 1850s standard-gauge track had yet to reach Swindon, so Great Western Directors decided that standard-gauge locomotives should be built and repaired at the Stafford Road works in Wolverhampton, and with the purchase of the West Midland Railway in 1863 the GWR's Northern Division became predominantly standard gauge; the broad gauge, concentrated on Swindon, survived on the old London–Bristol main line, the South Wales main line and in the West Country. As the standard-gauge network expanded, the company was effectively split into two for operational purposes, and, disheartened at this turn of events, Gooch finally stepped down as Locomotive Superintendent in 1864. With his resignation and the death of Brunel five years earlier the two main supporters of the broad gauge were gone, and within two years Swindon Works had built its last all-new broad-gauge locomotives.

Gooch's replacement was Joseph Armstrong, who had been a driver on the Liverpool & Manchester Railway in 1836 and had then worked on the Hull & Selby and London & Brighton lines before being appointed Locomotive Superintendent of the Shrewsbury & Chester Railway prior to its absorption by the GWR in 1854. Ten years as Superintendent of the Northern Division and as Gooch's assistant had given him extensive experience of the GWR's standard-gauge locomotives. As Locomotive Superintendent Armstrong had two main tasks — to oversee the further development of standard-gauge types and to maintain the existing broad-gauge fleet. In the short term, however, new broad-gauge designs were required to replace worn-out locomotives, and 26 'Hawthorn'-class 2-4-0 tender engines were followed by 14 0-6-0 goods locomotives of the aptly named 'Swindon' class.

The final new broad-gauge locomotives to be built for the GWR were six 0-6-0 tank engines of the 'Sir Watkin' class, which were completed in 1866. Armstrong was, however, best known for his 0-6-0 'Standard Goods', of which more than 130 were built. In a move that would have found favour with his old boss, he ensured that these locomotives included many standardised parts and fittings that were common to other designs, most notably his 'Sir Daniel' 2-2-2 passenger locomotives, which appeared the same year. When the decision was taken finally to phase out the broad gauge Armstrong began the task of overseeing the construction of replacement standard stock in readiness for conversion. Worn out by this work, he died 'in harness'

in 1877 and was replaced by his assistant, William Dean.

In the 25 years after he took office Dean had a similar yet perhaps more difficult task than Armstrong. Dean had already been at Swindon for nine years when he took over, and although the broad gauge still (just) survived, the main priority for GWR locomotive policy was clearly standard gauge. The phased replacement of the 7ft gauge meant that broad-gauge services were still running in many parts of the system, and locomotives still needed, so a goodly number of the 727 constructed under Dean before 1892 were 'convertibles', which could be rebuilt at a later date to run on the 4ft 8½in gauge. The declining reputation of the broad gauge, combined with a lack of funds, meant that no 'new' broad-gauge designs could be approved by the directors, although between 1878 and

Below: The highly polished 0-6-0 side tank pictured here was built not at Swindon but at the GWR's works at Wolverhampton, in March 1872. An example of the '633' class, it was fitted with condensing apparatus and was finally condemned in March 1934.

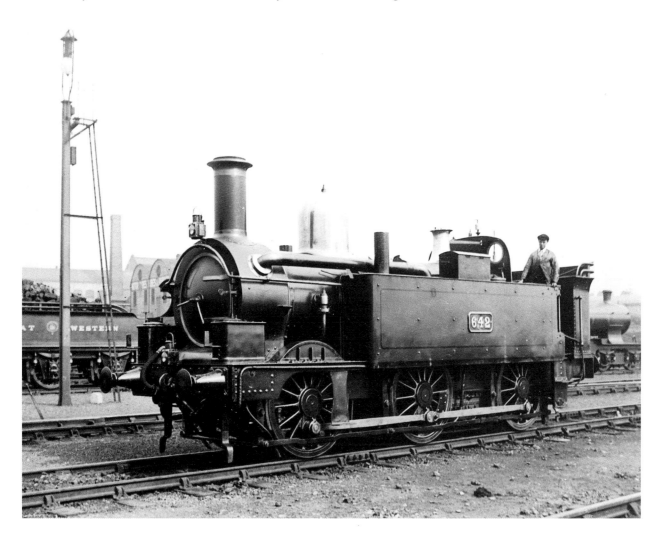

1888 13 Gooch 4-2-2s were 'renewed' — an accounting convention whereby the minimum number of original parts were incorporated into what was essentially a brand-new locomotive. The resulting 'Rover' class worked expresses on the GWR main line until the end of the broad gauge in 1892, a fitting postscript to the experiment planned and executed by Brunel and Gooch.

The building of 270 0-6-0 standard-gauge saddle tanks and 60 2-4-0 side tanks, both to Armstrong designs, for branch-line and suburban use, reinforced the notion of continuity, as did Dean's use of sandwich frames from the Gooch era on his 'Barnum' 2-4-0 tender engines in the 1880s. With the final abolition of the broad gauge in 1892 Dean began move forward; his Standard Goods design, which appeared in 1897, owed much to his predecessor's goods engine, and, whilst hardly revolutionary, having inside frames and cylinders, the locomotives were powerful, reliable and had a surprising turn of speed. They also proved extremely long-lived, the last surviving until 1957, having being used extensively by the War Department in both world wars. For many his '3031' ('Achilles')-class 4-2-2 express engines were the high point of GWR locomotive design in the 19th century. Harry Holcroft, who in his youth had worked on the engines, argued that nothing approached them in terms of 'beauty of line and artistic finish'; certainly the highly polished dome and safety-valve covers, outside frames and single driving wheels were a last hurrah for the old regime, and, as the 20th century approached, Dean and his assistant, Churchward, began to move away from the past and produce new designs that looked forward rather than back.

Great Western locomotive designs were changing, mainly because the company was changing. Management wanted faster and more powerful locomotives to haul trains, passenger and goods, on a network that was growing in size and becoming much busier. By the late 1880s William Dean's was beginning began to fail, and Churchward started to take a more dominant role both in running the Works at Swindon and in the design of locomotives and rolling stock; railway historians have debated long and hard as to when the younger man took over, and the precise details of this transitional period. We shall probably never know exactly what transpired, but in the years just prior to 1902, when Churchward was finally appointed Locomotive Superintendent, a series of increasingly modern designs began to emerge from Swindon. Large numbers of 4-4-0s — the 'Armstrong', 'Atbara', 'Badminton', 'City', 'County' and 'Flower' classes, all intended as express designs — were introduced. Apart from the 'County' class they were for the most part a mix of old and new, boasting a bewildering variety of boilers and outside 'sandwich' framing.

By the time the first of the 10 'City'-class locomotives appeared in 1903 their appearance may have seemed somewhat old-fashioned in comparison to the new 4-6-0, No 100 *William Dean*, which had appeared the year before. Nevertheless, the class was a great success, particularly as two of its number distinguished themselves by running at speeds not seen before on the railway. In July 1903 No 3433 *City of Bath*, in charge of a Royal Train, ran non-stop between Paddington and Plymouth via Bristol in just over 233 minutes at an average speed of 63.4mph. Topping

Below: *William Dean, Locomotive Superintendent of the GWR from 1877 to 1902.*

Right: *The final development of the broad- gauge single design, begun by Daniel Gooch. Eupatoria was technically known as a 'renewal' but was essentially a new locomotive, completed at Swindon in October 1878. These engines remained the mainstay of broad-gauge express services on the GWR until the abolition of the 7ft gauge in 1892.*

88mph on Dauntsey Bank, near Swindon, the train arrived 37 minutes early. The following year further fast runs were recorded on 'Ocean Mail' specials from Plymouth to Paddington. On 9 May 1904 the liner SS *Kronprinz Wilhelm* arrived at Plymouth after an Atlantic crossing from New York. More than 1,000 mail bags were loaded onto a special train hauled by No 3440 *City of Truro*, which left Plymouth at 9.23am and arrived in Bristol just over 64 minutes later. From Bristol the train was handled by a Dean 'Achilles', *Duke of Connaught*, departing at 11.30am and arriving at Paddington at 1.09pm. Total journey time was thus 3hr 46min — an average of 65½mph. This impressive run generated much publicity in the railway press, but what did not emerge at the time was the fact that *City of Truro* had broken the 100mph barrier on its leg of the trip. On Wellington Bank, in Somerset, the train was timed by Charles Rous-Marten, correspondent for *The Railway Magazine*, as reaching a speed of 102.3mph, a figure that has been disputed over the years; whatever the exact speed, GWR General Manager James Inglis was reluctant to publicise it in case it frightened the travelling public, then unused to such high speeds.

In stark contrast to the exploits of passenger locomotives on express services was the challenge the company faced in terms of the increasing coal traffic from South Wales, for which the 0-6-0 'Dean Goods' were now insufficiently powerful. In 1896 an experimental 4-6-0 goods locomotive, No 36 (nicknamed 'The Crocodile' by Swindon staff), was built specifically for running through the Severn Tunnel. Although powerful, the design

Above right: *Five years after the gauge conversion, the Great Western exhibited at the 1897 Diamond Jubilee Exhibition at Olympia. Pride of place went to broad-gauge survivors* North Star *and* Lord of the Isles. *This picture shows the exhibition set up at Swindon before its move to London. Less than a decade later the GWR would be searching for a home for both locomotives which did not really fit in with the new developments there. No institution would take them, and both would eventually be cut up, in 1906.*

Right: *The cab of 'Dean Goods' No 2340. Built in 1884, the locomotive is seen after withdrawal in 1954. The open nature of the cab is very apparent in this picture, meaning that in winter the crew had little protection, save a tarpaulin that could be stretched from the cab roof to tender in heavy rain.*

Right: *Record- breaking
Churchward 4-4-0*
City of Truro *stands at
Westbourne Park shortly after
construction in 1903.*

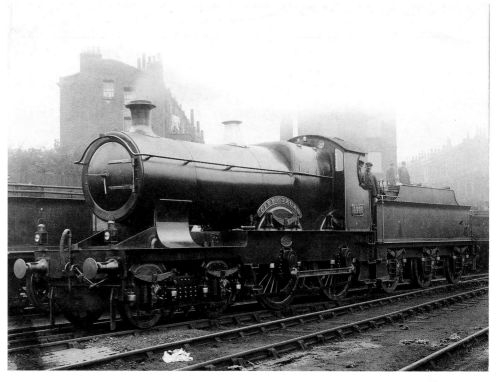

— scarcely the most handsome to emerge from the works — was not perpetuated. Instead an arguably even more graceless 4-6-0, the 'Kruger', was built three years later, with a domeless boiler. In due course 10 of these inelegant machines were built, but all had relatively short lives, eventually being replaced by 2-6-0s of the 'Aberdare' design.

Churchward's appointment as Locomotive Superintendent confirmed beyond doubt that the GWR had moved on from the broad-gauge era and away from the locomotive traditions begun by Gooch. Churchward had studied locomotive development in Europe and the United States and was happy to incorporate new ideas where required, even purchasing three 4-4-2 compound locomotives from French company De Glehn to test against his own designs. The 'Frenchmen', as Swindon staff called them, proved reliable but heavier on oil. A rather dismissive article in the *GWR Magazine* for March 1904, reporting the first

Right: *Many would argue that
the 'Star' class was
Churchward's finest
achievement. No 4006*
Red Star, *built at Swindon in
April 1907, stands at Old Oak
Common, ready to head a Royal
train. Note that, in addition to
the two large royal crests
carried on the side of the
smokebox, the locomotive boasts
two special Royal-train
headlamps. It would be
withdrawn in 1932 as 'Castle'
and 'Hall' designs began to
proliferate on the GWR.*

use of one of these locomotives on a scheduled train, noted that there had been 'various statements in the press as to running of the "Frenchman", but we are officially informed that although running satisfactorily, it is doing nothing exceptional, merely running ordinary trains at schedule times'.

Whilst standardisation was not new, particularly in the use of interchangeable parts like boilers, cylinders and valve gear on different locomotives, Churchward went much further. Following tests and experimentation Churchward devised a range of locomotives, each designed for a particular task. A limited number of standard boiler types, wheel sizes, cylinder blocks and other components were planned, ensuring that the GWR would be cope with the demands of the Traffic Department for many years to come. With this standard framework in place a steady stream of powerful and well-constructed locomotives was built at Swindon, passenger services being handled not only by the 4-4-0 designs but also ultimately by the ground-breaking 'Saint' and 'Star' 4-6-0 classes. Branch-line and suburban passenger services were handled by 2-6-2 tank engines, heavy freight by 2-8-0 tank and tender engines, and mixed-traffic duties by the elegant 2-6-0 tender engines of the '43xx' class. Amidst all the standardisation, one locomotive did not fit the pattern; the Great Western Railway's only Pacific, No 111 *The Great Bear*, built in 1908, clearly did not fit into Churchward strategy but was an obvious publicity coup for the company. However, the size of the locomotive meant it was confined to the main line between London and Bristol and had a short life, being rebuilt as a 'Castle', *Viscount Churchill*, in 1924.

When Churchward was replaced by C. B. Collett in 1922 it could be argued that it was 'business as usual' as far as GWR locomotive policy was concerned. It would nevertheless be a gross oversimplification to label Collett as merely Churchward's 'disciple', even though many of the designs he produced bore the unmistakable hallmarks of his predecessor's standard locomotive policy. Less than a decade after taking over as Chief Mechanical Engineer Collett had produced two of the most famous and powerful types to run on the GWR — the 'Castle' and 'King' 4-6-0 classes. Both were outstanding designs built to cope

with the ever-increasing demands of the Traffic Department and were used on the company's 'Blue Riband' expresses like the 'Cornish Riviera Limited' and 'Cheltenham Flyer'. In addition he updated the Churchward 'Saint' class by designing a new mixed-traffic 4-6-0, the 'Hall'. Experimenting with No 2925 *Saint Martin*, he fitted it with 6ft driving wheels, a successful innovation that resulted in the construction of no fewer than 258 similar locomotives. Collett continued the formula with the smaller 'Grange' and 'Manor' 4-6-0 classes, introduced in 1936 and 1938 respectively.

A design not contemplated by Churchward had been the 0-6-2 tank engine, although it had already been used extensively by companies in Welsh valleys, notably the Taff Vale and Rhymney, to haul coal trains from 'pit to port'. When these ageing pre-Grouping locomotives became worn out, Collett took a decisive step away from traditional GWR locomotive policy and introduced the '56xx' 0-6-2 tank engines in 1924 to replace them. Eventually 200 of these locomotives were produced, along with 54 '72xx' 2-8-2 tank engines, the latter rebuilt from Churchward 2-8-0 tank engines rendered surplus as a result of the slump in coal production in the Depression. These powerful locomotives, introduced in 1934, were used on longer-distance coal trains running from South Wales. Another key task completed by Collett was the assimilation of all non-standard types acquired by the GWR in 1922/3, the motley selection of locomotives inherited from the pre-Grouping companies being variously scrapped, sold or, wherever possible, rebuilt with standard GWR fixtures and fittings.

In addition to the onerous task of dealing with pre-Grouping locomotives, Collett and his team at Swindon found time to design many of the most famous and recognisable tank engines used on the GWR, including almost 1,000 pannier tanks and 95 0-4-2s used on branch and 'auto-train' services. The renewal of older 'Duke'- and 'Bulldog'-class 4-4-0s, which by the 1930s were becoming life-expired, generated more controversy. Collett's seemingly elegant solution was to combine the boilers of the former and the frames and motion of the latter, in the process creating a new 'Earl class. However, the antiquated appearance of these locomotives caused some annoyance amongst the nobility after which they were named, and the nameplates were quietly moved to more impressive 'Castle'-class 4-6-0s.

Despite the quantity and variety of the designs produced at Swindon between 1922 and 1941, Collett did not command universal respect and affection amongst GWR staff, and his diffidence and reserve did not enamour him to many Swindon workers. Many also felt that Collett, like Dean, should have retired earlier than he did. By the time he did leave the company, at the age of 70, Swindon was no longer the centre of innovation it had been under Churchward, and new locomotives built by the LMS and LNER were faster and more technologically advanced. Collett's cautious approach on refining and shaping existing Churchward designs also meant that

the ambitious and talented William Stanier, a GWR stalwart, was forced to move away from the GWR to obtain a CME position. Had he remained at Swindon, locomotive development might have been different; indeed, his move to the LMS in 1932 has prompted much debate amongst GWR enthusiasts and historians as to 'what might have been' had he stayed. Other staff, like Harry Holcroft, another Great Western man through and through, who worked with Churchward, also left the GWR and joined the Southern Railway.

The final holder of the post of Chief Mechanical Engineer for the GWR was F. W. Hawksworth, who took over in 1941. Hawksworth had the longest involvement with the company of any holder of the job, having 43 years of service under his belt. He

Right: C. B. Collett, Chief Mechanical Engineer of the Great Western Railway, 1922-1941.

Far right: F. W. Hawksworth, the last CME of the Great Western, sits at his desk at Swindon in 1949, shortly before his retirement.

Below: Collett 'Hall' No 4978 Westwood Hall, *built in February 1930, passes Woodley Bridge 'box with a local train in the 1930s.*

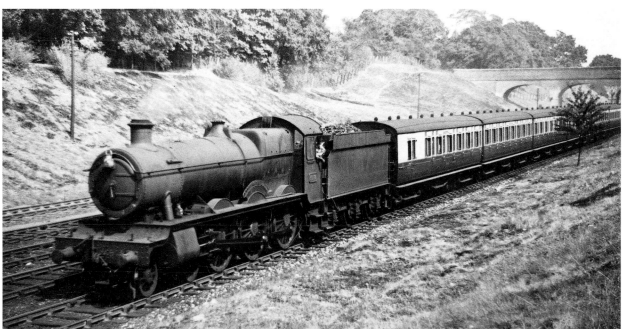

had the misfortune to be appointed at a period when the works at Swindon was heavily committed to war production and so had little chance to make any significant innovations until the end of hostilities. Unlike his predecessor, he demonstrated during the relatively short time he held the top job at Swindon that he was not afraid to step away from the Churchward template, but although the locomotives he designed before nationalisation had many innovations they still bore a strong family likeness to previous GWR designs. Hawksworth persisted with the 4-6-0 wheel arrangement for his first express-passenger type, the 'County', which was a two-cylinder design, a muscular-looking locomotive that was appreciated by enginemen. Three updated designs of pannier tank were produced, although the '15xx', '16xx' and '94xx' locomotives that resulted were rather ungainly.

On 'Hall'- and 'Castle'-class locomotives Hawksworth also introduced the use of high-level superheating, a practice used by other 'Big Four' companies, particularly the LMS, and in BR days most types would be so modified. From 1944 the 'Hall' class was expanded by the construction of a further 71 'Modified Halls' which featured important changes, their frames being extended through to the buffer beam to remove a weak point of the original design.

Nationalisation of the GWR in 1948 brought to an end an unbroken engineering tradition stretching back more than 100 years, although the post of Chief Mechanical Engineer remained until 1949, when Hawksworth retired, and construction of GWR-designed locomotives — 'Castles', 'Modified Halls' and 'Manors', as well as '16xx' and '94xx' pannier tanks — continued into the 1950s.

Above right: Although Collett was best known for his larger 'Castle' and 'King' classes, arguably one of the most important designs he produced was the '56xx' 0-6-2 tank engine, designed to replace elderly pre-Grouping locomotives on 'pit to port' coal workings in South Wales. This picture was probably taken in 1924, when the first batch was built.

Right: A striking head-on view of a Hawksworth '15xx' 0-6-0 pannier tank. The outside cylinders made them somewhat ungainly in comparison to many of their predecessors, but these powerful locomotives proved useful for empty-stock workings at Paddington.

CHAPTER TEN

GO GREAT WESTERN:
1930-1939

There is little doubt that the Great Western had endured difficult times in the years following the Great War, both labour difficulties and the decline of the coal trade taking their toll in the 1920s. As the company moved into a new decade under recently appointed General Manager James Milne considerable efforts were made to fight back and increase both the standing and the economic viability of the company. Although there had been large-scale investment on the Great Western Railway in the years before 1914, the resources needed to restore standards after the war, together with subsequent work on harmonising working practices of companies absorbed at the Grouping, meant that there had been little opportunity to consolidate work done in the early part of the 20th century. Even before the economic slump triggered by the Wall Street Crash of 1929 the Government had promised railways guaranteed loans to enable them to invest in new works which would alleviate unemployment. The GWR was quick to take advantage of the Development (Loan Guarantees and Grants) Act of 1929, and within two years 24 different schemes had been agreed.

The proposals put forward by the Great Western involved a capital cost of £4.5 million, and it was hoped that they would provide more than 200,000 'man months' of work for the unemployed. By this time more than a million men were out of work, so there can be little doubt that the various projects planned by the company represented a welcome development. Although aimed largely at improving its ability to handle passenger traffic on the railway as a whole, the schemes put forward broadly addressed two major difficulties faced by the company — first the requirement to upgrade facilities for passengers, some of the most important stations on the Great Western receiving major investment, and secondly the need to speed up train services by modernising cramped and outdated track layouts and building further 'cut-off' lines. Further sums were to be spent on upgrading and modernising locomotive sheds, goods depots and marshalling yards.

Three of the largest stations on the Great Western — Paddington, Bristol Temple Meads and Cardiff General — benefited from considerable investment. Although there had been much work done at Paddington in the years before the Great War, when the station was extended with the addition of another roof span, facilities for passengers still left much to be desired, and in the 1930s work centred on the area, known as the 'Lawn', between the Great Western Hotel and the buffer-stops. Until its redevelopment this had been used for handling parcels traffic, but conversion of the west end of the very long Platform 1 into a parcels depot saw the Lawn transformed into a much more usable and attractive circulating area, which also contained refreshment facilities and offices. Further capacity was added by lengthening platforms and awnings, allowing longer trains to be handled. The Bishops Road station, used by both GWR and Metropolitan suburban trains, was also enlarged, a process that involved the construction of a new approach road for cabs, suspended above a new four-platform complex on a massive girder structure — work that involved major engineering and excavation.

Bristol Temple Meads, always one of the busiest and most congested stations on the network, was also modernised. A description of the work, published in 1934, reminded passengers that whilst the familiar gothic clock tower and stone façade seemed unchanged, behind this frontage 'a great transformation is being effected. What is virtually a new station is appearing alongside the old one.' The overall aim of the work was twofold: to speed up the handling of trains, and to improve facilities for the travelling public. New platforms, complete with standard GWR awnings, were constructed outside the original Matthew Digby Wyatt trainshed, adding much-needed capacity and enabling the existing main platforms to be widened and provided with improved office and refreshment facilities. The existing refreshment rooms on the old up main line were also remodelled, being in their new form 'much admired by the travelling public', according to a writer in the *GWR Magazine*. The walls were lined with 'Napoleon' and 'Botticino' marble to dado height and elegant silver-grey wood panelling above; the new rooms were 'well thought out', the company argued, and would be 'cool in summer and comfortable in winter'.

A new, wide subway, served by lifts and lined with attractive art-deco brickwork, was excavated under the station to replace an old footbridge, and an additional subway was built, specifically for parcels traffic, serving the platforms and a new parcels depot built on the site of old carriage sidings. The running lines between Filton Junction to the north and Portishead Junction to the south were quadrupled, entailing the rebuilding of smaller suburban stations at Horfield and Ashley Hill to the north and Bedminster and Parson Street to the south. When the work was complete three trains could arrive and depart from the station simultaneously — a great improvement over the previous arrangement. Facilities for the Locomotive Department were also reorganised with the rebuilding of the old Bristol & Exeter shed at Bath Road, passenger locomotives henceforth being concentrated here, whilst goods engines were stabled at the nearby St Philips Marsh depot, accessible by a relief line.

Another important station, Cardiff General, was extensively rebuilt between 1930 and 1934, at a cost of almost £1 million. Alterations to train workings following the absorption in 1922 of the Barry and Taff Vale companies meant that there was greater interchange between lines than previously, so the station's track layout was remodelled to facilitate this and to include independent through lines for non-stop trains. The *GWR Magazine* for March 1931 reported that the station was in the process of being completely rebuilt; four 1,000ft platforms served main-line trains, two 800ft platforms were provided for Taff Vale traffic, and the old Riverside station was rebuilt and integrated into the complex to serve Barry-line trains. The platforms were connected by a new subway which led to new station buildings. West of the station was Canton Yard; here a new carriage shed and milk and fruit depot were built, and the locomotive shed was upgraded with the addition of a larger (65ft) turntable and a brand-new coal stage.

As the 1930s progressed other stations were rebuilt. The remodelling of Taunton in 1932 resulted in a new track layout complete with relief lines to allow through trains to pass the station without being obstructed by stopping services. The old Brunel overall roof was removed, and a new booking hall constructed on the north side of the line. On the new up island platforms another block of station buildings was provided, complete with commodious refreshment and dining rooms; a new subway replaced the old footbridge linking the platforms. In the years 1936-9 the scruffy wooden broad-gauge-era station at Leamington Spa was modernised by the

Below: The 'Lawn' at Paddington after its refurbishment and conversion into a spacious passenger circulating space.

construction of two new platforms, both more than 600ft long, one with bays for trains serving the Stratford line and stopping services to Birmingham; the new complex was completed by an elegant three-storey art-deco station building on the down side.

Although in the 1930s private car ownership was still in its infancy the GWR's holiday-train business was beginning to suffer competition from motor buses and coaches, which could provide quick and cheap transport to resorts in Devon and Cornwall. Any advantage in speed that the railway might have had over road transport was lost on busy summer Saturdays as a result of congestion at various points on the West of England main line. It was therefore natural

that the company should invest a good deal of the available Government capital in work to speed up holiday traffic at peak times. In a move mirroring the construction of 'cut-off' lines before the Great War, a substantial sum was invested in further avoiding lines at Frome and Westbury, in an effort to accelerate services on the West of England main line.

The first new cut-offs, completed in 1933, were relatively small and cost £220,000; the avoiding line at Frome was just 2 miles long, whilst the Westbury cut-off was slightly longer, at 2¼ miles. They did, however, improve timings for non-stop trains like the 'Cornish Riviera Limited' and, importantly, by cutting out forced deceleration of trains, reduced coal consumption and wear and tear

Right: Work on the modernisation of Bristol Temple Meads station is well underway in this 1934 photograph. The old footbridge is in the course of being removed, to be replaced by a large subway under the tracks.

Right: Cardiff station before modernisation. This gloomy view was recorded by the company photographer in 1910.

on locomotives. A further bottleneck was removed with the quadrupling of the 7½-mile stretch of line between Taunton and Norton Fitzwarren. The work was, according to the *GWR Magazine* for May 1932, designed 'to overcome the considerable difficulties in operation which have been experienced during busy periods, especially in the summer months'. Rather more extensive than the two schemes already described, it required major new earthworks and the building or rebuilding of 16 bridges, as well as seven new signalboxes. To avoid a complicated crossing at Cogload Junction a new flyover was also constructed where the Bristol–Exeter main line was joined by the newer West of England main line. The total cost of this major scheme, including rebuilding of the old broad-gauge-era station at Taunton and upgrading of signalling in the area, was £360,000.

Further money was spent on signalling at other locations on the GWR; new, state-of-the-art colour-light signalling, controlled by power 'boxes, was installed at Paddington, Bristol and Cardiff. At the same time the company spent its own money on extending its Automatic Train Control system to cover almost all of its fastest main lines. Before 1930 only 372 miles of track and 334 locomotives had been equipped, but an investment of more than £200,000, saw this extended to 1,700 miles of line and a further 200 locomotives, cementing the company's reputation for safe high-speed running.

Away from the major projects, further money was spent on the extension of marshalling yards at Banbury, Rogerstone and Severn Tunnel Junction, as well as new locomotive shed facilities replacing old and worn out pre-Grouping facilities in South Wales at locations such as Duffryn Yard, Landore, Port Talbot, Radyr and Treherbert. Another depot receiving funds via the Development (Loan Guarantees and Grants) Act was Didcot. The *GWR Magazine* for October 1932 reported that a new four-road shed, 210ft long, had been brought into use, along with other features which would 'greatly improve the locomotive accommodation at the depot'. These included a new lifting shop, coal stage and plant for calcinating sand. Money was also spent modernising facilities at both Swindon and Wolverhampton locomotive works; at the

latter location a new building, which included an erecting shop and wheel and machine shops, was constructed with the capacity to handle all types of Great Western locomotive — even the heaviest 'King' 4-6-0s, a number of which were allocated to the nearby shed. Although it had built locomotives many years before, Wolverhampton Works no longer undertook any new building but served as a modern and efficient repair facility, reducing the need to send locomotives back and forth to Swindon.

At Caerphilly the Great Western undertook a major reorganisation, the old Rhymney Railway works becoming a centralised facility for all GWR lines in South Wales; after the Grouping the GWR gradually closed all the smaller works and depots belonging to the pre-Grouping companies, concentrating staff and equipment at Caerphilly. A new three-bay erecting shop was constructed, and other workshops were modernised and re-equipped. O. S. Nock, in his history of the GWR, noted that once all the work had been completed Caerphilly was a 'self-contained factory in which tank locomotives of various sizes, types and weights were completely overhauled'.

The general slump in the coal and steel industry of South Wales in the aftermath of the Wall Street Crash led to a reduction in traffic for the company. Coal traffic from GWR ports dropped from 36.7 million tons to 19.6 million tons, and in July 1931 the company was forced to lay off staff at Caerphilly, those that remained working short time, a situation that continued until the autumn of 1936. In South Wales alone, more than 5,000 Great Western staff were made redundant during this period. In addition the Locomotive Department intensified its rationalisation of locomotives inherited from pre-Grouping companies; those not worn out were placed on sales lists, and many were purchased by industrial concerns for use as shunters. At the west end of Swindon Works, beyond the great 'A' Shop, was 'The Dump' — sidings where many of the withdrawn locomotives lurked, sometimes for years, before being either sold or scrapped. The 1930s was also characterised by an increasing locomotive standardisation, many older GWR classes being withdrawn, along with the distinctly non-standard types that originated with such as the Cambrian or

Top: *The frontage of Leamington Spa after modernisation, seen on a rainy morning in the late 1930s.*

Above: *Happy holidaymakers pose for the camera at St Ives station, deep in the heart of the Great Western's Cornish Riviera.*

MSWJR. Although efforts had been made to 'Westernise' such locomotives with taper boilers and GWR-pattern cabs, chimneys and safety-valve covers, most had been withdrawn by the late 1930s, replaced by standard Collett designs.

Leaving aside the trials and tribulations suffered by the Great Western between the wars, there is little doubt that the 1930s represented a high-point for steam traction, and the company was able to run some of the world's fastest and most famous express trains. As the decade progressed, the LNER and LMS managed to steal some of the Great Western's thunder, notably in 1938, when *Mallard* broke the world speed record for steam traction. Before this, Paddington's claim to fame was that the GWR operated the 'World's Fastest Train' — the 'Cheltenham Flyer'. From 1929 this averaged 66.2 mph from Swindon to Paddington, making it the fastest scheduled train in the world. By 1932 the average speed had been increased to more

than 70mph; on 12 September the 77¼-mile journey between Swindon and Paddington behind No 5016 *Montgomery Castle* was reduced from 70 to 65 minutes, giving an average speed of 71.3mph for the whole trip.

In 1934 the GWR even went to the trouble of producing one of its 'Books for Boys of All Ages', titled *The Cheltenham Flyer*, in which the author, W. G. Chapman, described the train and all manner of other new developments on the GWR. As befitted a book published for the company, Chapman put a positive gloss on the fact that although the train was called the 'Cheltenham Flyer' it was only on the Swindon–Paddington stretch that speed records were broken, arguing that trains to and from London tended to be named after their starting station. 'Anyway, Cheltenham Flyer she is and will probably remain', Chapman concluded, adding that the train had created a stir all over the world, encouraging 'Americans, Chinese, Frenchmen, Germans, Indians and visitors from other countries' to include a trip on the train in their itinerary.

The company also made much of the exploits of its 'Blue Riband' service, the 'Cornish Riviera Limited', featuring a 'King'-class locomotive in one of its most famous publicity posters, titled 'Speed to the West'. The 'Limited' dated back to 1904, when, claimed the GWR, the introduction of a 7-hour service from Paddington to Penzance 'created a sensation, for nothing like it had ever been attempted in a regular daily service before'. The 246 miles between London and Plymouth were covered non-stop at an average speed of over 55mph; recognising the importance of this achievement, *The Railway Magazine* organised a competition to find a name for the train, quoting other examples such as the 'Flying Scotchman' *(sic)* and the 'Wild Irishman'. Well over 1,000 entries were submitted, and General Manager James Inglis finally chose the name 'Cornish Riviera Express', although two other entries had used the phrase 'Riviera Limited'. To most GWR staff the train was always known as the 'Limited'. Until 1906, when the new West of England route was opened, the train was run in the summer months only, but subsequently it ran all year round, and the departure time was put back from 10.10am to 10.30am. When war broke out in 1914 train speeds were reduced, and the journey time to Penzance was increased by 30 minutes.

By the 1930s the 'Limited' was the epitome of everything Great Western, especially when haulage of the service was taken over by 'King'-class 4-6-0s. Leaving from Platform 1 at Paddington, what the *GWR Magazine* described as the 'aristocrat of railway trains' ran non-stop to Plymouth North Road station — a distance now of 225 miles — in just 4 hours; time for the complete journey to Penzance was reduced to 6hr 20min. In 1935 the company celebrated its centenary by constructing two brand-new 13-coach corridor trains for use on the 'Cornish Riviera Limited'. Although the 60ft carriages were of a standard size, the interiors were what the GWR called a 'distinct departure from previous practice'. There were two end doors only on each side, with two 'spacious vestibules'; large drop windows were fitted in each compartment, and the panelling in each First-class carriage was light oak and walnut, whilst in Third class it was mahogany and walnut. The upholstery was very distinctive, in brown, blue and green moquette, with matching carpets and rugs, which, the company noted, 'make the general appearance very pleasing'. The 'Centenary' stock was of the highest standard, being every bit as luxurious as a Pullman train, and was described by *The Times* as a 'triumph of British workmanship' — a fitting tribute both to the skill of Swindon workers and to the efforts of the railway over the previous 100 years.

By 1923 the GWR's Publicity Department, which as the Advertising Department had been established by James Inglis before the Great War, was already an enormous asset to the company and after the Grouping, with Felix Pole at the helm, went from strength to strength. It had begun publishing books in earnest as early as 1904 and after the war had continued this initiative, broadening its range of titles from purely travel guides to include what it called 'Books for Boys of All Ages', many of which dealt with technical subjects such as engineering (*Track Topics*) and locomotives (*The King of Railway Locomotives*). The publication of many prewar titles continued on a larger scale, the likes of *The Cornish Riviera* being revised and reprinted. *Holiday Haunts* continued to be incredibly popular, more than 200,000 copies being sold

annually between 1928 and 1931 — a tremendous achievement, in view of the economic slump affecting the country at the time. By the 1930s the book had also grown in size and ran to more than 1,000 pages, yet still sold for just 6d. Published annually in March, it was described by W. H. Jarvis, writing in 1933, as 'a never-failing harbinger of spring'; in that year it covered 534 resorts in the 32 English and Welsh counties served by the Great Western Railway.

The inter-war period also saw the development of more unusual forms of publicity. One of the best known was the issuing of jigsaw puzzles featuring scenic views of locations on the GWR network, historical events (such as the Vikings landing at St Ives) and railway topics such as the 'Cheltenham Flyer' or *King George V*. The first jigsaw was produced to publicise the appearance of 4-6-0 *Caerphilly Castle* at the British Empire Exhibition in 1924, and by the outbreak of World War 2 the Chad Valley Co in Birmingham had manufactured more than a million puzzles.

Below: Another development in the 1930s was the introduction of GWR camping coaches. Situated in sidings at stations in holiday areas like Devon, Cornwall and Wales, the fully equipped carriages provided a cheap alternative to more conventional boarding-house or hotel accommodation. This publicity image was probably taken at Swindon, and the print was a copy from the Drawing Office.

Bottom: The luxurious new rolling stock built for the 'Cornish Riviera Limited' is seen near Teignmouth on 24 July 1935.

Right: *Ex- Midland & South Western Junction Railway 2- 6- 0 No 24, nicknamed 'Galloping Alice' in MSWJR days and 'Galloping Gertie' in the GWR era, is seen at Swindon Junction station on a goods service. Heavily rebuilt by the GWR and 'Westernised' with Swindon fittings and tender, it was destined to be withdrawn in 1930.*

Below: *A copy of the GWR monogram used between 1934 and 1942. This Swindon picture of the crest, which may have been a reference transfer produced at the works, was photographed in November 1950.*

Representing a more unusual publicity device were the Lantern Lectures — in fact sets of glass slides featuring views of tourist destinations on the GWR that could be borrowed by the public for their own amusement and entertainment. In 1926 there were more than 20 different sets of slides, covering areas as diverse as North Wales, the Wye Valley, Shakespeare Country and Oxford. The last, advertised as 'a walk around England's greatest University City', ran to 107 slides. A 1920s company advertisement in *Holiday Haunts* asserted that Lantern Lectures were 'suitable for literary or scientific entertainments, scholastic purposes and bazaars etc'. The slides were supplied free of charge, but the company needed two weeks' notice to arrange delivery within GWR territory.

The Lantern Lecture for the 'Cornish Riviera' consisted of a set of slides showing pictures of resorts and beauty spots in the Royal Duchy, ranging from Polperro to Falmouth, St Ives and Land's End. These were accompanied by a 32-page booklet with a complete script which could be read by staff or interested amateurs. 'Holidays in the West,' began the first section of the script, 'in the land of flowers and sunshine, poetry and romance! Could anything more fascinating be imagined or desired?'. The commentary added that 'this story will occupy approximately one hour. Interest is enhanced, when desired, by the introduction of appropriate music and elocution!'

It is widely acknowledged that GWR poster design was largely uninspiring until 1924, when the company expanded its advertising department and changed its title to 'Publicity Department', appointing William Fraser as 'Publicity Agent'. In their book on railway posters Cole and Durack argue that in the 1920s the Great Western tended to place more emphasis on press advertising than on the use of posters, something which did not change until Fraser's retirement in 1931. His successor, Keith Grand (later General Manager of BR Western Region), changed what we would now call its 'corporate image', introducing the now familiar GWR 'shirt-button' monogram and for much of its printed matter adopting the use of the Gill Sans typeface, making its publicity material much more distinctive and visually less cluttered. A more imaginative approach to poster design was also adopted, and in the latter part of the 1930s the company produced some striking examples featuring the work of such well-known artists as Edward McKnight Kauffer, Ronald Lampitt and Claud Buckle. The Great Western also had a talented artist in its own ranks; Charles Mayo joined the Publicity Department in 1932 and produced not only posters but also other artwork, including book covers. It was Mayo who, in 1939, was responsible for what many consider the most famous GWR poster of all, 'Speed to the West', featuring a 'King'-class locomotive on a West of England express.

As well as producing promotional material like posters and books the GWR was very adept at generating positive publicity from local, regional and national press, and its publicity machine made much of the introduction of another new venture in 1934, when diesel railcars were brought into service. The company had began cautiously with No 1, a single railcar with a chassis built by AEC at Southall and a streamlined body built by Park Royal. Fitted with a single 121bhp engine, it proved rather underpowered, but GWR management was sufficiently impressed to order three more vehicles, this time equipped with two engines. This extra power enabled them to run at speeds of up to 75mph, and they were used on cross-country express services between Cardiff and Birmingham, their sleek shape and art-deco design making them popular with travellers.

Writing shortly after the railcars' introduction, W. G. Chapman described their novel streamlined design and argued that it reduced wind resistance by 20% compared with that of a square-ended vehicle. Their performance would be 'watched with keen interest', he concluded, but clearly any doubts about their suitability were soon dismissed, as further examples, this time with more curvaceous bodywork manufactured by the Gloucester Carriage & Wagon Co, were ordered from AEC in 1935. In April 1936 a specialised diesel parcels car was introduced used to carry mail, parcels and even milk churns between Paddington and the West London suburbs. Early railcars, intended to run as single units only, were built without proper buffers, but this soon proved too restrictive, and later examples featured conventional buffers and couplings, allowing them to haul trailer carriages for extra passenger capacity. A final batch of vehicles, authorised by directors in 1938 but not built until the early part of World War 2, were designed and produced at Swindon Works; these featured a more angular body design and running gear more suitable for work on branch lines, where it was hoped they could be a more economic alternative to steam.

The Great Western Railway was the only one of the 'Big Four' companies to reach its centenary by virtue of its unbroken history, even through the Grouping process. Although there had been events to mark the centenaries of both the Stockton & Darlington and Liverpool & Manchester railways, celebrating its 100th birthday represented an ideal opportunity for the GWR to strike a blow against its rivals and promote its services to the public at large. In a foreword to a special Centenary edition of the company magazine Chairman Viscount Horne told staff that the railway had reached 'a highly distinctive stage' and that 'its identity is now definitely established, with its own individual traits and characteristics'.

In the event it seems that the company failed to make as much capital from the celebration as it had hoped. However, on 31 August 1935, to mark the anniversary of the founding of the GWR, *The Times* published a special supplement which featured not only articles on its history and development but also extensive coverage of many of its new initiatives, such as air services and diesel railcars. The actual 100th birthday fell on a Saturday, and to celebrate it the company ran a special train from Paddington to Bristol, leaving the capital at 10am and taking precisely two hours to travel down Brunel's old GWR main line. A celebration lunch was held at the Great Hall of the University of Bristol, and in his speech to the assembled guests Viscount Horne announced another publicity coup for the Great Western, the inauguration of a brand-new express, the 'Bristolian'; this would appear in timetables from 9 September and would run non-stop from Paddington to Bristol Temple Meads in 1hr 45min — an improvement of 15 minutes on any existing service between the two cities. After lunch guests were whisked back to the capital at 4.30pm —the time allotted for the return working of the 'Bristolian' — behind No 6000 *King George V*.

Below: *A well-known publicity picture for the 'World's Fastest Train', the 'Cheltenham Flyer'. The locomotive seldom carried the wooden headboard seen here, which has survived and is now displayed at Swindon.*

Guests at the Bristol dinner (and a subsequent Centenary banquet held in London, on 30 October) were treated to a showing of a special centenary film, *The Romance of a Railway*, which featured contemporary footage along with specially staged reconstructions of key moments in Great Western history. 'Well-known *artistes* have impersonated famous personalities connected at various times with the Great Western Railway', reported the *GWR Magazine* in September 1935; much of the filming was done at the Merton Park Studios, under the direction of Charles Creighton. Whilst a reconstruction of the first meeting of the GWR in 1833 was re-enacted at the Merchants' Hall in Bristol, a later set-piece recreating the arrival of the first train at Maidenhead, in 1838, was filmed at a rather less salubrious location — waste ground at the west end of Swindon Works. The *North Star* broad-gauge replica locomotive was pressed into service, pushed along the track by a diesel shunter placed carefully out of shot. The actors playing the crowd were members of the Great Western (London) and Swindon operatic societies; all went well until one unfortunate extra gave the game away by looking at his wristwatch while on camera. The film also included 'cleverly contrived glimpses of several resorts served by the railway, and of traffic operations', as well as a lengthy sequence filmed at Swindon Works.

The London banquet was staged at the Grosvenor House Hotel and was a grand affair attended by more than 1,100 guests, including the Prince of Wales and mayors and lord mayors of many towns and cities served by the railway. Also amongst the guests were some staff, although most were representatives of trade unions, pension and provident societies and officers of the St John Ambulance Association. The Prince of Wales gave a witty speech praising the achievements of railways and reminding the assembled diners that his grandmother, Queen Victoria, had first travelled by train on the GWR in June 1842. He concluded his speech arguing that on the company's 100th birthday it was 'entitled to have its own trumpet blown, and I am very happy to give it a hearty and resounding blast'. Viscount Horne, responding to the speech, concluded that 'the company's identity remains, its individuality is preserved, its vigour is undiminished, its traditions ands reputation are high, and its place, pray Heaven, in the loyalty of the people it serves is securely established'.

The centenary was also marked by a BBC radio programme, broadcast on 30 August 1935, which aimed to recount the story of the early history of the railway in the form of a

Right: *Great Western diesel railcar No 18, built in April 1936, hauls a rather ancient-looking auto-trailer carriage which contrasts sharply with the modern appearance of the 70- seat diesel.*

journey from Paddington to Penzance via Bristol. Two narrators, Mr V. C. Clinton-Baddeley and Mr Robert Speight, talked to staff at Paddington, including the driver of No 6000 *King George V*, W. H. Sparrow. Discussing the Battle of the Gauges, they were able to talk to a retired guard, H. J. New, who reminisced about the broad gauge. The broadcasters also spoke to W. H. Bickham, who had been Mayor of Swindon in 1934, about the town and its works, as well as the relative merits of the 'Castle'- and 'King'-class locomotives. The saga of the refreshment rooms at Swindon led to a discussion with F. H. Shephard, a chef on the 'Torbay Express', who explained how he cooked meals in such a small kitchen at high speed. The programme also featured a recording of the pumps at the Severn Tunnel, indicative of the work required to keep the tunnel dry 24 hours a day, and when Cardiff was reached one of the company's divers, W. H. Laurie, told 'some amusing and interesting things' about his work on the GWR dock system. More Great Western staff were interviewed to tell the story of the railway and its construction in the West Country, the programme concluding with a whispered 'good night' from Mr M. Froude, a retired GWR guard from Penzance — a clever ending described by one national newspaper as 'a touch of genius'.

The positive publicity generated by the centenary was diminished somewhat on 10 January 1936 when the company suffered one of the more serious accidents of the inter-war period, the 9pm Penzance–Paddington express ploughing into part of a coal train that had become divided near Shrivenham in Wiltshire. The detached wagons had not been spotted by signalmen, and the express, headed by No 6007 *King William III*, struck them at 60mph, the impact killing the driver and one passenger and injuring a further 10 people.

In the years immediately after the GWR centenary there was an improvement in the position of the railway, business being better than it had been for some years. The Great Western and other 'Big Four' companies were, however, becoming more and more concerned about the rise of road competition and the problems caused by their historic role as common carriers (*i.e.* a legal obligation to transport anything offered to them — something not required of road hauliers).

Another cause for complaint was the heavy burden of rates payable on the property owned by the railways (road hauliers paying only a fraction of the sum demanded of the likes of the GWR), and a pamphlet published jointly by all the railway companies in 1938 included appeals entitled 'The Railways Ask for a Square Deal' and 'Give Railways Equality'. However, it was soon clear that not everyone supported their cause; indeed, in some quarters the only real solution to the problems faced by the railways was seen as nationalisation as a public or semi-public utility. This option not was welcomed by the GWR, in particular, which as a private company had managed to pay a modest dividend of not less than 3% every year since the Grouping, even in the challenging economic climate of the inter-war period. Ultimately the outbreak of World War 2 would interrupt the debate over the future of Britain's railways, but postwar a Labour Government was destined to seal their fortunes.

Above: A large advertisement, as produced by all 'Big Four' railways and pressing their case for a better deal from the government in the face of fierce competition from the road transport industry, erected at the west end of Paddington station.

Left: A scene from the GWR's centenary film, Romance of a Railway. *The station was a prop, built on waste ground at Swindon Works. Out of shot is a GWR diesel shunter, used to propel the train, as the broad-gauge* North Star *replica did not actually run.*

CHAPTER ELEVEN

OFF THE RAILS

Away from its extensive rail network the Great Western operated a number of ancillary services to support its business. The introduction in 1903 of its first bus service is often seen as a pioneering development by the railway, although it is less well known that the vehicles used on the new service from Helston to The Lizard had actually been purchased second-hand from the narrow-gauge Lynton & Barnstaple Railway; not surprisingly there was no mention of this in an article on the new buses published in the *Daily Telegraph* of 17 August 1903. However, the growing importance of the internal-combustion engine had clearly not been missed by management at Paddington, and Company Chairman Earl Cawdor reported to shareholders that the introduction of motor vehicles could 'open out country districts and may even be of material assistance to agriculture'. The introduction of the service from Helston was also clearly linked to the development of tourist business in Cornwall, and this particular route was an alternative to a potentially expensive light railway between the two places, which had been discussed.

It was said that the Lynton & Barnstaple buses had been sold because they frightened horses in their locality, but the GWR had no such concerns about equine safety, and the service inaugurated on 17 August 1903 employed two Milnes-Daimler 22-seaters, running three trips in each direction daily. Within months a further service, between

Right: A photograph marking the inauguration of the Great Western's first omnibus service from Helston to The Lizard on 15 August 1903. The vehicle is a Milnes-Daimler.

Newlyn and Marazion, was launched. The *GWR Magazine* of September 1903 noted that the 'present wise and politic measures of the Great Western' were due in no small part to 'the pressure of a most salutary competition'; it made no secret of its concerns about the lessons learned from the growth of tramways around London and Birmingham and the share of increasing passenger traffic they could lose, adding that whilst the idea of developing bus services 'may be due to baser necessities of commercial rivalry, its ultimate development may reach the levels of a great national advantage'.

The enthusiasm shown by the company for motor vehicles was confirmed in 1904 when it placed an order for a further 30 Milnes-Daimlers, and by the outbreak of the Great War it was operating more than 30 'Road Motor' services throughout its territory, at locations such as Abergavenny, Carmarthen, Redruth, Stroud and Stourbridge. Whilst many of the vehicles were used as feeders, linking GWR stations and outlying areas, they were also employed on tourist services in a number of areas. In the fourth edition of its own travel book, *Devon: Shire of the Sea Kings*, published in 1916, the company placed a full-page advertisement giving details of its services. 'All the year round' the GWR operated buses between Moretonhampstead station and Chagford, Kingsbridge station and Salcombe, Yealhampton station and Modbury and between the stations at Totnes and Paignton. Also advertised were tours by 'observation cars', which 'under normal conditions' ran in the summer months over Dartmoor, 'giving the opportunity for an attractive excursion amidst attractive scenery and in bracing air'. GWR motor buses could also be hired at a cost of 2 shillings per mile, and the *GWR Magazine* of 1909 noted that it was now possible for golfers arriving at Slough station to telephone for an 'omnibus' to take them to the nearby Stoke Poges course.

The bus services advertised by the company in the 1916 travel book would have been severely curtailed by World War 1, but by the early 1920s the company had begun once again to expand its services in this area. Marking the 20th anniversary of the introduction of motor omnibuses, in 1923, the company magazine reported that those small beginnings had been expanded to the point where vehicles from the Road Motor Department were running almost 40,000 miles a week and the 96 buses now in use carried almost 3 million passengers annually. The services were, it added, also used to run replacement services when lines were blocked, and to carry travellers to other events, like agricultural shows and race meetings, the transporting of racegoers from Windsor station to Ascot — a service that dated back to the days of horse-drawn vehicles — meriting special mention as a regular and lucrative business.

In the 1920s the Great Western invested heavily in new vehicles, replacing older buses with faster and more reliable modern designs; in 1928 alone it purchased 50 32-seat buses and a further 25 smaller vehicles for narrower rural roads. In typical GWR fashion, the chassis and running gear of older vehicles withdrawn from passenger service were not scrapped but rebodied for goods use. In August 1928 new Parliamentary legislation formally allowed railway companies to run road-transport services as part of a national network, formalising powers the GWR had developed in earlier years. The *GWR Magazine* reported that during the Parliamentary proceedings 'appreciative references were made on more than one occasion to the enterprise of the Great Western in developing road transport services'. However, what the new bill did was to allow railway companies to invest in other bus operators and to work much more closely with them to link road and rail services, and the Great Western duly began to invest in companies throughout its territory. A good example of this approach was a partnership with the National Omnibus & Transport Co to create the Western National Omnibus Co, which took over the running of Great Western bus services in Cornwall and parts of Devon. Similar agreements were subsequently concluded 'after many vicissitudes' to create the Western Welsh Omnibus Co in South Wales, Crosville Motor Services (in partnership with the LMS) in Cheshire and North Wales and the Midland Red operation in and around Birmingham. By 1935 the GWR was able to claim that, independently or in partnership with other railways, it held 'not more than 50% interest in each of the seven principal omnibus companies that are within the range of the Great Western Railway'.

Above: *A Great Western single-horse 'Parcels Collecting Van' used at the company's London terminus. Pictured in August 1909, the wagon was used around the capital until the introduction of motor vehicles.*

continued to be used in decreasing numbers, and, as Janet Russell notes in her book *Great Western Horse Power*, GWR records reveal that as late as 1947 there were still 245 in use in the Birmingham and Hockley areas.

Notwithstanding the continuing popularity of the horse, the GWR had in 1908 introduced a 'Country Lorry' service which involved the use of lorries based at rural stations used to collect and deliver goods, parcels and agricultural produce well beyond the usual radius of collection and delivery. The service was slow to take hold, and it was not until after the Great War that matters improved, aided no doubt by improvements to rural roads in the 1920s; by 1923 receipts for consignments from passenger trains had risen to £91,000, while those for goods trains amounted to a substantial £940,000. Competition from the new road-haulage industry that had sprung up after the Great War ate into the GWR's business, but the company made strenuous efforts in the inter-war period to generate income from its road-transport fleet. Issued in the 1930s, a 52-page booklet entitled 'Country Cartage Services' and aimed at 'all traders distributing goods in the area served by the GWR' claimed that 'Remote places and premises are brought into close touch with the centres of distribution'; the company tried to compete with its rivals by offering some expensive 'same day' services, although most customers were happy with

Whilst these new measures enabled the Great Western to take a step back from the direct operation so many bus services, it remained heavily involved in the use of goods vehicles to collect and move goods, parcels and luggage until nationalisation. Before the introduction of motor vehicles, horse-drawn carts had been used extensively to distribute goods and parcels from GWR stations and depots. In 1907 the Great Western owned more than 3,500 horses, used not only for cartage but also for shunting in depots and yards. Despite the introduction of motor vehicles, horses

Right: *The parcels van pictured here in one of the streets close to Paddington station was the kind of vehicle that would eventually replace the horse-drawn vehicles that were so widely used in the Victorian era. This particular van was built by the Birmingham company of Wolseley at its Adderley Park works in 1905.*

a cheaper 24-hour delivery for it called 'smalls' traffic, which used a combination of fast freight services and collection and delivery by lorry.

A successful and growing business in the 1930s was that of container traffic, a venture promoted by all the 'Big Four' companies. Although small by the standards of the large international shipping containers now in common use, the road/rail container service was advertised as being 'door to door', and the 1936 edition of *Holiday Haunts* featured the operation, arguing that the service removed any 'handling *en route*, thus eliminating the risk of damage'. It also noted that containers reduced the need for excessive packing, which meant that 'economy is further reflected in reduced carriage charges'. Different types of container were available to cope with different types of loads; perishable goods could be transported in insulated containers which were cooled initially by ventilation, then by ice and finally by the use of solid CO_2; the *Holiday Haunts* advertisement also offered specially adapted containers that could be used to transport bicycles.

Two years before the outbreak of World War 2 the Great Western owned 2,200 motorised delivery lorries and vans, as well as 3,000 horse-drawn delivery wagons and 1,000 horses. All this was necessary to cope with merchandise and livestock traffic, which in 1937 amounted nearly 14 million tons —

Left: *A 1930s poster advertising the GWR's house-removal service.*

a figure not previously attained since 1930. The outbreak of war brought new and additional strains on the Goods Department, and the continuing growth of the road-transport industry postwar led to a major reorganisation involving a 'zonal' system designed to integrate better the delivery of goods by road and rail.

Left: *Great Western Goods Department staff help unload one of its containers. The picture was taken at Bedford Park in Chiswick, not too far from the company headquarters at Paddington. Like all good removal men, they have unpacked the kettle first!*

It seems strange that, in an era when steam was still the dominant form of motive power, the Great Western should have introduced its own air services. Nevertheless, it was reported in the *GWR Magazine* that on 12 April 1933 the company had 'entered upon a new and historic phase of transport enterprise' when it inaugurated Britain's first railway-operated air service. Beginning with two flights daily between Cardiff and Plymouth, the the venture was clearly motivated by the ability to provide fast and flexible travel between two important commercial centres. To travel by rail between Cardiff and Plymouth might take a good part of a day, whereas the new GWR air service reduced the journey time to 1 hour 20 minutes. Three Westland Wessex monoplanes, in GWR chocolate-and-cream livery, with the company crest on the tail, were used for the service, air and ground crew being hired from Imperial Airways.

The launch of the service generated a great deal of interest from press and public alike; the

Below: The crew proudly stand in front of one of the De Havilland Dragon Rapide aircraft used on the Railway Air Services venture begun by all four major railways in 1934.

Bottom: Company officials, press and interested bystanders at Cardiff for the inauguration of the company's first air service in 1933.

company magazine devoted no less than seven pages to the event, reprinting a letter wherein the Prime Minister congratulated the company on its experiment. Its coverage concluded with comments from the pilot, who felt that 'full advantage of the service will be taken when the great saving of time is realised by business people and holidaymakers anxious to travel between Devon and South Wales'. Unfortunately his confidence was not shared by the public, who were probably put off by the high fares — a ticket costing £3 single or £5 return — and the added complication that only 35lb of luggage could be carried on each six-seater plane. The service was extended to include Birmingham as a destination, but inevitably the glamorous experiment lost money, although a report in the September 1933 *GWR Magazine* noted that, due to increased demand, the service had been extended for a further three weeks.

Following the cessation of timetabled flights at the end of September 1933 the GWR took stock of the situation and instead joined a consortium — Railway Air Services — formed by all the 'Big Four' railways and Imperial Airways. The new airline opened for business in May 1934, services being extended to include Liverpool, Bristol, Southampton, Portsmouth and Brighton. The aircraft used were larger De Havilland Dragon Rapides, which although faster could still accommodate only six passengers and two crew. Writing in *The Times* in 1935, a correspondent argued that 'the potentialities of transport by air within the British Isles are so far appreciated by few'; however, the embryonic experiments undertaken by the GWR were limited not only by lack of demand but also the underdeveloped nature of airfields and supporting facilities, and the interruption of World War 2 ultimately put paid to any real progress in this bold initiative on the part of the company.

Mention has already been made of the Great Western Railway's significant interests in both shipping and dock operations, particularly after the Grouping in 1922/3, when it acquired many of the most important docks and harbours in South Wales. The company's involvement in shipping stretched back much further, however, and can be seen to have begun as early as the late 1830s, when Isambard Kingdom Brunel put forward the

argument that his new railway was merely a link in a much more ambitious dream to connect London and New York. The first steamship designed by Brunel was indeed named the *Great Western*, but neither this nor the SS *Great Britain* (nor the SS *Great Eastern* that followed) were ever actually owned by the GWR.

With the opening of the South Wales Railway as far as Neyland, Pembrokeshire, in 1858 the company made arrangements with a shipping company to provide steamer services to Southern Ireland. A fortnightly service between Milford Haven and Cork and Waterford was run on the company's behalf until 1872, when it took over the operation itself, purchasing four ships (including the delightfully named *Vulture*) as part of the deal. In 1874 the company acquired new steamships — the *Limerick*, *Milford* and *Waterford* — and introduced daily sailings between New Milford and Waterford. These services continued until 1906, when operations were transferred from New Milford to the new port of Fishguard, Irish cross-channel sailings being handled by a fleet of three new triple-screw turbine steamers — *St David*, *St George* and *St Patrick*. These fast ships were joined two years later by the *St Andrew* and continued in use until the 1930s, when they were replaced by more modern vessels bearing the same names.

Although services across the St George's Channel to Southern Ireland often catered for the tourist trade they also handled a good deal of freight traffic, particularly cattle which, it was reported by many travellers, made journeys in the summer months quite unpleasant, the smell of the four-legged passengers being difficult to disguise. When demand on the Irish route was slower, particularly in the winter, some ships were moved to the other main focus of Great Western maritime operations, the Channel Islands route. In 1857, a year after it had reached the Dorset port of Weymouth, the GWR began operating shipping services to the Channel Islands through the Weymouth & Channel Islands Packet Co, a separate venture which was supported by GWR capital and counted both Brunel and Gooch among its shareholders.

The company did not actually have Parliamentary powers to operate its own shipping services until 1872, and although it subsequently began operating the Irish services already described, it did not take direct control of its Channel Islands route until 1889, beginning its new operations with three new ships — *Lynx*, *Antelope* and *Gazelle*. These new fast ships only intensified the rivalry that had persisted between the GWR and the LSWR, which also operated services to the Channel Islands. Matters came to a head in 1899 when the LSWR steamer *Stella* hit rocks off Jersey, sinking with the loss of 100 lives. This followed a less serious incident three years previously, when the Great Western steamer *Ibex* had hit rocks off Corbière while racing an LSWR ship. The tragedy was enough to force the two companies to pool their resources and share receipts from both routes. In summer months each company would operate six sailings weekly in each direction, the LSWR at night and the GWR by day; in the winter months sailings were reduced as demand fell. This co-operation formed the basis of arrangements after the Grouping, sailings being scheduled to avoid any possibility of crews' racing one another.

In 1925 the company invested in two new cross-channel steamers to replace the elderly *Ibex* and *Reindeer*, which had been used on the route since the 1890s. The SS *St Julien* and SS *St Helier* were built in Glasgow and could each accommodate 1,000 passengers and cruise at 19 knots. These modern vessels were joined by two further cargo ships, the *Roebuck* and the *Sambur*, which were built at Newcastle upon Tyne. A further ship, the SS *St Patrick*, was added in 1930, replacing the ship of the same name, used originally on the Rosslare route, that had been lost the previous year. The

Above: *Three fishermen watch as the GWR steamer* St Helier *sails into the harbour St Peter Port, Guernsey, in the 1930s.*

replacement vessel was used on both Irish and Channel Island services but had a lucky escape in 1932 when it struck the Corbière rocks off Jersey in fog typical of that endured by crews operating ferry services to the island. Although badly holed the ship did not sink and, after passengers had been safely disembarked, was towed back to Plymouth for repair.

Despite the outbreak of World War 2 sailings to the Channel Islands continued until the islands' occupation by German forces in July 1940. The *St Julien* and the *St Helier* were requisitioned by the War Department, and they, along with other GWR ships, went on to play a crucial role in the war, as will be described in Chapter 12.

The Great Western also operated a small fleet of smaller vessels at Plymouth to act as tenders, taking passengers and mail from the many transatlantic liners that called there. In 1929 the company finally replaced the most elderly of these tenders, the *Smeaton*, which had been built in 1883. Its replacement was the *Sir John Hawkins*, a 180ft vessel which, the *GWR Magazine* reported, was 'thoroughly up to date' and capable of accommodating up to 600 passengers at any one time. The ship was also equipped with a dining saloon, which may have seemed rather excessive, given that it was used mainly to ferry passengers to and from the port; however, it and the other tenders were also pressed into service in summer months to carry tourists and holidaymakers along the coast of Devon and Cornwall. The other three tenders were also named after West Country maritime figures, being the *Sir Francis Drake*, *Sir Richard Grenville* and *Sir Walter Raleigh*.

Travellers using the company's steamers to cross the Irish Sea from Rosslare to Fishguard might well have made use of the GWR hotel at the West Wales port. The Fishguard Bay Hotel was one of a number owned or run by the company during its existence, and although the portfolio of establishments changed over the years, with the addition of some smaller esablishments, the running of four major hotels dominated its business by the 1930s. By far the most luxurious was the Great Western Royal Hotel at Paddington, which after its refurbishment in the 1930s was described by the company as 'a noted landmark' and 'one of the most modern and comfortable hotels in London'; the 'Royal' name was added when Prince Albert visited in 1854, shortly after its opening. Initially, at least, the hotel was leased to a company consisting of GWR directors and shareholders including Brunel, but following expiry of this agreement, in 1896, it was managed directly by the company and was modernised on a number of occasions. Then as today, passengers could gain access to the hotel via an entrance on the 'Lawn' in front of the main platforms at Paddington.

The Fishguard Bay Hotel already mentioned had been acquired when the GWR built its new port there in 1906. The company's guide to its Refreshment & Hotel Department, published in 1932, boasted that 'it is difficult to overrate the convenience of this roomy, well-built and well-equipped hotel close to the

Right: *The SS* St David, *one of the new turbine steamers introduced by the Great Western when it opened its new harbour facilities at Fishguard in 1906. The ship is pictured on sea trials, prior to its use on services to Rosslare.*

Left: *Loading motor cars at Fishguard Harbour in May 1937.*

landing quay'. The hotel was intended not only as a stopping-off point for weary travellers from GWR Irish ferry services but also as a centre for tourists spending time in West Wales. It also had eight miles of private fishing, and the *GWR Magazine* reported in 1925 that these waters had been re-stocked with trout for visiting fishermen.

Given its preoccupation with running trains to the Cornish Riviera it was only natural that the GWR should have its own hotel there. The Tregenna Castle Hotel, situated close to St Ives, was leased by the company in 1878 and could accommodate up to 160 guests. Besides standard rooms, the hotel provided 'self-contained suites', each comprising a double bedroom, sitting room and bathroom. Visitors' servants could also be accommodated, at a cost of 13s 6d per day between May and September and 10s 6d out of the holiday season. The hotel had over 100 acres of grounds, which contained a nine-hole golf course and tennis courts.

The company finally managed to acquire a high-quality hotel in its other main holiday destination, Devon, in 1929, when it opened the Manor House Hotel at Moretonhampstead. Previously been the residence of Lord Hambledon, this Jacobean-style building had been constructed as recently as 1907. A contemporary GWR pamphletreported the availability of 'hot and cold running water in every room' and that

the cellars contained 'complete stocks of choice wines', while the grounds were the workplace of perhaps one of the more unusual GWR workers — a river-keeper employed to look after the six miles of 'good trout fishing' on two nearby rivers, the Bovey and Bowden. In June 1930 the company opened an 18-hole golf course within the grounds, although it also claimed that 'some of the finest scenery in "Glorious Devon" must at once appeal to a great number of visitors in search of rest and recuperation in health-giving moorland air'.

Below: *The Great Western Royal Hotel at Paddington pictured shortly after its refurbishment, which had stripped it of much of its Victorian decoration. The original designs had been by the architect P. C. Hardwick, in the style of a French château. The large building to the left of the hotel contained GWR offices, including those of the Superintendent of the Line.*

CHAPTER TWELVE

THE GREAT WESTERN AT WAR

The strategic importance of railways had been recognised by government as early as 1842, when an Act of Parliament allowing emergency powers over them had been passed. When Brunel's broad gauge was debated at the 1845 Royal Commission the difficulties of transporting the military across country and dealing with the 'break of gauge' was an important consideration. The passing of the 1871 Regulation of the Forces bill gave government the ability to take control of the railways but left the day-to-day operational control to the companies themselves. The Crimean War had had only a minor effect on the operation of the Great Western, and the Boer War campaign was the first military conflict in which the army had made significant use of railways. However, whilst the GWR ran a number of special trains, its neighbour, the London & South Western, bore the brunt of the work, moving most of the half million troops involved in the campaign from Waterloo to Southampton.

This hard-fought conflict was bloody and controversial, and the treatment of the Boers had left many feeling uneasy. However, whatever misgivings there may have been, Paddington was the scene of grand ceremonies staged to greet the return of military leaders involved in the campaign; when Lord Roberts, Commander in Chief, arrived in January 1901 it was in a train hauled by a GWR locomotive named *Roberts* and decorated with his coat of arms. Platform 9 had been dressed with shields and red, white and blue banners, and was, to quote the *GWR Magazine*, 'carpeted in crimson'. In July 1902 the return of General Kitchener was accompanied by a similarly lavish ceremony.

The station was cleared of all but 'privileged spectators', and only ticket-holders remained to see the general greeted by the Prince of Wales, the Duke of Connaught, the Maharajah of Jaipur and other distinguished guests.

When World War 1 broke out, in 1914, the railways of Britain were taken over by the Railway Executive Committee (REC), an organisation that had been created as early as 1912, as the clouds of war began to darken. Under the control of the President of the Board of Trade, the REC included the general managers of the 10 largest railway companies with Herbert Walker, General Manager of the LSWR, as its Chairman. Just over a decade after the outbreak of war it was reported that the REC had 'at once entered upon their arduous duties of operating the railways in accordance with instructions from the War Railway Council'. Within 15 minutes of the declaration of war, at 11.45pm on 4 August 1914, 'the government was in possession of the railways in readiness for the first day of mobilisation'. That same evening the hooter at Swindon Works had been blown 10 times, sombrely marking the beginning of a conflict that would change irrevocably the face of the GWR, its staff and the nation it served. Staff were informed of the news the following day in a memorandum telling them that 'the government have, for the time being, taken over control of the railway in connection with the mobilization of the troops and general movements in relation to Naval and Military requirements'.

The company noted that the purpose of government control of railways was 'to render them available to the fullest extent for military purposes'. It therefore comes as no surprise to learn that the new lines built before the war proved an invaluable asset to the military, particularly in handling the large numbers of coal, troop and ambulance trains required to support the war effort. Despite difficulties caused by the calling-up of reservists working for the company, the GWR rose to the challenge of assisting the despatch to France of the British Expeditionary Force and in the space of five days — 15-19 August 1914 — ran 900 military trains in addition to local services.

Most of the coal used by the British fleet was mined from the Aberdare and Rhondda districts of South Wales. When war began the Admiralty, having agreed contracts with collieries for the supply of coal, hired around 4,000 wagons to transport it. Initially trains moved coal to South Wales ports for despatch by ship, but once German submarines had made the moving of coal around the coastline almost impossible it was left to the GWR to move the coal north to Grangemouth, in Scotland, which in 1915 was designated as the main base for coaling the fleet. Since many of the collieries supplying coal were situated on the lines of companies like the Taff Vale, Rhymney and Vale of Neath, Pontypool Road on the Great Western was the main concentration point for Admiralty coal. The first northbound train left there on 27 August 1914, and by 1918 an average of 79 trains carrying 32,000 tons of coal were being worked by the company every week; towards the end of the war even this was not enough, and 30 more specials a week were run, the greatest quantity being 56,000 tons in a single week. The scale of the operation was enormous; by the end of World War 1 the GWR had run 13,361 loaded coal trains which, it estimated, would have contained well over 5 million tons — a figure that becomes all the more impressive when one realises that the company had to handle the empty return workings as well.

Although the GWR recorded the number of military and naval passenger trains it ran during the war, it could not estimate the numbers of military personnel or government officials who travelled on ordinary services. Special military trains run between 1914 and the end of 1919 totalled 37,283, the greatest number (9,076) being run in 1915. In the latter part of the war the company ran a large number of trains from Liverpool to the South Coast, carrying American soldiers who had disembarked in Liverpool and Glasgow on their way to Channel ports. The large numbers of servicemen travelling put a real strain on the Refreshment Department's facilities, and at many stations additional arrangements

Left: *The special refreshment and rest facilities provided for service personnel at Paddington, seen shortly before closure in 1919.*

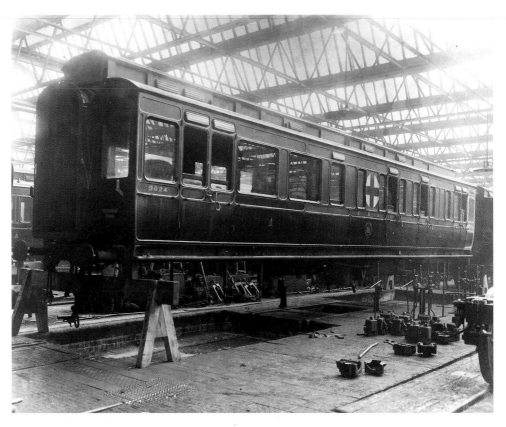

were made. At Banbury, through which many troop and ambulance trains passed, a 'Station Refreshment Fund' was established, and, thanks to public donations, provided refreshments supplied by Red Cross nurses and local people. Similar arrangements were provided at Birmingham, Exeter and other GWR stations. At Paddington a 'Soldiers' and Sailors' Free Buffet' was set up in April 1915 and operated 24 hours a day until June 1919, looked after by a staff of 80 'ladies' who over this period helped more than 3 million servicemen.

Aside from the troop trains, the GWR also ran more than 6,000 loaded ambulance trains carrying servicemen from South Coast ports to locations all over its network. Of these, 2,848 called at Great Western stations to unload sick and wounded troops; Bristol Temple Meads bore the brunt, handling 395 trains, followed by Paddington (351), Plymouth North Road (239) and Cardiff General (207). Although most wounded soldiers were taken to Dover or Southampton for repatriation, Avonmouth Docks was also utilised, especially for troops returning from the Mediterranean or the Far East, more than 25,000 men being received

there and moved by the GWR to hospitals in Bristol, London or Manchester. To help run these services the company had contributed four special ambulance trains converted at Swindon Works for 'home' use, as well as a further 12 which were sent overseas for use by British and American troops.

Swindon Works was pressed into service to assist the war effort and undertook work for the War Office, Ministry of Munitions and the Admiralty. The skill and adaptability of the staff at the factory was proved by the huge variety of tasks they tackled, often at short notice, two of the best known being the preparation of a number of 'Dean Goods' 0-6-0 and ex-GCR ROD 2-8-0 locomotives for service overseas and the conversion or construction of carriages for ambulance-train use. The list of other work carried out was, however, extensive, Edwin Pratt, celebrating the achievements of Swindon Works, commenting that 'a mere catalogue of the items would extend over many pages'. It included the manufacture of 327 six-pounder Hotchkiss guns, various large gun carriages, shell parts, fuses, shells, bombs and other ammunition components. Some idea of the scale of the work can be gained from the fact that, at the height of the war, the factory was turning out 2,500 shells per week. The Carriage & Wagon Department was also busy, building 1,100 wagons, 50 water carts, almost 3,000 stretchers and many other smaller items.

Whilst the contribution made to the war effort was clearly vital, it did mean that the normal prewar maintenance regime for GWR locomotives was disrupted, and a backlog built up. Accepted standards dropped, and the works, in the words of one of its historians, became 'very run-down'. To make matters worse, as one GWR source concluded, 'This valuable contribution to the war equipment of the nation was made without any financial profit accruing to the company.'

The Government also requisitioned seven of the GWR ships for use in the war effort. The steamers used on the Fishguard route — the *St Andrew*, *St David* and *St Patrick* — were converted into hospital ships, all the work being done by GWR staff at Fishguard. The remaining four ships — *Reindeer*, *Roebuck*, *Lynx* and *Gazelle* — came from the Channel Islands service; the *Roebuck*, renamed *Roedean* by the Admiralty, was sunk at Scapa Flow when it collided with a French battleship, but all the other ships survived the war, despite some narrow escapes. Amazingly, despite the dangers of mines and submarines in the St George's Channel, the GWR continued with its services from Fishguard to Rosslare throughout the war, carrying shiploads of cattle from Ireland to aid the food situation in Britain.

Although railway workers at Swindon and elsewhere on the GWR network were regarded as being in a reserved occupation, as the conflict dragged on more men were enlisted. By the end of the war no fewer than 25,479 had joined up, this total representing 32.6% of the railway's prewar establishment. The steady depletion of the workforce led to a substantial increase in the number of women employed by the company. Before the outbreak of war it had employed a total of just 1,371, of whom 497 were, it noted, 'employed on railway work proper', mainly as typists, 'shorthand girls' and telephone operators, a further 874 being engaged in a variety of other jobs, notably as waitresses, washerwomen, charwomen and waiting-room attendants. By August 1918 a total of 6,345 women were

Left: *Recruiting posters, seen at Paddington in 1915. 'Remember Scarborough' was a reference to the raid on the East Coast port by German battleships which killed 18 civilians in December 1914.*

working for the company, more than 5,000 on railway work. Most were employed in clerical positions, but there were also 346 porters, 323 ticket-collectors and 594 carriage-cleaners.

In 1916, as food shortages began to take their toll, the GWR offered its staff land alongside the railway for allotments at an annual rent of 3d, any land previously uncultivated being offered free to prospective gardeners. Arrangements were also made with local seed merchants to supply vegetable seeds on 'favourable terms'. Before the war 7,653 men had allotments, and by its end this figure had almost doubled, reaching 13,059.

Following the armistice the GWR counted the human cost of the 'War to end all Wars', and in 1919 it was recorded that no fewer than 2,524 employees had been killed, and many more injured. The contribution of the fallen was marked by memorials and rolls of honour at stations and depots all over the network. On Armistice Day 1922 more than 6,000 people attended the ceremony in which the Great Western Railway War Memorial was unveiled at Paddington station. Underneath the memorial, which consisted of a bronze figure of a soldier, the names of all those killed had been placed in a sealed casket, appropriately manufactured at Swindon.

★   ★   ★

Despite everything the Great Western had done to combat the effects of the economic depression, the uncertain international situation and increasing tension before and after the Munich Crisis of 1938 caused revenue to drop by almost £2 million. Although Prime Minister Neville Chamberlain had returned from Germany with the now infamous 'Piece of Paper' which, he proclaimed, would bring 'peace in our time', and tension was reduced somewhat, the Railway Executive Committee met once again and began formulating emergency plans that could be activated at short notice. The GWR also made its own preparations for a possible war; as well as planning air-raid precautions and blackout procedures it stockpiled vital supplies such as sleepers, rails and spare parts and early in 1939 purchased six extra breakdown cranes.

When World War 2 began, on 3 September 1939, the 'Big Four' companies (along with London Transport) were effectively nationalised, coming under the control of the Railway Executive Committee, as they had done in the Great War, through the issue of an order under the Emergency Powers (Defence) Act 1939. With this order the activities of the railways were transferred from peacetime to wartime conditions. Railways were guaranteed fixed annual payments from the Government, the Great Western receiving

£6,670,603. The LMS received the largest sum, an annual payment of £14,749,698, but the total amount paid by the Government to all the companies, £43million, was £13 million less than the 'standard revenue' figure estimated by the companies themselves — a source of resentment to the GWR, which had been a relatively prosperous business before war broke out.

The work carried out in the months before the war came to fruition when the GWR undertook the first major task of the conflict with the evacuation of almost 113,000 schoolchildren from London and other major urban areas to safer locations in the countryside. Evacuation plans had been prepared in advance by staff, and a 166-page timetable had been printed for some weeks by the time the GWR received an urgent Government request to implement a major evacuation within 24 hours on 31 August 1939. The first trains left London at 8.30am on the morning of 1 September, many leaving not from Paddington but from Ealing Broadway, on account of its better Underground links. The railway had already been able to practise the evacuation of large numbers of people when it carried out a smaller-scale operation during the Munich Crisis, running 200 special trains carrying school children and hospital patients.

Over the next four days thousands of children were moved to locations all over the West Country and Wales. In the end the number of evacuees moved was lower than estimated; on the first day 58 trains ran rather than the scheduled 64, but on that day alone more than 44,000 children were still moved to safety. What became known as 'The Exodus' ran largely like clockwork, GWR and local council staff being on hand to ensure that all went well. It must, however, have been an emotional time for parents and staff alike; staff were instructed not to divulge 'any information to the public as to the destination of an Evacuation Special' — an order that must have been particularly tough for parents waving goodbye to their children at the station.

Although much attention was paid to the evacuation trains that ran from the capital, the GWR ran similar trains on 1 and 2 September from Birmingham, from where 22,379 passengers were moved to stations in Wales and Gloucestershire. In the following days it organised another evacuation from Liverpool and Birkenhead which involved 35,606 evacuees. Two years later further evacuation trains were run by the GWR during the darkest days of the Blitz, when other towns and cities away from the capital were also being bombed. Bristol was particularly badly affected, and in February 1941 more than 7,000 children were evacuated from the city to Devon and Cornwall.

If the demands of moving evacuees were not enough, around the time of the 'Exodus' the Great Western moved many 'unofficial' evacuees fleeing the cities for safer rural locations. Although it proved impossible to count how many people were moved, one estimate put the figure at close to 2 million. Collie Knox, who wrote a moving history of the railway's wartime exploits, commented on these travellers' luggage, which ranged 'from beds to kettles and saucepans'. A further, more secret evacuation also took place in 1939, this being the transfer of much of the Great Western's own administrative staff to safer locations in the Berkshire countryside. By December the GWR had taken possession of purpose-built offices at Aldermaston, having used a number of requisitioned country houses and even occupied a number of restaurant cars at Newbury Racecourse station until permanent accommodation could be found.

The company had spent much time and effort on extensive air-raid precautions (ARP) and blackout measures, beginning this process

Below: The author has a family connection to the Great Western Railway evacuation operations. This family photograph shows his father (fourth from right) waving as he and his classmates leave Bristol for North Devon in 1941.

before the war. All staff received training in ARP; a GWR booklet issued in 1938 warned that 'the risk of attack from the air ... is a risk that cannot be ignored'. After the use of poison gas during World War 1 much attention was also paid to the wearing of gas masks and to decontamination procedures. Another booklet, published in 1945, recorded that across Britain's railways as a whole 626,339 gas masks, 205,925 oilskin suits and 333,280 pairs of 'gumboots' were issued to staff for anti-gas precautions. The biggest task was the blacking-out of railway property; the sheer number of lights and the difficulties of operating in a total blackout meant that safety and trains speeds were compromised.

Below: This well- known picture must have been taken early in World War 2, for the cab window of 'Castle' No 5085 Evesham Abbey *has yet to be blanked out with steel plate. The picture was, of course, taken to illustrate the use of gas masks.*

Wherever possible lamps were screened or dimmed to allow work to continue, but conditions for staff in places like goods yards were particularly difficult, as were those for engine crews. Locomotive cabs were blacked out with steel plating over windows, and tarpaulins masked the glow of the firebox, but it was not always possible to conceal all light from the locomotive, making trains an easy target for enemy aircraft.

Many staff joined ARP or Home Guard units or became firewatchers to help in the war effort, but the ferocity and frequency of air raids inevitably led to casualties amongst GWR staff. The scale and strategic nature of the Great Western Railway made it a target for enemy bombing, most of its principal stations being damaged in air raids, particularly during the Blitz of 1940 and 1941. The company's docks in South Wales and stations and goods depots in Bristol, Birmingham, Newton Abbot, Plymouth and Paddington were particularly hard-hit. Monthly reports submitted by the General Manager to the board when the Blitz was at its height are full of accounts of damage and destruction, and although the Great Western was not as badly affected as were other 'Big Four' companies, in particular the Southern, it nevertheless suffered 1,100 incidents between June 1940 and June 1943. Amazingly, only two GWR locomotives were completely destroyed by enemy action. The first, No 4911 *Bowden Hall*, was caught in a raid on Plymouth on the night of 29 April 1941 and had been stopped at Keyham near Devonport. A bomb fell close to the locomotive while the crew were sheltering under the steps of a nearby signalbox, damaging the locomotive so badly that it could not be repaired. Incendiary bombs had rained down on the nearby goods yard, setting fire to a wagon, which was full of pigs. The yard was full of other wagons containing oil and high-explosives, and it was only the prompt action of a GWR porter, Fred Harris, who climbed through the wagon full of terrified pigs to put out the fire, that prevented a major explosion, his bravery earning him a British Empire Medal. The only other GWR locomotive lost was a 0-6-0 pannier tank, No 1729, destroyed in an air raid on the Somerset junction of Castle Cary on 3 September 1942.

'The Principle adopted for transport in wartime is that the needs of war must come first,' warned a British Railways pamphlet

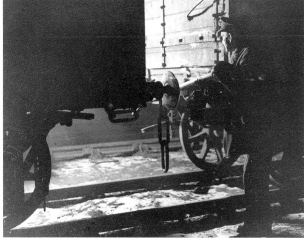

Top: *Some of the Great Western Railway Swindon Works Home Guard unit dressed in full anti- gas clothing. The picture, by local photographer L. Maylott, was taken in front of one of the workshops in the Carriage Works.*

Above: *Considerable damage was done on this air raid at Weymouth shed in January 1941. '43xx' Mogul No 8314 and 'Star' 4-6-0 No 4047* Princess Louise *are buried in the debris, although both would be repaired and returned to service without too much difficulty.*

Top: *The dangers inherent in carrying out shunting operations in the blackout are more than apparent in this picture of a Great Western Railway goods shunter at work in Bristol.*

Above: *A happier scene, featuring women permanent-way workers heading off to work in March 1943.*

issued in 1943. Within weeks of the outbreak of war the GWR had issued a new 'Emergency' timetable; not surprisingly, holiday trains were suspended for the duration, cheap tickets abolished, and the fastest expresses, like the 'Cornish Riviera Limited', curtailed or reduced. The now-familiar question 'Is Your Journey Really Necessary?' was first posed as early as 1939 but became more prominent two years later, when posters reinforcing the message appeared all over the GWR and the rest of Britain's railway network. With traditional resorts closed for the duration, holiday traffic declined, and the difficulties

experienced by railway travellers meant that most people made only essential journeys. Travelling by train in the blackout was a difficult enough proposition for railway staff and passengers alike, and blacked-out carriages, low train speeds and the removal of station nameboards and lighting made life particularly hard. It is thought that the blackout played at least some part in the tragic accident which occurred at Norton Fitzwarren on 4 November 1940. The driver of No 6028 *King George VI*, in charge of the 9.50pm Paddington–Penzance on the down relief line, believed that he was on the down main, not

Above: *Many Great Western ships saw action during World War 2. This photograph shows the SS* Roebuck *at Penarth Dock, moored for repairs following its involvement in the evacuation of Dunkirk and bearing the scars and bullet holes of battle.*

realising his mistake until overtaken by another train. By this time it was too late, and his train ran out of track. The resultant crash killed 27, including the fireman, and injured a further 56 passengers.

As the war progressed, the traveller faced more and more difficulties with the loss of the most basic comforts enjoyed before the war, which made a train journey problematic; in 1942 the General Manager reported that more than 8,000 towels had been stolen from trains, similar shortages being noted for necessities such as toilet paper and soap. Shortages of food saw the complement of restaurant cars reduced from 40 to 15, and refreshment rooms suffered similar problems. Crockery and utensils were also in short supply, so much so that the buffet at Swindon Junction was reduced to serving tea in jam jars.

There was constant pressure from the Ministry of Transport to reduce timetabled passenger trains to cope with far greater numbers of military personnel travelling to

and from bases all over the network and increasing numbers of war workers commuting to and from munitions establishments. Military staff travelling to and from their bases made trains very crowded, especially during holiday periods; it was recorded that in July 1942 alone more than a million servicemen were travelling 'under warrant'. One suggestion put forward by the REC in 1941 to reduce congestion on trains was the abolition of First class, but this was resisted by the railway, GWR General Manager Sir James Milne arguing that 'First-class passengers should have reasonable opportunity of travelling in the accommodation for which they have paid'. However, the increasing political power of the REC, backed to a certain extent by public opinion, meant that the GWR and other companies were forced to accept the compromise that First class would be abolished, but only on London suburban trains — a measure introduced in September

1941. Notwithstanding the inconvenience suffered by passengers, some idea of how traffic increased during the course of the war can be gleaned from the fact that, from 84,000 in 1939, the number of tickets issued by the GWR increased to well over 147,000 in 1944, dipping only slightly the following year.

In South Wales the docks played a vital role in the war effort, largely by dramatically changing their function. Not surprisingly, the war considerably reduced the export of coal, steel and tinplate from the docks, but their destiny was inevitably changed by the switch from East to West Coast ports prompted by the Nazi invasion of Europe. The Atlantic blockade meant that, as the war progressed, the dock facilities of South Wales were best placed as the first port of call for convoys that had made the hazardous crossing from the United States. By 1942 vast quantities of 'Lend-Lease' goods were being unloaded; berthed in South Wales ports in October that year were 29 ships, which had unloaded more than 57,000 tons of goods. As plans for the Allied invasion of Europe took shape the docks became the major centre for the import and storage of aircraft, landing craft, tanks and other armoured vehicles, as well as fuel and munitions. To cope with this increased activity there was considerable investment in new cranes, sidings, staff accommodation and storage facilities.

As had been the case in the Great War, the GWR shipping fleet was also pressed into action to assist with the war effort. Company ships were heavily involved in Operation 'Dynamo', the evacuation of Allied troops from Dunkirk, where the captain and crew of the SS *St Helier* braved mines and air attacks to make numerous trips into the harbour, eventually rescuing more than 11,000 troops and refugees. Great Western vessels were also involved in later campaigns as hospital ships; the SS *St David* was sunk off Anzio in July 1943 with the loss of 55 crew members, but the rest survived to assist in the D-Day landings.

At Swindon, Chief Mechanical Engineer C. B. Collett, who had been Works Manager during World War 1, is said to have been less than enthusiastic about the impact the new conflict was likely to have on his empire, given the disruption and backlog of maintenance and new building the last conflict had caused. However, pressure from the War Office

inevitably meant that the Works soon became heavily involved the war effort, and on a far greater scale than previously. Blacking out the huge 323-acre site proved problematic, but within weeks all the glass roofs of the factory had been covered with black paint, plunging the workshops into a permanent 'night shift' for the duration. Much of the works was turned over to war production, and the company carried out only the minimum of regular maintenance on its locomotives and rolling stock. Construction of new locomotives continued on a reduced basis, alongside the assembly of War Department engines. Swindon workers even built LMS-designed Stanier 2-8-0s, a move that must have gone against the grain for diehard GWR staff. The works also refurbished 100 ancient 'Dean Goods' 0-6-0s that had been requisitioned once again for use overseas; nine were so worn out that they had already been withdrawn, and were thus hurriedly reinstated. In an echo of the work undertaken during World War 1 the Carriage Works also built or converted coaches for ambulance trains used both at home and overseas.

The ingenuity of the Swindon workforce was also called upon to produce all manner of special equipment for the forces, often at short notice. After the Battle of Britain, for example, the factory produced 171,000 parts for Hurricane fighter planes, and in less than a month during March 1942 it machined 2,400 copper rings for shells destined for the Woolwich Arsenal. The works also manufactured unusual and sometimes highly secret items, including landing craft, midget submarines and gun mountings. Between 1941 and 1943, when the influx of munitions

Below: A movie camera is perched on the top of a car to record the handover of an ambulance train, converted for use by the United States Army, at Swindon Works on 24 March 1943.

from the United States began to ease the pressure on British manufacturers, the works produced bombs and shells of all shapes and sizes. In 1941 alone it turned out 60,000 mortar and aircraft bombs, and the following year it fulfilled an order for 2,000 500lb bombs, as well as larger 2,000lb and 4,000lb types.

Although staff were classified as being in a 'Reserved Occupation' the complement was eroded as the conflict wore on, just as it had been during World War 1. After the fall of France in 1940 it was estimated that within a year more than 2 million men and women would be needed in the armed forces and the munitions industry. More and more staff were conscripted into the services, and by the end of the war more than 15,000 were serving with the forces or in full-time civil defence. Although staffing levels were increased by more than 12,000 to make up this shortfall, the major problem for the company was the loss of skilled staff; many of the men conscripted had years of experience, and they could not easily be replaced; once again, it was only after the employment of thousands of women in railway service that any impression on the

staff shortages would take effect. The rapid integration of so many new female staff was not without incident, and conservative Great Western attitudes meant that some departments, like the Locomotive Department, were slow to take on women. A leaflet of the period which noted that 'women cannot be expected to lift such heavy loads as men' and a subsequent article in the *GWR Magazine* which claimed that requests for lighter parcels and loads were based on respect for the 'weaker' sex, who had come on to the railway for the duration. By 1941 it was reported that the GWR employed more than 8,000 women — a figure that was to double by the end of the war, female staff being employed as porters and ticket-collectors, permanent-way staff, machinists and carriage- and locomotive-cleaners. Altogether more than 124,000 women were employed on Britain's railways during World War 2 — a contribution that cannot be valued too highly.

In the period before D-Day the work that had been done by the GWR in upgrading its network over the years proved vitally important, and the further upgrading of two

Below: *A GWR Prairie tank hauls a trainload of tanks 'somewhere in England'. The contribution of the Great Western and other main-line railways to the Allied invasion of Europe was enormous and ensured that men, munitions and other material were delivered ready for D-Day and that supplies continued to flow after the landings had begun.*

key cross-country lines — the old Midland & South Western Junction and the Didcot, Newbury & Southampton — by lengthening loops and, where possible, doubling track, turned them into major routes. Both lines linked the Channel ports with the Midlands and the North of England and during the course of the campaign handled thousands of troop, munitions and fuel trains. Further wartime improvements included additional connections with the Southern in the Plymouth area and others at Thingley Junction (near Corsham), Oxford, Reading, Westbury and Yeovil.

In the weeks and months before the Allied invasion of Europe the GWR network was full of trains heading for the South of England; in the two months before D-Day the railways ran 24,459 trains for the movement of troops, ammunition and equipment and another 8,000 specials to move the stores, armoured vehicles and heavy equipment necessary to support the invasion. Following the invasion itself work continued, staff also dealing with a less welcome task, a steady stream of ambulance trains, handling 142 in June 1944 alone. A further unwanted but necessary job was the running of 167 prisoner-of-war trains between June and August 1944.

Despite the success of the landings the Great Western came under attack again in June and July 1944, when German 'V1' bombs fell on London and other British cities. As well as moving nearly 40,000 people on a series of Government evacuation trains on 6 July 1944 the GWR had to cope with thousands of passengers desperate to flee the capital. In the first week of the 'Flying Bomb' campaign more than 57,000 passengers were despatched from Paddington, but by the end of the first week of July this total had almost doubled, reaching 108,167. On the morning of the 29 July the company had to take the unprecedented measure of closing Paddington station for three hours after it became completely choked by thousands of people trying to escape to the West Country. The situation was improved only when, in response to urgent requests from the company, the Prime Minister's Office authorised the running of an extra 63 trains to relieve the congestion.

Within the year further more positive milestones were passed as an Allied victory drew ever closer; the threat of 'Flying Bomb'

Left: *Staff shortages meant that many Great Western footplate crew stayed on after their official retirement date. The* GWR Magazine *featured many of these veterans, and photographs appeared at regular intervals. This image features Driver Chaplain, pictured on 3 September 1945.*

attacks diminished, and in December 1944 the Great Western's own Home Guard units were stood down. In April 1945 the end of the blackout was greeted with huge relief by staff who had struggled through the war years in difficult conditions; a month later, the Swindon Works hooter blew for a full minute to celebrate the Allied victory in Europe. In September, VJ Day marked the complete end of hostilities, and GWR General Manager Sir James Milne, thanking staff for their efforts, reminded them that more than 15,000 employees had served with the forces during the war and that well over 600 had lost their lives in the conflict.

The losses suffered by GWR staff at home were not forgotten, 68 employees having been killed on duty, and a further 241 injured at work. Following the end of the war in the Far East the company ran extra trains to cope with the wave of 'demobbed' troops returning home and looked anxiously to the future; at its first postwar Annual General Meeting its new Chairman, Viscount Portal, told shareholders that there was much to do restore the railway to prewar standards. If this challenge were not enough, the spectre of nationalisation would prove a further battle — one the company would not ultimately win.

CHAPTER THIRTEEN

FROM CATTLE TO COAL: GWR GOODS SERVICES

Although commercial interests had been the driving force behind the establishment of the Great Western Railway in the 1830s, when the first section of line between Paddington and Maidenhead opened in 1838 no goods traffic appears to have been carried. Just over a year later, however, Brunel's railway began to handle freight when the line opened as far as Twyford, and by the time the Great Western had opened fully between London and Bristol the company had begun to earn a modest but increasing income from this source. A month after opening it issued a large handbill which provided a formal scale of charges for 'Merchandize, Cattle, etc', which divided goods into five main classes containing a weird and wonderful selection of items. First class included the heaviest traffic, such as coal, coke, lime, building materials and iron, whilst

Second class covered a multitude of commodities from flour and grain to turnips, beetroot and potatoes. Third-class goods included sugar, bacon and tallow, whilst among the items listed as Fourth class were wine and beer (in casks or barrels), eggs, sugar and cheese. Fifth class contained some of the most fragile and valuable loads, such as wine (in bottles), silks, glass, tea and books. The handbill also stated that the company could not be held responsible for the loss of 'jewellery, bullion, plate, clocks, watches, trinkets, rings, marbles, lace, furs, writing, paintings or other valuables'.

Nevertheless, passenger traffic dominated the company's balance sheet in the early years, and freight began to grow appreciably only when the company's expanding network finally reached areas with significant commercial and industrial activity. Until the opening of the line to Birmingham in 1853 freight business had been dominated by the agricultural nature of the landscape crossed by the Great Western Railway; an 1840 timetable noted that charges for goods were 18 shillings per ton between Paddington and Faringdon Road and 12 shillings per ton between Paddington and Reading, adding that 'Sheep, Beasts etc. are conveyed by the Goods Trains'. The commercial imperative of gaining freight business from industrial centres like Birmingham was not lost on the directors and shareholders of the GWR, and there was much criticism of the slow progress in generating income.

The biggest limiting factor to the expansion of GWR freight business was Brunel's broad gauge, particularly as the railway began to expand northwards and acquired standard

Below: The coming of railways revolutionised the transportation of almost every kind of commodity. Before the opening of the Great Western, goods were moved by the horse-drawn 'Bristol, Bath & London Wagon', pictured here.

gauge-lines like the West Midland Railway. There had been misgivings over the whole issue of the 'break of gauge' from the earliest days of the 7ft experiment, but Brunel had never been an advocate of the interchange of traffic over the whole of the British railway network, arguing that GWR goods wagons should stay on its lines only and that it 'would never pay to trust them in the hands of others'. Whilst the railway remained a small operation this parochial attitude was not a problem, but, within a decade of opening, problems were beginning to become apparent as the company's network grew ever larger. The transit of goods from stations on the broad-gauge Great Western to destinations with standard-gauge connections was not a simple one; goods would usually be subject to additional delays, as at some point during their journey they would have to be unloaded from broad- to standard-gauge wagons at a 'break of gauge' station — a process that could lead to damage through rough handling or even loss. Atkins and Hyde, in their history of GWR goods services, also revealed that invoices and paperwork were often mixed up in the course of transfer, leading to loads' being delivered to the wrong destination, adding to the delay and confusion caused by the gauge issue.

However difficult the transfer of goods and livestock, the most pressing problem caused by the gauge issue was the trans-shipment of coal. The company had acquired the South Wales Railway in 1863, and the rapidly expanding industrial heartland of South Wales was an increasing source of revenue. It was therefore not a surprise that one of the first railways to be converted from broad to standard gauge was the South Wales line, in 1872. Some measure of how rapidly the coal business increased can be gained from the fact that in 1865 the GWR carried 3,303,909 tons of coal and coke, a figure that had grown to 12,351,445 tons by 1875. It was only after this date that income from goods traffic actually exceeded that from passengers, yet by August 1910 the freight business was worth more than £3 million a year.

Before the Great Western took control of many South Wales companies at the Grouping in 1922/3 its coal business was substantial but nowhere near the scale it would later reach. To put its operation into perspective, in 1910 it

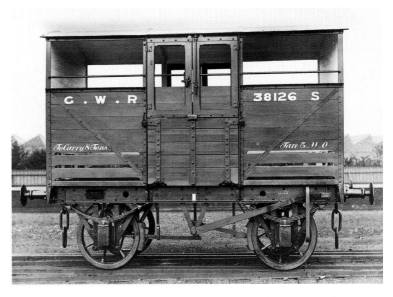

carried 15¾ million tons of coal mined from South Wales — a not inconsiderable amount, but 3 million tons less than that carried by The Taff Vale Railway, one of its much smaller competitors in the region. Nevertheless, the company made great efforts to speed up its heavy goods trains, particularly those running from South Wales to London. Despite the introduction of Churchward's powerful 2-8-0 freight engines, the operation of coal trains was not without difficulty; although the company had trumpeted the running of 100-wagon trains the average coal train tended to be somewhat shorter. In 1907 it was reported that the heaviest regular mineral train was a 70-wagon service between Banbury and London, and trains through the Severn Tunnel from Wales were limited to 56 wagons. The company called these services 'Big Engine' workings, but even with the powerful Churchward locomotives in charge they were still very slow trains. In 1907 trains from Wales could manage an average of just 16mph, a speed not helped by the fact that many of the wagons used were fitted with greased axleboxes, which tended to run hot on long and faster services and required checking every 40 miles or so. Matters improved only with the gradual introduction of newer, more modern wagons and, eventually, continuous braking.

Following its acquisition, at the Grouping, of both the general goods and coal traffic of South Wales companies like the Rhymney and Taff Vale railways the GWR's domination of

Above: An early short-wheelbase GWR cattle wagon, built at Swindon in 1888.

the coal business changed the whole scale and nature of its operations in the region. The report of the directors issued to shareholders in February 1934 reveals that receipts from 'goods train working' had leapt to more than £13 million annually, the coal business still being worth more than £5 million despite the Depression. The Great Western now owned not only the lines previously operated by the pre-Grouping companies but also the docks and trans-shipment facilities that went with them. It also took over responsibility for a large and complex train-control system that had evolved over many years. Company staff at Control Offices co-ordinated and organised the running of trains from pithead to port, liaising between collieries, docks and the railway itself, ensuring that there were enough rolling stock, siding space and locomotive capacity to run trains promptly. To keep costs down the GWR worked to ensure that light-engine working and shunting was kept to a

minimum and that empty wagons were returned to collieries as soon as possible. On their return workings otherwise empty wagons were often loaded with wood for use as pit props. The scale and complexity of this traffic is hard now to comprehend, given the huge decline of the coal industry in South Wales; the valleys echoed to the sound of steam locomotives hauling trains to and from the collieries that were the life blood of the region. Giving some idea of just how busy these lines were, it was estimated that during the heyday of the coal industry a loaded coal train or empty return working passed Pontypridd every eight minutes, day and night.

Writing in 1923, W. G. Chapman observed that the previous 20 years had seen a speeding-up of goods services due to the introduction of vacuum-braked goods stock, an initiative in which the GWR had taken a lead, marking 'an epoch in freight train

Below A view of the first 100-wagon train run on the Great Western, at Acton Yard in 1913. The picture is more interesting for the huge variety of GWR goods stock seen in the sidings of the yard itself.

services'; along with the construction of specially designed heavy-goods locomotives this had led to a vast improvement in the operation of what he called 'trains that pass in the night'. These developments were matched by a corresponding increase in the speed of goods trains; previously the old loose-coupled trains had rattled along at around 15mph, an average speed that increased to over 45mph. Chapman added that as loads had also increased, by almost 100%, this meant that the company was carrying 'twice the load at three times the speed!'. He went on to highlight a special train nicknamed 'The Grocer', which, not surprisingly, carried commodities such as tea, coffee, cocoa and margarine and ran from London to the North of England. What he claimed to be the finest and fastest freight train in the United Kingdom left Southall at 11.55am, running north via the GW/GC joint line to Leamington and on to Wolverhampton and Crewe; continuing via the LMS, the train arrived in Aberdeen at 8am the following day.

'The Grocer' was just one example of the express freight services run by the GWR; by 1929 there were so many that the company was moved to print a list in a booklet, issued to traders, called 'How to Send and How to Save'. The list extended to 75 trains, and many of the names had been provided over the years by staff, some dating back to the broad-gauge era, although a number had been added when the *GWR Magazine* organised a competition amongst staff for further suggestions. The names adopted over the years were a real mixture, revealing not only the wry humour of railway staff but also a glimpse of the geographical spread of the company itself. It should thus come as no surprise to discover that the 12.05am Paddington–Worcester was known as 'The Sauce' or that the 8.20pm Kidderminster–Paddington service was 'The Carpet'. The 9.05pm Birkenhead–Cardiff service was, logically, 'The Mersey', while, in acknowledgement of its Wiltshire origins, the 4.20am Westbury–Wolverhampton was known as the 'Moonraker', this being a nickname of inhabitants of that county.

Most of these trains ran overnight, as Chapman notes, largely to avoid slowing daytime express passenger services. The practice also enabled the company to offer its customers 'next day' delivery; it was able to charge premium rates for such a service and

Above: *Cardiff Newtown goods depot, photographed in 1924. At this time the use of horses for both shunting and delivering and collecting goods was still commonplace.*

Opposite top: Porters at Paddington manhandle the large Express Dairies milk churns out of wagons. The six churns perched on the closest wagon would have been very heavy and awkward to move.

Below: A classic view of a GWR goods combination. An unidentified Great Western 0-6-0 pannier tank and crew wait at Banbury with its shunter's truck – a small wagon used by goods-yard staff to shunt wagons around the sidings.

during the 1930s at least could still boast an advantage in speed over its road-haulage rivals, which did not yet enjoy the benefits of good-quality roads or vehicles to match the non-stop rail services. The introduction of these fast vacuum-braked trains for perishable goods like fish, meat, fruit and vegetables was, of course, ideal for the rapid transit of items requiring delivery quickly, but smaller single-wagon loads were catered for by 'pick-up' local goods services. These trains would call at smaller stations on a regular basis, collecting and depositing wagons in each yard. The process of shunting and sorting wagons was, not surprisingly, slow, compounded by an additional sorting carried out at larger marshalling yards. For even smaller consignments the GWR operated what it called a 'Station Truck' system; this involved the use of a wagon attached to the back of a local slow goods train, which called at each station along a predetermined route of up to 20 stations to allow smaller consignments to be loaded and unloaded — another time-consuming process.

A feature at many rural stations was a cattle dock, used to load and unload livestock. Until the growth of road transport the railways provided the only safe and reliable method of moving farm livestock over long distances. Although many cattle wagons and horse boxes were shunted onto local slow goods the company also ran regular cattle trains, loaded with cattle landed from Irish cross-channel steamers, from Fishguard to Acton. In 1907 it was noted that these trains were run during the day, when traffic was busiest, meaning that trains speeds were low and that the journey from West Wales to the capital took a staggering 14 hours.

Another feature of rural station working was the collection of milk. The rapid growth of Britain's urban centres led to a huge demand for dairy produce and a consequent growth in dairy farming in the years before 1900. Initially milk was transported in large (17-gallon) milk churns, often carried in passenger guards vans, but these were replaced by smaller and more manageable 10-gallon churns, transported in distinctive 'Siphon' wagons complete with louvred sides to improve ventilation and cooling. Following World War traffic grew to the point where the GWR was running 75 special milk trains daily, with more than 1,000 wagons in use. By the 1930s the milk churn was being phased out, and milk

transported instead in a fleet of 3,000 glass-lined milk tankers. Chapman noted that each new tanker took the place of three vans filled with churns, saving a 'dead weight of 58 tons'. In addition to the four- and six-wheeled milk tankers the company employed flat wagons on which road milk tankers could be transported.

Mention of the 'Siphon' wagon is a reminder that the GWR used an elaborate and somewhat idiosyncratic system to identify its fleet of goods wagons, which by the outbreak of World War 1 amounted to more than 88,000 vehicles. The Drawing Office at Swindon Works identified each type by diagram number, but a further code name was used for communicating by telegraph; this was so that a clerk in a goods depot could request a particular wagon for a particular load without having to waste vital words describing it. Thus a 'Crocodile' was a wagon for carrying heavy items like boilers or oversize metal castings, rather than one to carry exotic reptiles as the name might suggest. Other names were more obvious; the 'Tadpole' and 'Bloater' wagons carried fish, and the 'Fruit' vans were used for the movement of bananas and other fruit. Thousands of tons of bananas were imported through Avonmouth Docks at Bristol, from where special trains were run to London using ventilated vans which in summer allowed the bananas to ripen; in winter steam heating could be used to hasten this process. The operation was carried out with military precision to enable the fruit to be delivered as soon as possible to London markets; in 1910 the *GWR Magazine* reported that more than 200,000 bunches of bananas had been shifted in a single week.

Much of the fruit and vegetable traffic handled by the Goods Department was seasonal; special trains were run on the new Honeybourne line in Gloucestershire to handle the autumn harvest of apples and plums from the Vale of Evesham. Such was the level of traffic at Evesham that, in the 1920s, more than 200 wagons per day were shifted during harvest time. Given its long-standing historical connections between the railway and the Duchy of Cornwall, it is not surprising that the GWR paid particular attention to the shipping of broccoli to London and the major markets there. At its height this traffic was particularly lucrative for

the company, the annual crop amounting to more than 30,000 tons; in the 1930s more than 200 special trains would be run in the early spring to get the harvest to market in the freshest condition, and for a few hectic weeks sleepy rural lines like the Helston branch would be transformed into busy goods routes. Similar important seasonal loads were shipped from the warmer climes of the Channel Islands and the Isles of Scilly. Great Western steamers brought thousands of tons of spring flowers, new potatoes and tomatoes from Jersey and Guernsey, whilst Scilly Islands flowers shipped to Penzance were then transported by the GWR to Paddington and other major urban centres. A *GWR*

Above: One of the most dangerous loads to be carried by the Great Western was that of gunpowder or explosives. These 7-ton steel wagons were lined inside with timber to reduce the possibility of stray sparks causing an explosion. Not surprisingly, special care was taken in shunting such stock and when marshalling them in larger trains.

Above: A posed but atmospheric view of fish traffic being loaded at Neyland in West Wales at the beginning of the 20th century. Fast specials were run to get the fish to Paddington and the restaurants of London as quickly as possible.

Magazine article of 1904 reported that almost 300 wagon-loads of flowers had been shifted through Penzance between January and May that year.

Mail had been carried on the GWR as early as February 1840, when the company began to transport this important load between Paddington and Twyford, and when the line opened fully in 1841 the fastest train on the London–Bristol route was the down 'Night Mail' — a service that covered the 118¼ miles from Paddington in 4hr 10min. On 1 February 1855 the company introduced what company historian E. T. MacDermot called 'the first Postal Train in the world', a special train run exclusively for the Post Office. This innovation followed complaints in Parliament about the national postal system as a whole and, initially at least, was a very lightly loaded train, consisting as it did of two sorting carriages and another coach, hauled by one of Daniel Gooch's 7ft 'Lord of the Isles' locomotives. The development of what is now known as the Travelling Post Office was advanced in 1866 when a pick-up apparatus was installed at Slough, allowing mail to be picked up and sorted *en route* — a system that would be fully adopted only by the GWR and the LMS.

By the 1930s, however, more than 80% of mail was carried by rail, and as well as this 'bread and butter' business the company derived much income and publicity from its 'Ocean Mail' traffic. From the early years of the 20th century transatlantic liners bound for Southampton had made a brief call at

Plymouth to allow mail to be unloaded (and passengers disembarked) for a more rapid journey to the capital. The well-chronicled race between the GWR and LSWR had led to increases in train speeds between Paddington and the West Country, and by the 1920s the whole Ocean Mail operation run by the GWR had become very slick. An official GWR account related that the Post Office kept in close touch with liners via 'wireless' to confirm their arrival time so that Great Western tenders based at Plymouth Docks could be ready to take off mail as soon as the ship dropped anchor. In 1927 the GWR had invested heavily in new electrical conveyors at Plymouth Millbay station which ensured that the mail bags could be loaded quickly onto special trains, with the result that in 4 hours 'or less' the mail had been transported to Paddington for handover to the Post Office.

Just how much our world has changed is apparent from the words of W. G. Chapman when he noted in 1934 that it was taken for granted that newspapers 'should be delivered by the time we come down to our eggs and bacon in the morning', adding that the 'London dailies are handed to the railways when people of this country are normally in dreamland'. In the internet age not only has the sheer number of newspapers printed diminished significantly, but also road transport has taken over a business that was once the sole preserve of the railway. Between midnight and 2am Paddington station was a hive of activity, more than 100 vans arriving from Fleet Street and depositing 145 tons of newspapers for despatch; in the early hours of Sunday this figure increased to 330 tons. Newspapers were transferred to trolleys, weighed, checked and then loaded onto the newspaper specials. The company boasted that the world's fastest newspaper train was the 1.20am Paddington service, which covered 133½ miles to Cardiff in 137 minutes, despite speed restrictions in the Severn Tunnel. The 1.40am train travelled as far as Taunton, Exeter and Newton Abbot, and a later (2.30am) departure delivered papers to Bristol, with connections to Oxford, Swindon and Gloucester.

The huge variety of loads carried by the Great Western was due not only to its commercial enterprise but also the fact that it, like other main-line railways was a 'common

Left: *The scale of the broccoli traffic in Cornwall can be seen from this image, taken at Penzance on 8 April 1942. The company has utilised its own lorry to collect the vegetable from local farms, although the yard is full of other vehicles, including a horse-drawn cart.*

carrier', bound by an Act of Parliament — the Carriers Act 1830 — to transport any traffic offered it. The rates charged for each type of goods were laid down in an exhaustive 'Classification of Goods', which in the 1930s ran to more than 400 pages and prevented railway companies from competing on price, something their road-transport rivals were free to do. A campaign to abolish this legal burden was interrupted by the outbreak of World War 2, and after nationalisation road competition made further inroads into the railways' freight business. All the GWR and other companies could do to minimise the impact of the legislation was to generate as much publicity as it could from the movement of the large, awkward or unusual loads it carried, even if the work itself could hardly have covered its costs. The *GWR Magazine* therefore regularly covered the transshipment of large machines, ships' boilers and even an entire circus, confirming that, whatever the load, the Great Western could handle it!

Left: *A 1938 picture taken by Swindon Works to illustrate the movement of goods en route. Complaints were often received by customers when their goods arrived damaged, and the GWR made great efforts to reduce such occurrences. The wagon shown here was a fitted shock-absorbing goods van, built at Swindon in 1937.*

CHAPTER FOURTEEN

WESTERN REGION AND BEYOND: 1945-2010

The wave of optimism generated by the end of World War 2 led to a hope that in peacetime the four main-line railways and London Transport could be restored to something of their prewar glory. In 'It Can Now be Revealed', a booklet published in 1945, the railway companies stated a determination to 'regain and surpass their peacetime standards of public service' with the aim of providing 'the finest railway service in the world to be offered to the British public'. GWR Chairman Sir Charles Hambro informed shareholders in 1945 that it was the view of the company that 'the main-line railways should continue as four separate entities' and that it was proceeding with its postwar plans on that basis. There was certainly much to do; leaving aside damage from enemy action, day-to-day maintenance of permanent way, rolling stock and buildings had declined sharply as the war continued, leaving the company a postwar legacy of maintenance work costing more than £13 million.

Immediate progress on tackling the backlog was limited by the more serious uncertainty surrounding the future of the railway itself. Even during the dark days of war in Europe there had already been rumours about the future of Britain's railways when victory was finally achieved. Some railway staff had seen the advantages of centralised control that had been so successful during the war under the Railway Executive Committee and were keen for it to continue. Not surprisingly, Great Western management and directors were firmly against the idea of nationalisation; O. S. Nock reported that senior staff on other 'Big Four' railways joked that the 'broad-gauge' mentality was alive and well on the GWR,

although the more cynical on the Great Western also argued that those companies that had struggled in the years before the war were now the keenest to embrace nationalisation.

What was dubbed the 'Khaki General Election' was held on the 5 July 1945, only months after VE Day. Because of the huge number of postal votes cast by military personnel stationed overseas the result was not announced until 26 July. The momentous outcome was a surprise to many at home and abroad: Churchill and his Conservative Party were defeated in a landslide victory for Labour. Clement Atlee and the Labour Party had campaigned on a manifesto that committed them to state ownership not only of the railways but also of the coal-mining, iron and steel industries; as a result the GWR lived under the shadow of nationalisation, with all the uncertainty that brought.

Postwar recovery was also limited by the period of extreme austerity suffered in Britain after 1945. Given the Allied victory, the shortages and rationing seemed undeserved, but the fact remained that Britain had borrowed heavily to fund the war effort, and the millions owed needed to be paid back. In order to obtain foreign currency the Government had restricted supply of the best South Wales coal from newly nationalised pits, sending most of it for export. As a result GWR had great difficulty in obtaining enough good-quality coal for its locomotive fleet and was forced to rely on imported American coal which did not always suit Swindon-built locomotives designed to run on Welsh steam coal, and crews often struggled to maintain boiler pressure as fireboxes filled with clinker. The difficulties encountered in maintaining adequate supplies of coal meant that some express services, like the 'Cornish Riviera Limited', were temporarily suspended, although in the case of the 'Limited' traffic was merely transferred to the next scheduled service at 11am, which was hardly a huge inconvenience to passengers. To make matters worse for company finances, however, the price of coal had increased significantly during the war, with the result that by 1946 it cost twice as much as it had in 1939.

The problems experienced in obtaining coal were made worse by the icy winter of 1946/7. Two very cold spells in December 1946 and January 1947 were followed by a prolonged freeze that lasted from 21 January to 16 March. As the temperature hardly rose above freezing the whole country ground to a halt. The severe weather took its toll on GWR services, which were delayed not only by deep snowdrifts in rural parts of Wales and the West Country but also when the freezing conditions caused brakes and water troughs to ice up.

Given this difficult backdrop, GWR management actively sought new and alternative sources of fuel to run their trains. Before the war the company had carried out a feasibility study to explore the possibility of electrifying the main line west of Taunton; the cost of modifying bridges, permanent ways and signalling, coupled with the capital required to provide new 164 electric locomotives, amounted to more than £4 million. The savings in running costs when compared to steam traction were minimal, and not surprisingly GWR directors had decided in 1938 not to proceed with the scheme. Postwar there was little enthusiasm for reviving the idea, besides which the GWR, like the other 'Big Four' companies, had no significant funds to invest heavily in electrification, having instead to 'Make Do and Mend' and continue with steam traction.

Despite enormous difficulties in obtaining materials and fuel, Swindon Works made welcome progress in 1946, constructing 80 new locomotives and completing heavy repairs on more than 700 others. Having diesel railcars already at work on its network, the GWR placed an order with outside contractors for 17 diesel shunters — a move prompted by the fact that diesel oil seemed easier to obtain. With this in mind the company, with Government approval, also began a scheme to

convert some of its steam locomotives to oil firing. An experiment was tried using 20 heavy-freight '28xx' 2-8-0s, which, somewhat ironically, were used on the South Wales coalfield lines. Once the technology had been tried and tested the trial was extended to include five 'Castles' and 11 'Halls'. The converted locomotives were found to steam freely, and the lack of ash and clinker meant that maintenance and cleaning costs at sheds were reduced. Given the fierce criticism faced by the Government over its handling of coal supplies for railways, the success of the GWR experiment encouraged the Ministry of Transport to authorise the conversion of a further 1,217 locomotives on all 'Big Four' lines, hoping it would reduce coal consumption by more than a million tons a year overall. However, O. S. Nock noted in his history of the GWR that the scheme ultimately became a 'colossal fiasco', as difficulties in maintaining an adequate supply of fuel, combined with a lack of currency to buy it from sources abroad, led to abandonment of the idea, all the GWR locomotives being converted back to coal firing by 1950.

An even more unconventional choice of motive power was made by the Great Western in 1946 when the company ordered a gas-turbine locomotive from the Swiss firm of Brown-Boveri. Shortly afterwards, with nationalisation looming, the company ordered more powerful locomotive from the British Metropolitan-Vickers company. It was hoped that gas-turbine technology would provide an

Below: *Snow-clearing operations at Dowlais Top, in South Wales. Experiments were carried out using a jet engine to blow away the snow, which it did, but it also blew away the ballast — an unintended consequence that led to the idea's being discontinued.*

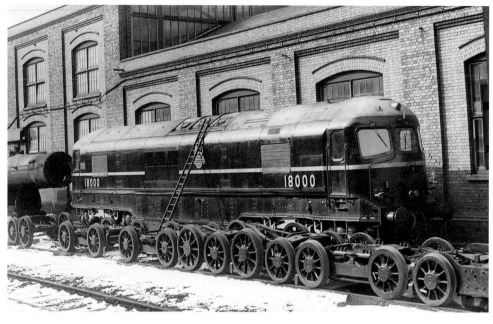

Right: *The first Brown-Boveri gas-turbine locomotive, seen outside Swindon Works on 6 March 1955. When the engine was first introduced at a special ceremony at Paddington, it had an inauspicious start when its powerful exhaust dislodged soot from the roof at the station, causing it to rain down on the assembled VIP guests below!*

Above: *The first style of British Railways crest, as applied to Great Western locomotives following nationalisation on 1 January 1948.*

effective alternative to the diesel-electric locomotives being introduced in large numbers in other parts of the world. The locomotives were not delivered until 1950 and 1951 respectively and, although powerful, were not reliable and spent much time under repair at Swindon Works. Nock reported that one of the biggest problems was that the steam-heating boilers often did not work in winter months, making the locomotives particularly unpopular with the travelling public.

Finally, in the autumn of 1946, the Government announced that it would introduce a bill to Parliament which would bring railways, canals and long-distance road haulage under state control. The process began in November, and, buoyed by public support for nationalisation, the Labour Government was in no mood to back down. The political temperature ran hot, and the situation was not helped by some intemperate remarks from Chancellor of the Exchequer, Hugh Dalton, who argued in a Parliamentary debate that the railways were 'a disgrace to the country'; for GWR staff who had worked so hard to recover from the damage and disruption of World War 2 this criticism was hard to bear. The company began a well-organised campaign to oppose nationalisation, but to no avail; despite much debate inside and outside Parliament, the bill establishing the British Transport Commission — the organisation set up to run the

nationalised railways and other forms of inland transport — was passed on 6 August 1947. What was especially galling to the management at Paddington was that, unlike the other 'Big Four' companies (in particular the LNER), the Great Western was in good financial shape, in its final year even paying its shareholders a divided of 5%.

The last few weeks of 1947 were a time of both regret and apprehension for GWR staff, from senior management to the most junior porter; contrasting with the situation on the other 'Big Four' railways, which had been created only 25 years previously, men and women working for the GWR could trace their company's history back to 1835. On 1 January 1948 the Great Western Railway became British Railways (Western Region) and the traditional 'blow in' of the New Year at locomotive sheds all over the network was tinged with sadness as the railway entered a new era, 113 years after its foundation. As mentioned above, the nationalisation process created an umbrella organisation, the British Transport Commission, which was responsible for canals, docks, London Transport, public road transport and railways, the last grouped together in what was known as the Railway Executive. British Railways consisted of six Regions, the Western Region equating largely to the territory of the old GWR.

Having fought so robustly against the nationalisation process, the old Great Western

WESTERN REGION AND BEYOND: 1945-2010

Railway had little representation within the offices of the new British Transport Commission and Railway Executive. In a final act of defiance Sir James Milne, the GWR's last General Manager, had declined an invitation to chair the Railway Executive, and Sir Allan Quartermaine, the Chief Civil Engineer, also refused the chance to be a member of the Executive. These decisions may have been as a result of LMS staff being promoted over them but also stemmed from a dislike of the centralised system introduced at nationalisation. In the event the only representative of the old company was David Blee, the former Goods Manager; whilst the resentment of the new arrangements was understandable, it did put the new Western Region in a weaker position.

There was, however, some continuity at management level, K. C. Grand, previously assistant to Sir James Milne, becoming Chief Executive Officer of the Western Region, the title 'General Manager' being seen as a relic of the old regime and abolished. Important though the new position was, it had been downgraded in comparison to the old General Manager role, as responsibility was transferred into the upper echelons of the Railway Executive. To the passenger there seemed at first to be only minimal change. Ex-GWR locomotives continued to appear in Brunswick green, carriages were repainted in the familiar chocolate-and-cream livery of the prewar railway, and stations also acquired a chocolate-brown colour scheme recalling the old company. The Railway Executive gradually began to exert a tighter centralised influence on the running of the railway, but this was fiercely resisted by Western Region staff at every level for many years. Under Grand, staff attempted to maintain as much Great Western tradition as was feasible, preserving old working practices and opposing the spread of standardisation which Grand publicly described as 'the end of progress' and 'a fetish on British Railways'.

One of the most difficult issues to resolve was the instruction by the British Transport Commission that the Western Region should adopt its Automatic Warning System (AWS) for train safety instead of the old GWR Automatic Train Control (ATC) system. Ex-GWR men were convinced that their system had a far better pedigree and made comparisons with the safety records of other pre-Grouping companies, arguing that the other Regions should adopt their Automatic Train Control system. The number of serious accidents on the railway in the previous two decades or so appeared to back them up, but AWS eventually won out. A related issue was the long tradition of using lower-quadrant signals on the GWR and the practice of distant signals' being held at Caution ahead of speed restrictions — a custom abolished in 1949 to bring Western Region into line with the rest of British Railways. Another difference lay in the fact that Great Western locomotives were driven from the right-hand side of the cab, which made life very difficult for footplate staff when BR Standard designs with a left-hand driving position were introduced.

The effects of nationalisation were also felt strongly at Swindon Works, especially when F. W. Hawksworth finally retired in 1949. The post of Chief Mechanical Engineer was then abolished, and new departments — Carriage & Wagon, Mechanical & Electrical and Motive Power — were set up. The close-knit workforce at the Swindon factory began to change with the appointment of newcomers, largely from the old LMS. Not surprisingly for a railway community with traditions stretching back more than a century, there was great opposition to what many saw as 'Midlandisation', and a feeling that old scores were being settled. Despite these changes Swindon practices were still hard to break, and until the end of steam in the 1960s the works continued to operate in much the same way it had since the days of Collett.

The decision to build further 'Castle' 4-6-0s in 1946 and 1948 could be characterised as either complacency or defiance — or both. Whilst on other Regions new developments were being pioneered, Swindon management appeared happy enough to build locomotives that featured only minor changes to a design dating back to 1923. The 'Castle' was seen as perfectly adequate to handle the size of trains then being contemplated, as well as being economical and well liked by enginemen, so the construction of more of the same was entirely logical to management. In 1948 the Railway Executive held a series of Locomotive Exchange Trials, mirroring similar exchanges that had taken place between the 'Big Four' in 1925. Tests were conducted for three types of

locomotive — express passenger (in which category the Western Region was represented by a 'King'), mixed-traffic (represented by a 'Hall') and heavy freight (represented by a '28xx' 2-8-0). Loading-gauge restrictions meant that the GWR designs were limited in the 'foreign' routes they could use, and a combination of poor coal, cautious running by locomotive crews and lack of enthusiasm on the part of WR management meant that the Swindon products did not impress, although later trials produced better results, and when BR Standard locomotives were designed their boilers owed much to Swindon practice.

Whatever misgivings there might have been among traditionalists at Swindon, the factory had little choice but to turn out considerable numbers of these BR Standard types, even though many had a clear LMS pedigree. It was truly the end of an era for the works when, in March 1960, it completed Class 9F 2-10-0 No 92220, the last steam locomotive built for British Railways and thus the last to be built at the works in Swindon. Although classed as a heavy-freight locomotive, which should have been turned out in black, it emerged in fully lined Brunswick green and, amidst great ceremony, was formally named *Evening Star*, complete with GWR-style brass nameplates which, like the name itself, recalled the era of Daniel Gooch and broad gauge.

By mid-1950s , the Government was finally in a better position to address the updating Britain's railways. The Modernisation Plan of 1955 promised £1,240 million over a 15-year period, much of this to be spent on new locomotives and rolling stock. Whilst other Regions adopted diesel-electric types, the Western Region continued on an independent path by constructing instead a series of diesel-hydraulic locomotives, built under licence from German manufacturers. These new locomotives promised to be lighter and more powerful than diesel-electric types and when working well proved a great success. All the classes eventually introduced did, however, suffer from unreliability. The first to appear was the 'D6xx' 'Warship' class, built not by BR at Swindon but by the North British Locomotive Co. The inaugural run, on 17 February 1958, was not auspicious, one of the two locomotives, No D600 *Active*, failing on its run from Paddington to Bristol. The 'D6xx' locomotives were soon followed by the lighter 'D8xx' 'Warships', while the smaller mixed-traffic 'Hymek' type appeared in 1961. December of that year saw the debut of the largest diesel-hydraulic design, the D1000 'Western' class, construction of which would be shared between Swindon and Crewe works. Although the 'D6xx' class was relatively short-lived, most of the other diesel-hydraulic designs remained a major part of the Western Region locomotive fleet until the early 1970s, when diesel-electric types began to replace them.

However hard Grand and the Western Region staff may have attempted to preserve GWR practice, outside factors had a more serious effect on the fortunes of the railway. Road competition continued to grow steadily, and the financial crisis gripping British Railways meant that drastic measures were inevitable. Grand's successor, J. R. Hammond, although a Western man, could do little to save the railway from the effects of the Beeching report of 1963. The wholesale closure of many of the Western Region's cross-country routes and branch lines changed for ever the character of what had been the old GWR network. In any case, the Western's 'Indian Summer' of nominal independence had ended in 1962 with the appointment as General Manager of Stanley Raymond. Concerned with reducing the losses being suffered by the Western Region, he had little interest in GWR custom and practice and made major changes, modernising the main offices at Paddington and having the old GWR exhibits and paintings that had hung there for many years removed. Although staff remember historic material being thrown away, fortunately most still survives either in the collections of the STEAM Museum or the National Railway Museum. Whilst many disagreed with Raymond's lack of sentiment for GWR tradition, his actions, along with the cuts made as a result of the Beeching report, ensured that large parts of the old GWR network survived. Under his successor, Gerard Fiennes, General Manager from 1963 to 1965, matters improved somewhat. Respecting at least some old Great Western traditions, he had a number of Brush Type 4 diesels named after early GWR locomotives. The introduction of diesels had led to the slow but inexorable decline of steam on the Western Region, and the end came on 31 December 1965, nearly three years before the complete abolition of main-line steam traction on British Railways. Any GWR-designed locomotives still working had been transferred to the London Midland Region, although for a time No 7029 *Clun Castle*, which in 1965 had hauled a number of 'Farewell to Steam' specials around the WR network before being sold for preservation, continued to see unofficial use in the Birmingham area.

The introduction of Inter-City High Speed Trains onto both the West Country and Bristol–London main lines in 1976 improved travelling times significantly, and passengers were able to speed along Brunel's old main line at 125mph. By May 1977 there were 27 trainsets at work on Western Region, replacing locomotive-hauled services on the London–Bristol and London–South Wales routes. This

Right: *BR Western Region permanent-way staff ride to work on their Wickham gangers' trolley, complete with trailer.*

Right: *The 'A' Erecting Shop at Swindon in September 1966, with two 'Hymeks' and a 'Western' visible. The picture was taken to record the installation in the workshop of modern fluorescent lighting.*

Right: *'Castle' No 7029* Clun Castle *is prepared for departure after making a stop at Bristol Temple Meads during the 'Farewell to Steam' tour in 1967.*

Far right: *The rise in importance of air travel led to the introduction of a coach link between Reading and Heathrow Airport. One of the hostesses initially employed waits for departure on 11 September 1970.*

innovation ultimately ended the use of diesel-hydraulic power on the Region, the remaining 'Western' workings being taken over by Class 50 diesel-electrics displaced by HSTs.

The number of staff employed at Swindon Works had diminished steadily over the years, and by the time of the completion of *Evening Star* in March 1960 there were only 5,000 at the factory. The town council had made great efforts to rid itself of the 'Railway Town' tag, attracting larger employers to the area so that the railway factory was no longer the dominant force it had once been. Lack of investment from British Railways and the later parent company, British Rail Engineering Ltd, meant that the factory was badly in need of updating and short of work. By 1973 the staff complement was as low as 2,200, and despite a brief renaissance in the late 1970s, when, under Works Manager Harry Roberts, numbers rose again, it came as no surprise to some when, in 1984, BREL announced that the workshops would close for good in 1986. For many others, including the 4,000 staff employed there, the announcement was a real blow; the fact that the works had survived for so long meant that its demise was all the more shocking. Despite a vociferous and well-supported campaign the closure went ahead, and the famous works hooter sounded for the last time on 26 March 1986.

For enthusiasts the closure announcement cast a shadow over plans for a year-long celebration in 1985 to mark the 150th anniversary of the founding of the Great Western Railway. BR Western Region had seen the anniversary as a great opportunity to publicise not only the past but also the progress being made in the present. The most immediate casualty of the closure was a major 'GWR150' exhibition which was to have been held at Swindon Works and would have featured a stellar line-up of preserved GWR locomotives and rolling stock from museums and preservation groups across the country. However, BR continued with other activities, including the running of a special 'GWR150' exhibition train which during the course of the year visited various locations on the WR network. There were a number of other important developments: the Science Museum commissioned the construction (by Resco Railways) of a full-sized replica of broad-gauge 4-2-2 *Iron Duke*, and the

locomotive made its first public appearance on a piece of track laid in Hyde Park, close to the Albert Hall, in the spring of 1985, later appearing at Didcot, Old Oak Common, Tyseley and York. Another major event was the restoration of one of the most famous and best-loved GWR engines, 4-4-0 *City of Truro*. In 1984 the locomotive was removed from the old GWR Museum in Swindon after a 22-year stay and moved to the Severn Valley Railway for restoration. There was more than a little excitement on 1 April 1985 when *Steam Railway* announced that the locomotive would be returned to steam in BR black (a livery it had never worn, having been withdrawn in GWR days), the outraged enthusiasts who complained about this failing to notice the date. When the locomotive did return to traffic it appeared in its Edwardian splendour, in lined-green livery with brown frames.

The 150th-anniversary celebrations were also seen as an opportunity for locomotives like *City of Truro* to return to the main line. Most steam enthusiasts will agree that the resulting programme run during the year was not universally successful. The first official special, run from Bristol to Plymouth on 7 April 1985, was a disaster, Nos 6000 *King George V* and 7819 *Hinton Manor* both suffering hot axle boxes and failing *en route*, requiring diesel power to complete the run. Meanwhile, during the summer, BR ran a series of specials between Swindon and Gloucester, and these, along with other specials, notably between Birmingham and

Below: *Steam slowly rises in the Spring Shop at Swindon Works. Although the author took this picture on a summers afternoon in 1983, the equipment and methods still in use could had changed little over the previous 50 years. Within three years the furnaces in the Spring Shop were cold and the works was closed for good.*

Right: An Inter-City 125 train speeds through Sonning Cutting in the 1980s.

Stratford, were rather more successful. Aside from a repeat of the Bristol–Plymouth special, run in October to compensate passengers who had been disappointed in April, the final steam working of note took place on 10 September, when '28xx' 2-8-0 No 2857 made a main-line run from its home at the Severn Valley Railway to Newport hauling a rake of restored GWR wagons in order to demonstrate the progress made in the freight business.

The 1993 Railways Bill called for the wholesale privatisation of British Railways, and when it was passed and the new organisational structure came into being on 1 April the following year there were hopes that a new company could be created that would reflect the practices and traditions of the old GWR. The arrangements finally adopted, however, resulted in the creation of separate train-operating and railway-infrastructure companies, meaning that there would be no return to an operation like the old GWR. Today the trains running on the old GWR network are operated by a company called 'First Great Western', but its operating practices and ethos are very different from those of the original company. It was no coincidence, however, that the parent company of the train operators maintained the 'Great Western' name, at least.

More than 60 years after the Great Western ceased to exist as an independent company it is still held in great esteem by many, not all of them railway enthusiasts. Some of this interest and affection may be due to the fact that much original Great Western infrastructure still survives. Many of the stations and civil-engineering structures that made the GWR famous still exist, including Brunel's Paddington station, Maidenhead Bridge, Box Tunnel, Bristol Temple Meads station and the Royal Albert Bridge at Saltash. Many other smaller stations, like the Brunel designs at Charlbury and Culham, are still in daily use, as are many other solid Victorian and Edwardian GWR buildings. Following its closure in 1986 the Swindon Works complex has gradually been refurbished for other uses; English Heritage now occupies what was the General Offices building, while shoppers now stroll through the Great Western Designer Outlet Village in what was once 'V' Boiler Shop.

The Swindon site is also home to STEAM — Museum of the Great Western Railway, a fitting tribute to the men and women who worked for the Great Western and BR at Swindon and on the railway as a whole from the 1830s onwards. The collection was moved from a smaller museum, created in the last days of steam, when Swindon Borough Council and the British Transport Commission combined to open the Great Western Railway Museum. Located in an old Wesleyan chapel in Faringdon Road, the museum opened in 1962 and featured some famous locomotives, including broad-gauge replica *North Star*, Churchward 4-6-0 No 4003 *Lode Star* and the only surviving 'Dean Goods' 0-6-0, No 2516. Following the closure of the works in 1986 plans were made to create a larger and more comprehensive museum in one of the workshops, a process which took the best part of 15 years to complete, the new museum finally opening in 2000. A number of the locomotives on display, including No 4073 *Caerphilly Castle*, are on long-term loan from the National Railway Museum at York, where other famous GWR designs forming part of the National Collection are on display.

Away from the formal setting of a museum the spirit and legacy of the Great Western lives on in the many heritage railways that are located on old GWR lines and operate restored Swindon locomotives, carriages and wagons. The continuing existence of so many Great Western engines after the demise of steam on BR is for the most part due to their survival at the now-famous Woodham Bros scrapyard at Barry, in South Glamorgan. Ex-GWR locomotives had been sent there on a regular basis, but scrapping ceased in September 1965, when Billy and Dai Woodham began to concentrate their efforts on wagons, leaving a growing stockpile of locomotives. The last ex-GWR locomotive to arrive at the yard was No 7802 *Bradley Manor*, in July 1966, and at one time there were more than 200 engines stored there. During their stay they suffered from the effects of the salty sea air and the stripping of more valuable non-ferrous parts either by Woodham's or thieves.

Most of the ex-GWR locomotives at Barry were subsequently purchased by preservation societies, the first — Churchward '43xx' 2-6-0 No 5322 — leaving on 8 March 1969. Although it went initially to a location in South Wales for restoration, this locomotive formed the core of a collection based at what is now known as Didcot Railway Centre. Twenty minutes east along Brunel's main line from Swindon, the Didcot site is the home of the Great Western Society and is centred on the old 1932 GWR locomotive shed. It has the largest collection of GWR locomotives and rolling stock in Britain as well as a small but well-displayed museum of small relics such as GWR memorabilia and posters. Visitors can also see working

signalboxes, a broad-gauge running track and many more Great Western treasures.

The preservation of so many ex-GWR designs by Dai Woodham ensured that on heritage lines like the Cholsey & Wallingford, Dean Forest, East Somerset, Gloucester–Warwickshire, Llangollen, Severn Valley, South Devon, Swindon & Cricklade and West Somerset railways, as well as at steam centres such as those at Buckinghamshire and Tyseley, passengers can travel behind a Swindon-built locomotive and recapture something of the atmosphere of 'God's Wonderful Railway'.

Left: *A Great Western legend emerges from the old Great Western Railway Museum on the night of 14 July 1984.* City of Truro *was then taken to the Severn Valley Railway for restoration, its place being taken by GWR diesel railcar No 4.* Author's collection

Below: *To mark the beginning of the Great Western Railway 150th-anniversary celebrations in 1985 the replica* Iron Duke *was steamed on a short section of track close to the Royal Albert Hall in London.* Author's collection

BIBLIOGRAPHY

General

Adams, W. (Ed): *Encyclodædia of the Great Western Railway*

St John, D and Whitehouse, P. B.: *The Great Western Railway — 150 Glorious Years* (David & Charles, 1985)

Railway Correspondence & Transport Society: *Locomotives of the Great Western Railway* Parts 1-13.

The *Great Western Railway Magazine* 1895-1947

1. Brunel's Great Western: 1835-1841

The Great Western Railway Magazine — A Miscellany of Fact and Fiction Vol II: London (George Burns & Co, 1864)

Barman, C.: *Early British Railways* (King Penguin, 1950)

Bryan, T.: *Brunel — The Great Engineer* (Ian Allan, 1999)

Channon, G.: *Bristol and the Promotion of the Great Western Railway* (The Historical Society, Bristol Branch, 1985)

Chapman, W. G.: *Track Topics* (GWR, 1935)

Gooch, Sir Daniel: *Diaries of Sir Daniel Gooch Baronet* (Kegan Paul, 1892)

Kelly, S., and Kelly, M. (Eds): *Brunel: In Love with the Impossible* (Bristol Cultural Development Partnership, 2006)

Editorial: (*The Railway Times* Saturday 3 July 1841)

Vaughan, A.: *Grub, Water and Relief* (John Murray, 1985)

Williams, Alfred: *Brunel and After: The Romance of the Great Western Railway* (GWR, 1925)

2. Engineering Excellence

Body, G.: The Severn Tunnel (Avon Anglia, 1986)

1859-1959 Centenary: Royal Albert Bridge, Saltash (British Railways Western Region, 1959)

Brunel, I: *The Life of Isambard Kingdom Brunel, Civil Engineer* (Longman, 1870)

Chapman, W. G.: *Track Topics* (GWR, 1935)

'Great Western Progress 1835-1935' (supplement to *The Times*, August 1935)

'The Company's Greatest Engineering Feat: The Construction of the Severn Tunnel'. (*GWR Magazine* September 1935)

Kelly, S., and Kelly, M. (Eds): *Brunel: In Love with the Impossible* (Bristol Cultural Development Partnership, 2006)

Vaughan, Adrian: *A Pictorial Record of Great Western Engineering* (OPC, 1977)

Walker, T. A. C.: *The Severn Tunnel: Its Construction and Difficulties* (third edition) (Bentley & Son, 1891)

3. The Broad-Gauge Empire: 1841-1892

Awdry, C.: *Brunel's Broad-Gauge Railway* (OPC, 1992)

Cole, F., and Rice, I. (Ed): *A Broad Gauge Album* (Newton Abbot GWR Museum, 2000)

Day, L.: *The Broad Gauge* (Science Museum, 1985)

Gooch, Sir Daniel: *Diaries of Sir Daniel Gooch Baronet* (Kegan Paul, 1892)

Kentley, E. (Ed): *Brunel: Recent Works* (Design Museum, 2001)

MacDermot, E. T.: *A History of the Great Western Railway Vol 2: 1863-1921* (Ian Allan, 1964)

Rolt, L. T. C.: *Isambard Kingdom Brunel* (Longman, 1957)

Williams, Alfred: *Brunel and After: The Romance of the Great Western Railway* (GWR, 1925)

Editorial: *Engineering* 3 June 1892

Untitled article: *The Times* 20 May 1892

4. Passenger Comforts

Acworth, W. M.: *The Railways of England* (John Murray, 1889)

Cattell, J., and Falconer, K.: *Swindon: The Legacy of a Railway Town* (HMSO, 1995)

Chapman, W. G.: *The Cheltenham Flyer* (GWR, 1934)

Hotels and Catering Services: General Arrangements & Tariffs (GWR, 1937)

Through the Window: Paddington to Penzance (GWR, 1924)

Chapman, W. G.: *The 10.30 Limited* (GWR, 1923)

Hebron, C.: *Dining at Speed — A Celebration of 125 Years of Railway Catering* (Silver Link, 2004)

'The Modern Engineering Moloch' (*The Mechanics Magazine* 1 January 1842)

'The Last of the Broad Gauge, 1892' (article in the *STEAM Museum Cuttings Collection*)

'From Ordeal to Luxury' (*Great Western Railway Magazine* August 1935)

5. The Giant Awakens: 1892-1914

Bryan, T.: *The Golden Age of the GWR* (PSL Books, 1991)

The Cornish Riviera (GWR, 1904)

Fishguard 1797-1908 (GWR, 1908)

Harrison, D.: *Salute to Snow Hill* (Barbryn Press, 1982)

Home, G.: *Peeps at Great Railways: The Great Western Railway* (Adam & Charles Black, 1913)

Kingdom, A. S.: *The Great Western at the Turn of the Century* (OPC, 1976)

Norris, J., Beale, G. , and Lewis, J.: *Edwardian Enterprise* (Wild Swan, 1987)

Williams, Alfred: *Brunel and After: The Romance of the Great Western Railway* (GWR, 1925)

6. Swindon Works

Swindon Works (British Railways Western Region, 1954)

Swindon Testing Station (British Railways Western Region, 1950)

Bryan, T.: *Return to Swindon* (Avon Anglia, 1990)

Cattell, J., and Falconer, K.: *Swindon: The Legacy of a Railway Town* (HMSO, 1995)

Durrant, A. E.: *Swindon Apprentice* (Runpast, 1989)

Gibbs, K.: *Swindon Works Apprentice in Steam* (OPC, 1986)

Swindon and its Part in Great Western History (GWR, 1935)

Hayward, J. S.: 'A Factory Life At Swindon, Part 3' (*North Star* Vol 11, No 3, 2009)

Peck, A. S.: *The Great Western at Swindon Works* (OPC, 1983)

Richens, F. R.: *Manuscript Notes on Swindon and the GWR* (STEAM Library Collection)

'Swindon Works' (*British Machine Tool Engineering* Vol XXXII, No 160, April 1950)

Williams, A.: *Life in a Railway Factory* (Duckworth, 1915)

7. Great Western Swindon

Swindon Railway Village Museum Guidebook (Thamesdown Borough Council, 1980)

Cattell, J., and Falconer, K.: *Swindon: The Legacy of a Railway Town* (HMSO, 1995)

Cockbill, T.: *A Drift of Steam* (Quill Press, 1992)

Darwin, B.: *A Century of Medical Service* (GWR Medical Fund Society, 1947)

Grinsell, L. V. (Ed): *Studies in the History of Swindon* (Swindon Borough Council, 1950)

Richens, F. R.: *Manuscript Notes on Swindon and the GWR* (STEAM Library Collection)

8. Great Western Inheritance: 1918-1929

The General Strike, May 1926 (GWR, 1926)

The Great Western Railway of England: The Quickest Route: New York to London (GWR, 1927)

The Lines Absorbed by the Great Western Railway (bound volume of *GWR Magazine* articles) (GWR, Paddington 1923)

Potts, C. R.: *The GWR and the General Strike* (Oakwood Press, 1996)

Rees, P.: *The Royal Road* (Avon Anglia, 1985)

Semmens, P. W.: *History of the Great Western Railway, Vol 2: Consolidation* (Allen & Unwin, 1985)

The Book of the Great Western (*The Times*, 1970)

9. GWR Locomotive Design

Bryan, T., Hyde, D., and Semmens, R. : *Swindon's Finest* (Thamesdown Borough Council, 1990)

Chapman, W .G.: *The King of Railway Locomotives* (GWR, 1927)

Griffiths, D.: *Locomotive Engineers of the GWR* (PSL, 1987)

Holcroft, H.: *An Outline of Great Western Locomotive Practice, 1837-1947* (Ian Allan, 1971)

Peck, A. S.: *The Great Western at Swindon Works* (OPC, 1983)

Russell, J. H.: *A Pictorial Record of Great Western Engines* (two volumes) (OPC, 1975)

Summers, L. A.: *A New Update of Swindon Steam* (Great Western Society, 2007)

10. Go Great Western: 1930-1939

Body, G.: *Riviera Express: The Train and its Route* (Avon Anglia, 1979)

Chapman, W. G.: *The Cheltenham Flyer* (GWR, 1934)

Cole, B., and Durack, R.: *Railway Posters 1923-1947* (Laurence King, 1992)

The Cornish Riviera Limited — A Silver Anniversary (GWR, 1929)

A Lantern Lecture: The Cornish Riviera (GWR, 1932)

Harris, M.: *Decades of Steam: 1920-1969* (Ian Allan, 1999)

Nock, O. S.: *A History of the GWR, 1923-1947* (Ian Allan, 1967)

Clear the Lines! (Railway Companies' Association, 1938)

Rees, P.: *The Royal Road — 150 Years of Enterprise* (Avon Anglia, 1985)

Vaughan, Adrian: *A Pictorial Record of Great Western Engineering* (OPC, 1977)

11. Off the Rails

Atkins, T., and Hyde, D .J.: *GWR Goods Services — An Introduction* (Wild Swan, 2000)

Chapman, W. G.: *Twixt Rail and Sea* (GWR, 1927)

'The New Motor Service' (*GWR Magazine*, September 1903)

Devon: Shire of the Sea Kings (GWR, 1916)

Holiday Haunts (GWR, 1936)

Hotels and Catering Services: General Arrangements & Tariffs (GWR, 1937)

Russell, J. H.: *Great Western Horse Power* (OPC, 1995)

12. The Great Western at War

Baker, M. H. C.: 'Wartime Incidents' (*Great Western Echo* No 182, Summer 2008)

It Can Now Be Revealed (British Railways Press Office, 1945)

Bryan, T.: *The GWR at War, 1939-1945* (PSL, 1995)

Knox, C.: *The Unbeaten Track* ([*(Publisher?)*,] 1944)

Transport Goes to War (Ministry of War Transport / HMSO, 1942)

Pratt, E.: *The War Record of the Great Western Railway* (Selwyn & Blount, 1922)

Wragg, D.: *Wartime on the Railways* (Sutton, 2006)

13. From Cattle to Coal: GWR Goods

Atkins, T., and Hyde, D .J.: *GWR Goods Services — An Introduction* (Wild Swan, 2000)

Timetable: Reading, Steventon and the Faringdon Road (GWR, July 1840)

London to Cirencester, Bath, Bristol, and Bridgewater — Merchandize, Cattle, etc. Scale of Charges (GWR, 30 July 1841)

115th half-yearly general meeting: Report of the Directors (GWR, 3 August 1910)

Report of the Directors and Financial Accounts and Statistical Returns for the Year ended December 1933 (GWR, 12 February 1934)

Page, J.: *Rails in the Valleys* (Guild, 1989)

Roberts, T.: 'Goods Train Working' (proceedings of the GWR [London] Lecture & Debating Society, 14 February 1907)

14. Western Region and Beyond: 1945-2010

Allen, G. F.: *The Western since 1948* (Ian Allan, 1979)

It Can Now Be Revealed (British Railways Press Office, 1945)

Steam to Diesel: The First Western Region Main-line Diesel Locomotives (Friends of Swindon Railway Museum, 2008)

Nock, O. S.: *A History of the GWR, 1923-1947* (Ian Allan, 1967)

Simpson, A.: *Barry: The Transitional Years* (unpublished manuscript, written 2008)

STEAM: Museum of the Great Western Railway (guide book) (STEAM, 2000)

INDEX

King'-class locomotive No 6000 King George V *stands at the portal of Middle Hill Tunnel near Box in a publicity picture taken prior to its visit to the United States in 1927.*